Shaping India's Future

Abid Hussain
(1926-2012)

Shaping India's Future

Essays in Memory of Abid Hussain

Editors

Deepak Nayyar

Rana Hasan

ACADEMIC FOUNDATION

NEW DELHI

www.academicfoundation.org

First published in 2017
by

ACADEMIC FOUNDATION
4772-73 / 23 Bharat Ram Road, (23 Ansari Road),
Darya Ganj, New Delhi - 110 002 (India).
Phones : 23245001 / 02 / 03 / 04.
Fax : +91-11-23245005.
E-mail : books@academicfoundation.com
www.academicfoundation.org

Cataloging in Publication Data--DK
Courtesy: D.K. Agencies (P) Ltd. <docinfo@dkagencies.com>

Shaping India's future / editors, Deepak Nayyar and Rana Hasan.
pages cm
ISBN 9789332703841

1. Economic development--India. 2. Public administration--India. 3. India--Economic policy. I. Nayyar, Deepak, editor. II. Hasan, Rana, editor.

HC435.S53 2016 DDC 338.954 23

Typeset, printed and bound by The Book Mint, New Delhi.
www.thebookmint.in

For

Trilok Karki Hussain

CONTENTS

Part 2: Tributes

About the Contributors

ESSAYS

Dipankar Gupta is Distinguished Professor, Shiv Nadar University. His previous positions include Director, Centre for Public Affairs and Critical Theory, Shiv Nadar University and Professor in the sociology departments of Jawaharalal Nehru University and University of Delhi. He has held a number of visiting positions including Leverhulme Professor at the London School of Economics and Fulbright Professor at the University of Massachusetts. He has also served as Director, Reserve Bank of India and Director, National Bank for Rural Development. He has written numerous journal articles and authored and edited 18 books including, *The Caged Phoenix: Can India Fly?* (Stanford University Press). In 2010, he was awarded Chevalier De L'Ordre des Arts et des Lettres (Knight of the Order of Artes and Letters) by the French Government.

Rana Hasan is an economist with a multilateral development institution. His research has focused on understanding how market-oriented economic reforms affect labour market outcomes and industrial performance, and the relationship between growth, poverty, and inequality in the Asia-Pacific region. He has worked previously as Fellow at the East-West Center (USA). His research has been published in various journals including *Journal of Development Economics, Review of Economics and Statistics*, and *World Development*. He has also co-edited two volumes on trade and labour related issues. He holds a PhD in Economics from the University of Maryland

and a Masters' degree in Economics from the Delhi School of Economics, University of Delhi.

Abid Hussain (1926-2012) belonged to the Indian Administrative Service (1951-1985) and served as India's Ambassador to United States of America; Member, Planning Commission; and Secretary, Ministry of Commerce; and Secretary, Ministry of Heavy Industries. He chaired a number of important committees set up by the Government of India including those covering trade policy reforms; restructuring of the Council of Scientific and Industrial Research; and small scale industry. He was also a member of the committee for reviewing India's Constitution. He held senior positions in various think tanks and institutions including serving as Vice Chairman, Rajiv Gandhi Foundation and Chairman, Indian Institute of Management, Bangalore. He was deputed by the Government of India to work for various United Nation agencies. He was awarded the Padma Bhushan.

Rajiv Kumar is Chancellor of the Gokhale Institute of Economics and Politics in Pune, Senior Fellow at the Centre for Policy Research in New Delhi and the Founding Director of Pahle India Foundation. He was previously Secretary General of Federation of Indian Chambers of Commerce and Industry; Director & Chief Executive of Indian Council for Research on International Economic Relations (ICRIER); and Chief Economist of Confederation of Indian Industry, 2004-2006. He worked at the Asian Development Bank from 1995 to 2005 and in the Government of India from 1989 to 1995. He is a leading columnist and has published extensively. His latest book, *Modi and his Challenges* was published in May 2016 by Bloomsbury. He has a DPhil in Economics from Oxford University and a PhD from Lucknow University.

Pratap Bhanu Mehta is President, Centre for Policy Research, New Delhi. He has also been Professor at Harvard University, New York University, and Jawaharlal Nehru University. He has published widely on political theory, society and politics in India, and constitutional law. He is co-editor of the *Oxford Handbook of the Indian Constitution* and has also served on the Board of the National Institute of Public Finance and Policy and the National Council of Applied Economic Research among others. He is the recipient of the Infosys Prize and the Malcolm S. Adisheshiah Prize. He has published widely in the fields of political theory, intellectual history, constitutional law, politics and society in India and international politics. He is on the Editorial Board of numerous journals including the *American Political Science Review* and *Journal of Democracy*. He holds a PhD in Politics from Princeton University.

Rakesh Mohan is Distinguished Fellow at Brookings India and teaches at Yale University as Senior Fellow in the Jackson Institute for Global Affairs. He has served as Deputy Governor of the Reserve Bank of India; Secretary, Ministry of Finance and an Executive Director on the Board of the International Monetary Fund. He was also Chairman of the National Transport Development Policy Committee of the Government of India with rank of Minister of State, and Senior Adviser, McKinsey Global Institute, McKinsey and Company. He is also a Non-Resident Senior Research Fellow of Stanford University. His latest book, *Growth with Financial Stability: Central Banking in an Emerging Market* (Oxford University Press) was published in August 2011.

Sudipto Mundle is an Emeritus Professor at the National Institute of Public Finance & Policy (NIPFP), New Delhi, and a Visiting Senior Fellow at Centre for Policy Affairs and Critical Theory, Shiv Nadar University, New Delhi. He is also a member of the governing bodies of NIPFP and the Institute for Human Development, New Delhi. Prior to this, he was a member of the Fourteenth Finance Commission, a member of the Reserve Bank of India Monetary Policy Advisory Committee and member and acting Chairman of the National Statistical Commission. He was with the Asian Development Bank for a number of years and has also held senior faculty positions in academic institutions in India and had visiting assignments at the University of Cambridge, Yale University, Institute of Social Studies, and the Netherlands & Japan Foundation. He was also an Economic Adviser in the Ministry of Finance, Government of India. He has published extensively in professional journals and authored several books.

Deepak Nayyar is Professor Emeritus at Jawaharlal Nehru University, New Delhi, and an Honorary Fellow of Balliol College, Oxford. Earlier, he has taught at the University of Oxford, the University of Sussex, the Indian Institute of Management, Calcutta, and the New School for Social Research, New York. He was Vice Chancellor of the University of Delhi from 2000 to 2005. He also served as Chief Economic Adviser to the Government of India and Secretary in the Ministry of Finance from 1989 to 1991. His research interests are primarily in the areas of international economics, macroeconomics and development economics. Prof Nayyar has published more than 75 papers in academic journals and 15 books. His latest book, *Catch Up: Developing Countries in the World Economy*, was published by Oxford University Press, Oxford.

Yaga Venugopal Reddy served as Governor of the Reserve Bank of India and Chairman of the Fourteenth Finance Commission, Government of India. An officer of the Indian Administrative Service, he has held the positions of Secretary (Banking) in the Ministry of Finance, Government of India and Principal Secretary in Government of Andhra Pradesh. He served as an Executive Director at the International Monetary Fund. He has written numerous scholarly papers and authored several books, including *Economic Policies and India's Reform Agenda: New Thinking* published by Orient Blackswan. He was Distinguished Professor of the Indian Institute of Technology Madras and has been a visiting fellow and professor at numerous prestigious institutions including the London School of Economics, Osmania University, and Administrative Staff College of India. He is a recipient of the Padma Vibhushan.

TRIBUTES

Jagdish Bhagwati is a University Professor at Columbia University and Director of the Raj Center on Indian Economic Policies. He was Senior Fellow in International Economics at the Council on Foreign Relations. He has been Economic Policy Adviser to Arthur Dunkel, Director General of GATT (1991-93), Special Adviser to the UN on Globalisation, and External Adviser to the WTO. He has served on several high-level expert groups and advisory committees and has published numerous scholarly articles. Five volumes of his scientific writings and two of his public policy essays have been published by MIT press. He has also received several prizes and honorary degrees, including awards from the governments of India (Padma Vibhushan) and Japan (Order of the Rising Sun, Gold and Silver Star).

Nitin Desai is an Indian economist and international civil servant. He has held numerous prestigious position in the Government of India including Special Secretary in the Planning Commission and Secretary and Chief Economic Adviser in the Department of Economic Affairs, Ministry of Finance. He has also served as Under-Secretary-General for Economic and Social Affairs of the United Nations. He has written extensively, contributing to major reports at international and national levels.

Arvind Panagariya is the Vice Chairman of Niti Aayog of India and Professor of Economics at Columbia University. In the past, he has been the Chief Economist of the Asian Development Bank and a Professor of Economics and Co-Director, Center for International Economics, University of Maryland at College Park. He has written numerous scholarly articles in leading technical and policy journals and has written/edited 10 books. He has been an editor of the *India Policy Forum*, jointly published by the Brookings Institution, Washington, D.C. and the National Council on Applied Economic Research, New Delhi. He holds a PhD from Princeton University.

Jairam Ramesh is an Indian economist and politician belonging to Indian National Congress. He is a Member of Parliament representing Andhra Pradesh state in the Rajya Sabha since June 2004. He has served the Government of India in various capacities including as Minister of Rural Development and Minister of State (Independent Charge) at the Ministry of Environment and Forests. He has also served in the Planning Commission, Ministry of Industry and other economic departments of the Government of India. He has has been a columnist for the *Business Standard, Business Today, The Telegraph, Times of India* and *India Today*, sometimes under the pen-name "Kautilya".

DEEPAK NAYYAR AND RANA HASAN

Introduction

I

ABID HUSSAIN: A LIFE

Abid Hussain was a distinguished civil servant, a consummate diplomat, and a concerned citizen of India who contributed to the public sphere in India and elsewhere across a wide range of activities. Above all, he was a wonderful human being, who was respected, loved or admired by those who knew him. Born in Hyderabad, on 26 December 1926, Abid came of age at a time when India's destiny was being shaped as never before. Like many youngsters in the 1940s, his imagination was captured by the freedom struggle led by Mahatma Gandhi and the vision of a modern India that was being forged by Jawaharlal Nehru along with other leaders of the freedom struggle. However, as is true for all individuals, Abid's family and circle of friends, combined with the education he received, were instrumental in shaping his personality and world view.

Family Influence

Hyderabad, like the rest of India, could not remain insulated from the raging currents of the socio-political movements and the nationwide demands for independence led by Mahatma Gandhi. There were many stalwarts of the national movement from Hyderabad, including some from Abid's family itself. Among the notable political

The authors would like to express their sincere gratitude to Narendra Reddy and Trilok Karki Hussain for contributing inputs and insights on various aspects of Abid Hussain's life.

activists in the family, his maternal uncle, Abid Hasan Safrani, 15 years his elder, served as secretary to Netaji Subhas Chandra Bose in the Indian National Army (INA). The greeting "Jai Hind" was coined by him and adopted by the INA before it became a national greeting. Another of Abid's uncles, Badrul Hasan, assisted Gandhi regularly in bringing out his publications and was known to have burnt his silk shop on Abid Road at his mentor's call to boycott foreign goods. Mrs Sarojini Naidu, a distinguished poet, speaker, activist, and administrator in the national movement, was a close friend of the family. Abid's strong nationalist outlook stemmed from these family traditions and networks.

Abid's grandfather, Sirajul Hasan, originally came from UP and settled in Hyderabad after pursuing studies at Oxford. He was a judge of the state's High Court, besides being a renowned anthropologist, having worked and published on the tribes of Telangana. Abid's father, Ghulam Panjatan, a colourful member of the judiciary and a Sessions Judge in Hyderabad state had built his professional reputation as an advocate for the legal rights of marginalised people and political activists in the state. Among them were several members of the Telangana movement of 1949-50 whom he defended forcefully and did so pro bono. As a parent, Mr Panjatan had a laissez faire approach in the upbringing of his children. In keeping with his unconventional ways, he sent his daughter to Scotland for higher studies, whereas his sons would be admitted to local educational institutions. However, he kept an excellent library at home, encouraging the younger lot to read, think, and take decisions on their own. Not surprisingly, the children pursued their own inclinations and paths. Tassaduque, the daughter, became a professor of sociology, Riaz also took to teaching, while Safdar joined the private sector. Turab, closest to age in Abid, joined the civil service, while Haseen went into medicine and Irshad became a professional actor and leading exponent of the art of mime. Askari, the youngest son, joined a reputed business family of Hyderabad. The bond among the brothers never slackened. Indeed, an enduring image seared into the memories of the later generations of the Panjatan family is that of the brothers, sitting together with their whiskey's, usually at Turab and Naseema's Banjara Hills residence where an exuberant welcome was extended to all and sundry, debating the various issues of the day and with the conversations punctuated by wit and Urdu poetry.

It is no exaggeration to say that a common cultural inheritance played a significant part among several other influences on Abid. Justice P. Jaganmohan Reddy, an illustrious Hyderabadi, who later became a judge of the Supreme Court of India described those times most aptly in his memoirs: "The state of Hyderabad was famous for its composite culture. It was a city in which Hindu, Muslim, Telugu, Marathi, Kanadese, Tamil and to some extent western culture intermingled. In fact, it was the *Sangam*—the meeting place of cultures of the north, south, east and west."[1] Abid imbibed and relished the different vignettes of this composite culture. Indeed, these were to serve him well later in life when he later took up senior positions in India and abroad.

Nizam College and Friends

In addition to family influences, Nizam College in Hyderabad played a profound role in shaping Abid's outlook and personality. Nizam College was established in 1887 to impart modern education to the youth of the state. It was one of the most esteemed institutions of higher education in south India. It had many firsts to its credit, including being the first to introduce English as the medium of instruction, allow co-education, and also the first to explore frontier scientific fields of the time. The college used to invite eminent persons to address its students, which contributed to their exposure to current affairs. Apart from the instruction by eminent teachers, the college also instituted weekly debates on current topics by students through their student union, an independent entity and not influenced by partisan politics of the times. This provided students an opportunity to develop debating skills and be up to date on current issues. It was no surprise therefore that Abid's years at Nizam College developed in him an abiding liberal outlook and sharp awareness of the world at large.

1. *The Revolution I Have Lived Through*. 1993. Printwell.

Abid's friendships at Nizam College would also play an important role in shaping his life. A noteworthy friendship was with Asif Ali Khan, who remained close to Abid throughout. An upright, principled man, he rose to senior executive levels in the nascent corporate sector of the country. Another particularly close bond was with Rasheeduddin Khan who went on to became a distinguished professor at the Jawaharlal Nehru University, a leading expert on federalism, and a member of the Rajya Sabha, the upper house of India's Parliament. Rasheed's influence on Abid went well beyond the latter's outlook and awareness of political and social dynamics. In fact, several years after both Abid and Rasheed had moved on from Nizam College and found themselves in New Delhi—Rasheed as a research fellow at the newly founded School of International Studies (located at the time in what was called Sapru House) and Abid as an Indian Administrative Service (IAS) officer deputed to the central government—Rasheed would introduce Abid to Karki, a young scholar at the School from a Nepali Hindu family settled in Bhopal. Impressed with not only her scholarship, but also her progressive social views, Rasheed did not hesitate to play the role of Cupid. A short while later, on 18 July 1958, Abid would wed Karki, a most happy and cherished union that brought much brightness into both lives.

Another distinguished and brilliant alumnus of Nizam College was Prof A.M. Khusro. A year older than Abid, Khusro was the president of the college Student Union for many years. He would go on to specialise in economics at the University of Leeds and was subsequently selected by the legendary Dr V.K.R.V.Rao to join his newly-formed Institute of Economic Growth at Delhi. Khusro would become the Vice-chancellor of Aligarh Muslim University—one of the founders of which was an ancestor of Abid, Nawab Mohsinul Mulk—and also served as India's Ambassador to Germany. There were other friends from Nizam College who also made a name at Delhi such as Vasudev Pillai and an older cousin of Abid, Kaokab Durry who started the cultural organization, Syam-a-Gazal which survives to this day.

Public Service

Nizam College had set the stage. But there were other influence too. Abid decided to pursue a career in public service, rather than journalism or politics, which were his initial interests in college. Abid joined the Hyderabad Civil Service in 1947-48, around the time of India's independence, and then the newly formed Hyderabad Administrative Services. With growing conflict between the Nizam of Hyderabad and the Union Government, this stint proved short-lived. Abid decided to take the entrance exam for the newly formed Indian Administrative Service and qualified to join the IAS in 1951.

Abid served as Sub-Collector, first in Mehboob Nagar and then in Hyderabad. A focus of his work was on 'community development'. Despite all the academic and cultural facilities available to the elite in Hyderabad city, there was wide-spread and stark poverty, juxtaposed with feudalism in the interior districts of Hyderabad state where there were practically no educational facilities.

The Telangana movement found an easy space to spread there and at the time when Abid had just joined the state government service, the communist party had given a call for armed rebellion. They had formed "Dalams" in every village recruiting youngsters and training them in guerilla warfare to work to emancipate the poor farmers. They attacked the landlords including *razakars* and police stations.[2]

At his first posting, Abid took up the implementation locally of the community development programme that was being rolled out nationally, and the foundations of which were laid by the dynamic minister of rural development at the time, Mr. S.K. Dey. Abid was subsequently brought to the Department of Community Development Administration in the Government of India, at Delhi, by Mr Dey, whom Abid had the opportunity to interact with and impress with his work as a sub-collector. In this new environment, he found an ideal mentor in Mr J.C. Verma, who was a close confidante

---

2. After the army action in 1948, initiated by the Government of India in response to the Nizam of Hyderabad's intention to keep Hyderabad State an independent entity, the movement subsided and in the first general election held in India, one of the key leaders of the Naxal movement, Mr Ravi Narayana Reddy, contested a Lok Sabha seat and polled the highest number of votes in the country, even more than Jawaharlal Nehru in his constituency!

of Mr Dey. Mr Verma would continue to play a significant role in Abid's professional and even personal life.

This was the time of his wedding to Karki. The sojourn in Delhi also provided Abid with an opportunity to grow in his profession. It enabled him to gain more expertise on issues of community development, building on what he had learnt at the grass roots level. He was subsequently sent on a deputation to the United Nations in Turkey where he served as an advisor to the Turkish government on community development issues (1962-1964).

After Turkey, Abid was appointed as the District Collector of Vishakapatnam, also known as Vizag, where he served from 1965 to 1968. His years as District Collector proved to be especially important. Given the posting in Delhi and deputation to Turkey, Abid was to be one of the older District Collectors. With his experiences in Delhi and Turkey—and the travels in Europe and Middle East—Abid brought with him an experience and perspective that would not be found in somebody younger and less travelled. In the first place, Abid's active involvement in political issues in the 1940s, and the efforts at bringing people together to build schools, roads, etc., as part of the community development programme had given him an appreciation of the complexities involved in developing a region and fostering a cooperative spirit among people. At the same time, the exposure to Europe had also impressed on him an appreciation of the need for local economies to diversify and industrialise.

Abid distinguished himself as collector of Visakapatnam. He became close to its citizens, both its elite as well as its less fortunate. Uncommon for the times, he believed that by helping the rich to grow one could make them help the poor and needy. Abid gave meaning and substance to the phrase 'city of destiny' and presented an optimistic vision of a future that would be luminous and rewarding for all. Vishakapatnam was to become an abiding memory in his life. On Abid's part, the entrepreneurial spirit of the people in Vizag, their academic and ideological interests, and zest for good living were traits to nurture and cherish. In an enduring personal touch his daughter Vishaka was named after the city.

A number of everlasting friendships and associations ensued from the posting. These included colleagues at work as well as many others from different walks of life. A noteworthy bond was formed with the entrepreneur Atluri Jairam. A self-taught man with little formal education, Jairam made a deep impression on Abid as he combined many different persona into one: an entrepreneur with a keen sense of the market, a voracious reader with immense intellectual curiosity, a nationalist with a liberal vision for his country, and a deeply sympathetic man who stood ever ready to help both the unfortunate as well as the young, be they aspiring entrepreneurs or promising students who were short of funds for college. Another close bond that developed in Vizag would involve the transformation of familial ties into deep friendship. A young cousin, Peter Hassan landed his first job at Coromandel Fertilisers and came to stay with the Hussain household. Two traits of Peter were evident from early on and would resonate with Abid: an uncanny capacity to connect with people and bring them together in a common pursuit of creating something new or better, and the ability to celebrate life with warmth and generosity. The friendship blossomed and remained till the end.

From 1968 to 1970, Abid worked as Director and then Secretary in the Department of Industry in the Government of Andhra Pradesh. In 1971, Abid was given a posting in New Delhi as Joint Secretary in the Ministry of Industry, Government of India. For a year, Abid was sent on deputation to the United Nations to Fiji as an advisor on industry. From 1974-1981, Abid was Chief of the Industry Division in ESCAP, United Nations, at Bangkok. He returned to India in July 1981 to serve as Secretary to the Government of India to the Ministry of Heavy Industry and subsequently as Secretary to the Ministry of Commerce. His retirement from the civil services in December 1984 was followed by five years as a Member of the Planning Commission from 1985-1990 and two years as India's Ambassador to the United States from 1990-1992. He went on to be the first Vice Chairman of the Rajiv Gandhi Foundation and led the newly founded Rajiv Gandhi Institute for Contemporary Studies. Retirement never really followed, however, as Abid continued to serve in various committees, including prestigious and important ones such as that on the Review of India's Constitution on which he was appointed member by the National Democractic Alliance (NDA) government of Prime Minister Atal Bihari Vajpayee and the 1997 Report on Small Scale Industries on which he served as Chairman.

In many of his assignments, Abid had the honour of serving India at critical junctures and was able to bring an important personal imprimatur to various elements of policy. His role in strengthening India-US relationships from 1990-1992 is an important example. Abid also lectured extensively on a variety of topics spanning the role of bureaucracy in Indian democracy, science and technology, and attributes of a good society.

The Policy Maker

In the 1980s, Abid served as Chairman of two Committees— one on restructuring of the Council of Scientific and Industrial Research and the other on restructuring the textile industry. Both led to landmark decisions. But, his most enduring legacy is the role he played in making the case for, and pushing India's liberalising reforms that gained momentum in the 1980s. Abid was an early proponent of economic liberalisation in India. In 1984, he was Chairman of the Committee on Trade Policies which advocated measures to rationalise and simplify trade policies and recommended a focus on export expansion. The report led to much simplification, the announcement of export-import policy on a three-year cycle instead of every year, and the introduction of several East Asian style export incentives. Along with a large depreciation of the rupee, these measures more than doubled India's exports in the second half of the 1980s. Abid was also among the first to push for industrial policy reforms. He was associated with the broad-banding of the industrial licensing regime in the mid-1980s. Some years later, while at the Planning Commission, he coordinated a policy paper making the case for, and anticipating, the industrial de-licensing reforms of 1991.

In a similar vein, The Abid Hussain Committee Report on Small Enterprises (1997) provided an intellectual foundation and road map for ending the policy of reserving product lines for small-scale industries. The report recommended the abolition of the policy and argued for support to small and medium enterprises through alternative, promotional instruments, and this marked the beginning of the process of reducing the number of product lines reserved for the small-scale sector.

There can be little doubt that Abid's instincts as a liberaliser were developed by his travels and work abroad. An important example is Abid's almost seven year assignment at UN ESCAP in which Abid saw first hand the rise of the East Asian Tigers and the start of the nascent reform efforts in China. Indeed, for Abid, these experiences were instrumental in shaping a vision of industrialisation in which engagement with the global economy was crucial. This vision recognised the important role of the state in encouraging industrialisation. But, it also incorporated a recognition of the stifling effects that a bureaucracy could have on individual initiative and creativity.

On this last point, however, Abid's personality and mental make-up were probably just as important. Like many of his contemporaries working on issues of industrial development in the late 1960s and early 1970s, Abid believed in the importance of a vibrant industrial sector as key to India's prosperity. Where he seems to have differed from many of his contemporaries was in his views on the importance of relying on individual creativity. From today's standpoint, this distinction may seem banal. However, in the context of India's industrial licensing regime—which Abid worked under in various capacities including Director in the Department of Industry in Government of Andhra Pradesh—Abid's stress on the individual was actually quite remarkable.

A telling story recounted by Abid is on how he dealt with the issuance of industrial licences in the Department of Industry in Andhra Pradesh. He noted that he was both quick and liberal in his decisions on, and assessments of individual cases. Perhaps even worse from the perspective of the mindset that made up the "License Raj", Abid was seen as friendly with business men, and was known to socialise with them. Soon enough, eyebrows were raised and the question of whether Abid was examining licences carefully and impartially came up. As it turns out, Abid had an approach which began with his realisation that an entrepreneur seeking a licence for producing a particular product typically had far more knowledge about both the production process involved as well as market conditions than he. Instead of seeking technical details on a proposed project, Abid believed that a more fruitful line of inquiry would focus on understanding the entrepreneur's motivations. In particular, he engaged in dialogue with the entrepreneur to understand the entrepreneur's vision for himself and his vision for the country. If these were progressive, Abid would back the entrepreneur's application with little hesitation.

Did Abid Hussain regret this approach? His answer, always, was an unequivocal no. Whether or not his approach was as effective as Abid believed it to be is difficult to prove or disprove. But, the approach was perfectly in line with three traits of Abid: sense of pragmatism about the feasible, humility regarding the limits of his own knowledge and abilities, and optimism about, with a faith in, his fellow human beings. A fourth trait was wit and humour, that Abid used with great effect to convey powerful ideas, dis-arm the opposition, and persuade the reluctant fence-sitters.

Throughout his life, Abid was committed to the idea of a prosperous, liberal, and secular India, convinced that a bright future lay ahead for the country. This was in part due to an innate optimism that was a defining feature of his personality. But, it was also due to an appreciation for the spirit, ability, and creativity he found in so many of his contemporaries and fellow citizens from all walks of life. Indeed, his passion for people, dialogue, and debate; and openness to the ideas of individuals from different persuasions, ideologies, and backgrounds—economic and social—were perhaps instrumental in enabling him to 'see further' than many.

The Family and Friends

This story about the life of Abid Hussain would remain incomplete without reference to the family, which was a critical anchor in his non-stop professional life. The affection and the sentiment for the family was an integral part of his being.

Karki, his wife, was the love of his life. She was the companion. She was the mother of his children. She was the keeper of the extended family. She was a sounding board for ideas. She was a source of sagacious advice. And she was the reality check. Abid and Karki had three children. The eldest, Suhail, shared his mother's interest in politics and father's ability to read socio-economic trends. For his profession, however, he opted for engineering and today specialises in research and design of IT hardware in Silicon Valley. Vishaka, Abid and Karki's only daughter, trained as a lawyer and has for some years now been professionally associated with the US-India Business Council. Her passion for bringing people together in the pursuit of a common goal and good is reminiscent of Abid. Rana, the youngest, studied economics. Abid drew immense satisfaction in drawing him in arguments which he as an amateur would quite often win against his more formally educated son.

For Abid, of course, his sense of family extended way beyond the nuclear family. Abid's extended family from Hyderabad was family. Karki's extended family from Nepal and Bhopal was family. Lifelong friends were family and so were their families. Friends and colleagues from different stages of his professional life were family. The dinners at their home to celebrate his birthday, or lunches to celebrate Eid, were an ever-widening circle to which people were always added but none were ever subtracted. His deep affection for children was endearing and close rapport with young people was admirable.

It needs to be said that friends were as much an integral part of Abid's personal and professional life. Over a period that spanned more than half a century, this circle of friendships became wider and grew larger. The idea of India, embedded in pluralism and secularism, was the common bond and the shared aspiration. The diversity and range of these friendships was indeed striking. From the early days, there were friends from across the political spectrum. Soon thereafter, this extended to the civil service fraternity in Hyderabad and Andhra Pradesh. Once he moved to New Delhi, there was a natural progression in friendships to administrators from different parts of India, followed by people in the United Nations system. But there was far more to come. Abid had close friends not only among academics and journalists, but also in industry and civil society. There were a few persons from the world of arts and letters too. Many of the economists in government were part of his close circle. And so were some diplomats. These friendships might have started in his world of work but continued even after that association was over to become cherished life-long friendships. The close relationship with so many people much younger than him was rare in our social milieu. It was attributable to the unusual personality and the human qualities that Abid was endowed with. He was egalitarian in a hierarchical world. And he nurtured younger people in whom he spotted talent or promise. All these friends were precious for Abid. But it was the diversity and longevity of these friendships that made Abid so special.

He was social beyond imagination, whether it was entertaining at home, or going to three parties in one evening. In this social dimension of Abid's life, he owed much to his wonderful wife, Karki, who kept open house for more than five decades, as friends from near and far dropped in for a chat, a drink or a meal. This hospitality was forever. But even Karki drew a line with Abid's hectic social life. In later years, she was not willing to go to more than one dinner party in an evening!

II

ROAD MAP TO THE VOLUME

This volume seeks to honour Abid Hussain's lifelong passion and commitment for a better India.

In Part 1, nine essays, including a previously unpublished essay by Hussain, deal with contemporary issues that were not only held to be important by Hussain, but which are also likely to shape India's future over the coming decades.

Part 2 consists of six tributes, most of which were published in major newspapers in the country soon after he passed away in July 2012. Taken together, these short pieces reprinted here show Abid as a man of many parts, to capture his multi-dimensional persona, which no single tribute could possibly have done.

A theme that ties the essays of Part 1 together is that to be successful, India's quest for high and inclusive growth requires not only a particular set of economic policies, it also requires that these policies be implemented in the context of a just and efficient structure of governance and a society which shares progressive social and cultural norms. Accordingly, the essays are organised in two sections. The first deals with issues related to the economy and state, while the second to issues of governance and society.

Economy and State

Chapter 1, by Deepak Nayyar, examines the economic role of the State in countries that are latecomers to development, including India. Nayyar notes enormous diversity in the nature of the state across different countries, ranging from a strong reliance on markets and openness at one end to strong state intervention and controlled openness at the other. Thus, there are alternative paths to development. Crucially, the success of the different models has in part depended upon the ability of countries and their governments to make course corrections. For example, minimising market failures is the key for countries that stress markets and openness. Conversely, minimising government failure is the key for countries that stress State intervention with moderated, calibrated or controlled openness. Turning to India, Nayyar notes that real question is no longer about the size of the State or the degree of State intervention. It is about the nature of State intervention and the quality of the performance of the State. In addition to outlining areas where the government must continue to play a key role (such as physical and social infrastructure), the essay emphasizes that the government must endeavour to change the nature and the quality of its intervention in the market, consciously differentiating between the functional, the institutional and the strategic aspects. The conclusion drawn is that India needs a developmental State to shape its future.

Chapter 2, by Y.V. Reddy, examines the role of three institutions with a major role—past, present, and/or future—in economic policy making in India. These are the Planning Commission, its successor, the NITI Aayog, and the Finance Commission. Reddy makes the point that the Planning Commission's replacement by NITI Aayog captures the new realities of macroeconomic management and of Union-State relations, especially the need to foster a spirit of competitive federalism within the context of a broader environment of cooperation. He also describes how the recommendations of the Fourteenth Finance Commission, in particular, are relevant for NITI Aayog, as they enable India's states to be drawn into a partnership with the Union Government for transformation and development. Crucially, he identifies the areas and a path that would allow the two institutions to enhance the quality of planning in India in future.

Chapter 3, by Rajiv Kumar, begins by noting that India, unlike any other country, has chosen to undertake simultaneously three distinct transitions: social, political and economic. The enormous challenge of simultaneously carrying forward this 'triple transition' is exacerbated by India's continental size and diversity. After a discussion of the main contours of the three transitions, Kumar focuses on the preconditions for accelerating economic growth and sustaining it over the next three decades. He also argues that with nearly 12 million entrants into the labour force each year—comprising young people as well as those seeking to shift from agriculture and low productivity jobs elsewhere—employment maximisation must be chosen as the principle, if not the exclusive and overarching policy goal that provides the necessary analytical framework for policy making in India. However, policy prescriptions are not enough. Implementation of the ideas or statutes already in place and greater efficiency in the delivery of public services are critical.

Chapter 4, by Rana Hasan, starts with the idea that India's success in creating productive and well-paying jobs holds the key for meeting its goal of achieving inclusive growth. This implies an urgent need for India's policymakers to focus on raising productivity in agriculture and expand employment opportunities outside that sector. One sector with continued potential to create reasonably productive and well-paying jobs is manufacturing. Hasan notes that notwithstanding the de-licensing and trade reforms of the 1980s and 1990s, the sector continues to operate under difficult conditions. Public investments in infrastructure; regulatory reform; and tackling market failures through appropriate elements of industrial policy are needed. Fortunately, the government's recognition of the importance of a dynamic manufacturing sector and its "Make in India" programme provide a much needed platform for transforming Indian manufacturing and enabling it to meet its full potential.

Chapter 5, by Rakesh Mohan, focuses on the transportation needs of the country over the next couple of decades, and what needs to be done to satisfy these. Both the quantum as well as the types of investment are crucial if India is to achieve growth rates of 8-9 per cent per year and reach middle income status by the early to mid-2030s. Moreover, the choices made on transport systems will also have implications for energy efficiency and transport-related emissions. Two issues are singled out by Mohan as priorities for policymakers. First, there needs to be a step up in public investment in railways. Second, a coherent and integrated strategy for the transport sector will require breaking of silos and a tendency toward planning and programming approaches that are project centric. The need for a modernised integrated logistics system that enables efficient and economic inter-modal transfers requires an integrated system based approach. This in turn requires the creation of coordinating policy and planning institutions with the requisite technical expertise.

Governance and Society

Chapter 6, by Dipankar Gupta, takes up the issue of citizenship in the context of the development of a nation state. Gupta argues that citizenship must remain the guiding principle of the democratic nation-state and that a liberal democracy is the best guarantor of creating citizenship. Moving to the experience of India, Gupta notes that unlike most other nation-states that emerged after the Second World War, India embraced liberal democracy from the start. However, it is not enough to stop there. Liberal democracy demands relentless vigilance and must always strive to higher expressions of citizenship. This is challenging, no doubt, given that the many languages, histories and traditions of a country as vast as India may sometimes work at cross-purposes. However, ideas such as non-violence—a centre-piece of Gandhi's thinking—and the debate and discussion it allows form the bedrock of guaranteeing citizenship rights to people of diverse provenances. These are part of the Indian tradition and adherence to them must be strengthened.

Chapter 7, by Pratap Bhanu Mehta, is a natural complement to the essay by Gupta. It first discusses various laws, including archaic ones, introduced early in the Republic of India's history that have inadvertently served to restrict freedom by encouraging the formation and perpetuation of certain identities over the creation of a common citizenship with the primacy of individual rights. These need to be repealed or amended given the way they have sometimes functioned. Mehta then goes on to argue that none of the pathologies of certain laws will be addressed if we do not reconceptualise India as a Zone of Freedom—in line with India's constitutional ambition to liberate individuals from the burden of compulsory identities—rather than a Federation of Communities. The idea of a zone of freedom does not argue that these identities will vanish, only that they will be largely private matters.

Chapter 8, an unpublished essay by Hussain and delivered in parts as speeches and in debates in various forums a few years before his demise in 2012, is concerned with the role of bureaucracy in a democratic society such as India's. The chapter notes that a key challenge a bureaucracy faces is the establishment of a smooth and good working relationship with the political leadership. In India's case, a healthy synergy between the bureaucracy and political leadership evolved easily, much to the country's advantage. However, there has been for many years now a general disenchantment with the bureaucracy. Bureaucracy must become more effective and efficient in its core area of enforcing law and order and assume a prominent and active role as a provider of public goods and services to the common man. It must recreate the sense of pragmatic idealism which was once its hallmark and should become more mission-oriented with a sense of pride in doing service to the people. Achieving this will not be easy, and will require creative solutions acceptable to all stakeholders involved. However, the pay-offs to doing so will be immense.

Chapter 9, by Sudipto Mundle, discusses issues relating to two very different aspects of governance: governance as viewed from the lens of service delivery and the issue of corruption. On the former, the essay proposes a metric for rating performance based on the specific context of service delivery by sub-national governments. Such metrics are important as they can be a powerful tool in promoting better governance. On the issue of corruption, the essay proposes that effective action to contain corruption might actually have to be initiated outside government, for example, by an institution against corruption established by business or the non-government sector. It then goes on to discuss what might be the core elements of such an institution. In both aspects of governance considered by the essay, the success or failure of the proposals will depend on the prevailing socio-political context and values. However, as the essay notes, there are encouraging developments ranging from a tendency for political parties, particularly at sub-national levels, to compete on the basis of performance in addition to traditional identity politics at one end, to the greater fiscal autonomy of states at the other.

Part 1

Essays

Economy and State

1

DEEPAK NAYYAR

The State and the Economy

The theme of this essay was the subject of many engaging conversations and serious discussions that I had with Abid Hussain over three decades of a long association and a close friendship. It is, therefore, an appropriate choice for a volume in his memory. The object of the essay is to analyse the economic role of the State in countries that are latecomers to development situated in the wider context of the world economy. In doing so, it draws upon economic theory and economic history, leading into a discussion on India at the present juncture with reference to the past and the future.

The structure of the chapter is as follows. Section I examines the evolution of thinking about the degree of openness (of the economy) and the degree of intervention (by the State in the market) in the process of development, over the past six decades, to set the stage before the play begins. Section II starts with economic theory to explain how and why both governments and markets are susceptible to failure leading to outcomes that are inefficient or undesirable. Section III draws upon economic history and development experience over the past two centuries to develop an understanding of the economic role of the State in historical perspective. Section IV shifts the focus to India and highlights the polar opposite views about the State in the economy that have dominated the discourse at different times. It argues that the time has come to redefine the economic role of the State, which is critical for the future of development in India.

Openness and Intervention

It is essential to recognise that the degree of openness vis-à-vis the world economy and the degree of intervention by the State in the market always were, and continue to be, the critical issues in the debate about policies and strategies for development.

At the beginning of the post-colonial era, it was widely accepted that developing countries must industrialise, starting with import substitution in the manufacturing sector, fostered by a supportive or leading role for the State in the process. Both represented points of departure from the colonial era characterised by open economies and unregulated markets. This Development Consensus of the early 1950s was dominant until the early 1970s.

The actual industrialisation experience of economies in Asia, Africa and Latin America during the quarter century from 1950 to 1975, led to questions. For orthodox economics, the main conclusion was that industrialisation policies, which protected domestic industries from foreign competition and led to excessive or inappropriate State intervention in the market, were responsible for the high cost and low growth in these economies. Inward-looking policies driven by import substitution, particularly in the sphere of trade, were seen as the prime culprit. The prescription followed from the critique. More openness and less intervention would impart both efficiency and dynamism to the process. And outward-looking policies, particularly in the sphere of trade, were seen as the prime saviour. Thus, trade policies were perceived as critical in the process of industrialisation and development.

It needs to be said that this approach to trade and industrialisation was narrow in its focus. For it was not recognised that there is more to trade policies than the distinction between import substitution and export promotion, or inward and outward orientation, just as there is much more to industrialisation than simply trade policies (Helleiner 1992 and Nayyar 1997). In fact, the emphasis on import substitution or export promotion, and inward or outward orientation, differed across countries and changed over time in a process of state-led industrialisation. It was also not recognised that this phase, when protection or promotion was provided to domestic industry, witnessed rapid industrialisation in developing countries, with rates of growth in manufacturing output that revealed a sharp contrast with their past of de-industrialisation during the second half of the 19th century and the first half of the 20th century, when they practiced free trade. Indeed, during this period, which coincided with the golden age of capitalism, industrial growth in the developing world kept pace with that in industrialised countries.

Even so, this approach came to exercise a strong influence on thinking about development. And the beginnings of a change were discernible by the late 1970s (Nayyar 2008). Many countries in the developing world, to be followed by transition economies a decade later, began to reshape their domestic economic policies to integrate much more with the world economy and to enlarge the role of the market vis-à-vis the State. It was, in part, a consequence of perceptions about the development experience in the preceding 25 years, often associated with inappropriate or excessive state intervention, which did not lead to expected outcomes in development. This was juxtaposed with the impressive economic performance of a few countries in East Asia, which was attributed to markets and openness. These success stories—Hong Kong, Singapore, South Korea and Taiwan—were portrayed as role models in development. The process was reinforced by the reality that unfolded. The earlier success stories turned into the East Asian miracle, which spread to Malaysia, Thailand and, in the perception of some, even Indonesia. The debt crisis surfaced in Latin America, moved to sub-Saharan Africa, and ultimately caught up with South Asia. The new orthodoxy was readily accepted by economies in crisis where the International Monetary Fund (IMF) and the World Bank exercised enormous influence through their stabilisation and adjustment programmes. The political collapse of communism reinforced the process. For the advocates of this worldview, the erstwhile centrally planned economies of Eastern Europe and the USSR represented failure, while the open market economies of East Asia epitomised success. The disillusionment with the Development Consensus was complete. And, by the early 1990s, the Washington Consensus, which stressed virtues of markets and openness to advocate generalised prescriptions across countries on the presumption that one-size-fits-all, acquired a near-hegemonic status in thinking about development.

This hegemony did not last long. It was eroded by the financial crises in Asia and elsewhere. Development experience during the 1990s also belied expectations. Economic growth was slower and more volatile. The orthodox prescriptions were subjected to increasing question (Amsden et al. 1994, Stiglitz 1998 and Easterly 2001). The real dampener, however, was unfolding reality (Rodrik 2005, Taylor 2007 and Nayyar 2008). Countries that were conformists and liberalisers underperformed or did not perform, whereas countries that were non-conformists without being liberalisers were the performers. Most countries in Latin America, sub-Saharan Africa and Eastern Europe adopted the reform agenda of the Washington Consensus almost in its entirety. But their performance, in terms of economic growth, industrial development and distributional outcomes, was not only much worse than other parts of the world, but was also distinctly worse than their own performance in the preceding three decades. In sharp contrast, countries in Asia modified, adapted, contextualised and paced their reform agenda, to use unorthodox or heterodox policies for orthodox objectives in much the same way as the small East Asian countries had done earlier. They turned out to be star performers in terms of growth and industrialisation, even if not in terms of distributional outcomes.

The belief system underlying the faith in markets was shaken badly by the financial crisis that surfaced in the United States in late 2008. It led to a sharp contraction in trade, output and employment, which spread rapidly across the world economy through contagion. The Great Recession that followed in its aftermath persists even now. Recovery is slow, uneven and fragile (Nayyar 2011). There is a growing recognition that markets are no magic wand, that the invisible hand of the market is not visible because it is not there, and that markets are good servants but bad masters. It is no surprise that the Washington Consensus on development is dented if not discredited. This dramatic transformation in the international context provides an opportunity to rethink the role of the State and the market in the pursuit of national development.

Government Failure and Market Failure

Ideologues, both on the right and on the left, often pose the problem simply as a choice between government failure and market failure. This is inappropriate if not misleading. Economic theory shows clearly why, or how, governments and markets are both prone to failure, leading to outcomes that are inefficient or undesirable.

Government failure takes many forms and is attributable to many factors. Governments make mistakes because they do not have adequate information about a problem or do not understand the nature of the problem. Without adequate information and necessary understanding, governments are neither able to predict not able to control the consequences of their actions. Hence, government intervention may not resolve the problem it seeks to, leading to unwanted effects or unintended consequences. Moreover, there are divergences between the conception and the design, or between the design and the implementation, of government intervention.

However, people are not concerned with such abstractions. Their perceptions about government failures are based on observation or experience. Sometimes, management of the economy by the government leaves much to be desired if inflation rates or unemployment levels are too high. Governments are usually bad managers of state enterprises in the public sector. Governments are frequently sectarian in their actions, so that their interventions seek to promote or protect the interests of classes or groups whom they represent, if necessary, through corruption and nepotism. The interface of the citizen with government offices or public services could often be a source of frustration, if not harassment or despair.

Most people are far less conscious about market failures because they are difficult to recognise in terms of cause-and-effect. Yet, market failures are not natural events. There are underlying reasons. And there are several manifestations.

Textbooks in economics focus on some market failures that are cited often. First, in the absence of adequate competition, where there is monopoly (one producer) or oligopoly (few producers), efficient market solutions characterised as optimal do not emerge. Thus, the amount of a product manufactured by a monopolist or an oligopolist may be too little and the price charged may be too high compared with competitive situations. Economists describe such conditions as imperfect markets to highlight the contrast with their theoretical construct of perfect markets. Second, an economic activity may impose costs on society which are not reflected in the cost incurred by individual producers (pollution caused by a chemical plant), or may create benefits for society which are not reflected in the price received by producers (skills acquired by workers in a factory). Economists characterise these effects, which matter to society but are not reflected in market prices, as externalities. Third, there are goods and services that are considered desirable, even essential, from the viewpoint of society. But these will not or cannot be supplied by private markets because they are not profitable enough or cannot be easily charged for (street-lights). Economists call them public goods. Similarly, there are goods and services, which are socially desirable, but individuals may not wish to pay for them even if it serves their own interests (museums or seatbelts in cars). Economists term these as merit goods.

There is another dimension of market failure that receives less attention than it deserves. Markets tend to under-produce information, access to which cannot be limited or priced. But that is not all. Markets are characterised by asymmetric information. Important players in markets can manipulate access to information, suppress information, or even create misinformation. Such failures, which affect the functioning of markets by shaping outcomes, are described as information failure.

In many economic situations, where the whole is different from the sum total of the parts, market decisions may widen the divergence between private and social costs or benefits. The pursuit of profit-maximising behaviour by firms, or utility-maximising behaviour by households, might lead to over-production or over-use of goods (too many cars on the roads or too much of pesticides in agriculture), which could impose substantial costs on society in the form of environmental problems. In a similar mode, the atomistic pursuit of self-interest by individuals may lead to undesirable social outcomes where cooperative solutions would lead to unambiguously superior outcomes (private tube wells or community water harvesting). Insofar as such market failures arise at a macro level, are discernible only over time, or impose costs on society-at-large, they may go unnoticed by individuals who are not directly affected. But the failures are for real and so are the costs they impose on society.

There are other, just as important, market failures at the macro level. A reliance on markets leads to unemployment rather than full employment. Unfettered markets tend to increase inequality and accentuate poverty. Under-regulated financial markets can lead to scams and crises where the costs are ultimately borne by people as taxpayers. Market solutions may lead to under-investment in some sectors (infrastructure, education and healthcare) or under-provision for R&D or innovation in other sectors.

It is essential to recognise that the juxtaposition of government failure and market failure, or judgements about which is worse, as if there a choice to be made, is misleading because it diverts us into a false debate. Both market failure and government failure are facts of life. For neither markets nor governments are, or can ever be perfect. Indeed markets are invariably imperfect and governments are without exception fallible. Markets as much as governments are human institutions, which need correctives. Their failures are seldom absolute and a reasonable degree of correction is possible in either case. It is obviously important to learn from experience but it is just as important to avoid over-reaction in learning from, and correcting for, mistakes. Striking the right balance is critical for an economy. It is possible only if our rethinking recognises that the State and the market are complements rather than substitutes, and that cooperation rather than conflict should define the relationship between these two institutions. Such a premise would ensure that the State and the market provide effective checks and balances vis-à-vis each other to introduce correctives whenever necessary ensuring that neither institution acquires a dominance which can only turn out to be counterproductive for the economy.

Economic History and Development Experience

Economic theory provides an essential starting point. But an understanding of the economic role of the State also needs to draw upon economic history. The history of capitalism among the early industrialisers during the 19th century and the more recent experience of the late industrialisers during the second half of the 20th century, which continues in the early 21st century, suggest valuable lessons.

Economic historians tracing the evolutionary course of the market under early capitalism repeatedly noted that the market could become the organising principle of capitalism only when it was embedded in the regulatory mechanism of the nation state. The very extension of the scope of the free market necessitated, at each stage, the imposition of new regulations by the State to ensure the further growth of the market (Polyani 1944). Thus, any characterisation of the State and the market in opposition to one another is a misreading of history. Instead, it is more useful to think of the relationship as being governed by an adaptive principle in which neither the State nor the market become destructively dominant to cripple the other institution.

An important illustration of the economic role of the State in the early stages of development, among latecomers to industrialisation, is provided by the protection of infant industries through import tariffs or other means. The government protects domestic entrepreneurs or firms in the private sector from international competition in the domestic market, without which its potential comparative advantage in manufacturing might never be realised. Thus, the State and the market complement one another. Of course, if the objective is to be realised, after a time, the State must progressively withdraw the protection, undergoing an adaptive change in its role, so that infant industries grow up and ultimately become competitive in the world market. Studies in economic history reveal that no country has succeeded at industrialisation as a latecomer without a sustained period of protection for its infant industries in the manufacturing sector (Chang 2002 and Reinert 2007).

The story about a proactive economic role of the State begins with Britain that pioneered industrialisation under capitalism (Nayyar

2013). Its military success overseas and its mercantilist dominance during the era from 1688 to 1780 played a vital role. The extension of empire, later in the 19th century, which provided markets for manufactures and sources of raw materials overseas, was driven by this mercantilist urge to use power in order to secure plenty (Findlay and O'Rourke 2007). Hence the origins of the Industrial Revolution were closely connected with the state-driven international trade and overseas expansion in the preceding era. But that was not all. In 18th century Britain, before the Industrial Revolution, the State provided patronage for science and technology and helped to promote the mining and adoption of coal. Most important, perhaps, trade policies that protected domestic industry performed a critical role (Bairoch 1993 and Chang 2002).

In countries such as France, Germany and the United States that were latecomers following in the footsteps in Britain, the process of industrialisation was also supported by State intervention through tariff protection and industrial policies. It is no surprise that the origins of the infant industry argument were in the United States (Alexander Hamilton in 1791) and in Germany (Friedrich List in 1841). During the period 1870-1913, much after their industrialisation began average tariff levels were in the range of 15-20 per cent in France, 10-15 per cent in Germany, and 40-50 per cent in the United States (Bairoch 1993).

The story was similar in Japan that was the last among these early industrialisers. The development of industrial capitalism in Japan,which began after the Meiji Restoration in 1868, and gathered momentum after the Second World War in 1945, followed a similar path. State action that ranged from creating initial conditions, through establishing economic institutions, to using trade policies that protected domestic industry, and providing patronage for science and technology, performed a critical leading role in the process (Johnson 1982).

It would seem that industrial protection and state intervention provided the essential foundations in the now industrialised countries at earlier stages of their development. The storyline is similar for countries in the developing world that were latecomers to industrialisation during the second half of the 20th century.

Four small East Asian countries—Hong Kong, Singapore, South Korea and Taiwan, of which two are city-states without rural hinterlands—are portrayed by orthodox economics as role models of markets and openness. But, except for Hong Kong, their characterisation as success stories of economies that approximated to free trade and laissez-faire is partial, if not caricature, history. For one, their export-orientation was not the equivalent of free trade. For another, their development was more about the visible hand of the State than the invisible hand of the market, particularly in South Korea and Taiwan but perhaps even in Singapore (Amsden 1989, Wade 1990 and Chang 1996).

In a longer time horizon, however, the industrialisation experience of the developing world extends much beyond this narrow focus, even if success was concentrated in Asia, limited in Latin America and absent in Africa. During six decades, 1950-2010, there was a significant catch up in terms of output, manufacturing and trade, but this was concentrated among a few countries: Argentina, Brazil, Chile and Mexico in Latin America; China, India, Indonesia, Malaysia, South Korea, Taiwan, Thailand and Turkey in Asia; and Egypt and South Africa in Africa (Nayyar 2013). In fact, the economic significance of these countries, termed the Next-14, in the developing world was overwhelming in terms of their size, reflected in GDP (gross domestic product) and population, their engagement with the world economy, reflected in trade, investment and migration, and industrialisation, reflected in manufactured exports and industrial production.

There was enormous diversity among, and significant differences between, countries in the Next-14. Yet,there are possible clusters in terms of development models, which range from a strong reliance on markets and openness (Argentina, Chile, Mexico, South Africa, Malaysia, Thailand and Indonesia), through state support with moderated openness (Brazil, Egypt and Turkey), or strategic intervention and calibrated openness (South Korea and Taiwan), to state intervention and controlled openness (China and India). The differences are more than nuances. Moderated openness was largely open economies with few restrictions in some spheres. Calibrated openness was asymmetries in openness by design manifest in strategic trade policy that was open for the export sector but restrictive for other sectors, with limits on openness to foreign capital and tight curbs on foreign brand names. Controlled openness was much more extensive not only in trade but also with respect to foreign investment and foreign technology.

Even so, the Next-14 had much in common in terms of factors that put them on the path to sustained industrialisation. It is possible to identify three such factors: initial conditions, enabling institutions and supportive governments (Nayyar 2013).

There were two aspects of initial conditions. The first was the existence of a physical infrastructure. The second was the spread of education in society, where primary education provided the base and higher education provided the edge. In both, a critical minimum was necessary to kick-start industrialisation and development.

The framework of enabling institutions was put in place by proactive governments. It was all about industrial promotion and industrial investment whether through the use of industrial, trade and technology policies or through the establishment of planning offices, industrial boards, financial institutions and development banks. The object was to create production, investment and innovation capabilities in domestic firms with countries opting for different emphases on the public and the private sector.

The observed outcomes were attributable, in important part, to development strategies and economic policies in the post-colonial era that laid the essential foundations in countries that were latecomers to industrialisation. It is clear that the role of the State in evolving policies, creating institutions and making strategic interventions, whether as a catalyst or a leader, was also central to the process (Stiglitz 1989, Shapiro and Taylor 1990 and Bhaduri and Nayyar 1996). Thus, industrialisation was not so much about getting-prices-right as it was about getting-state-intervention-right. Supportive governments were, in fact, a key factor underlying success (Evans 1995, Wade 1990, Chang and Rowthorn 1995, Lall 1997 and Nayyar

2013). This was even more so in the Next-14, although there were differences in the nature and purpose of their role (Amsden 2001 and Nayyar 2013). For countries that stressed markets and openness, it was about minimising market failure. The emphasis was on getting-prices-right and buying the skills or technologies needed for industrialisation. For countries that stressed State intervention with moderated, calibrated or controlled openness, it was about minimising government failure. The emphasis was on getting-state-intervention-right and building the skills or technologies needed for industrialisation. Of course, this role was not defined once-and-for-all but evolved with development (Nayyar 1997).

Economic Development and the State in India

The second half of the 20th century witnessed a complete swing of the pendulum in thinking about the role of State in the process of development. This swing was perhaps more pronounced in India, as compared with elsewhere, with the possible exception of the centrally planned economies in Eastern Europe and the former USSR. It would seem that we moved from a widespread belief, prevalent in the 1950s, that the State could do nothing wrong, to a strong conviction, fashionable in the 1990s, that the State could do nothing right. These are, of course, caricatures of perceptions, even if the reality is more nuanced or complex, but it does reflect disillusionment with the role of the State. The dramatic change in thinking was attributable to past experience (inappropriate or excessive intervention) and the conjuncture in time (collapse of communism), reinforced by the dominant political ideology of the times (markets and capitalism). This ideology is now subject to question almost everywhere, in the wake of the market-driven financial crisis and persistent recession in the world economy. It is no longer dominant in the world outside. In India, however, the belief in markets remains strong among the literati and the influential, partly because of rapid economic growth and partly because of little faith in governments. Even if the limitations or failures of markets are recognised, concerns about inept or corrupt governments are larger than life.

In India, as in Eastern Europe, our perceptions have been strongly influenced by the counterproductive role of State intervention in the past. This has led to over-reaction, or over-correction, in a quest for minimum government. Consequently, the possibilities of a creative interaction between the State and the market are simply not recognised. It is forgotten that the *neta-babu-raj* has remained the same. This *raj* is no less at corrupting market forces than it was at corrupting government intervention. We would do well to remember that a government that fails in intervention is also bound to fail in liberalisation. For the same reason, a State that cannot provide governance or run enterprises cannot regulate, let alone guide or govern, markets. Indeed, efficient markets need effective governments.

More-of-the-same or business-as-usual is obviously neither acceptable nor desirable. In India, it is time to rethink and redefine the role of the State in a market economy in a very different national context, 70 years after independence, and a profoundly changed international context. Such rethinking can be set out in terms of two simple propositions (Bhaduri and Nayyar 1996). First, the State and the market are, by and large, not substitutes; instead they must complement one another in many spheres. Second, the relationship between the State and the market cannot be specified once-and-for-all in any dogmatic manner; instead the two institutions must adapt to one another through cooperation, rather than conflict, as the economy develops. Given that the entrepreneurial talents of the private sector and the capabilities of the government sector, as also the needs of the economy, change over time, this relationship must be flexible and adaptive. In such a milieu, the State and the market can provide mutual checks-and-balances that function as institutionalised self-correcting mechanisms when things go wrong. Indeed, the history of capitalism suggests that success at economic development is observed mostly in countries where governments and markets complement one another and adapt to one another as circumstances and times change.

In the earlier stages of industrialisation, State intervention alone can create the initial conditions for the development of industrial capitalism, by building a physical infrastructure with government investment in energy, transport and communication, and by developing human resources through education. These tasks remain unfinished in India although it is almost seven decades since independence. Clearly, the State must not only continue to perform this role in the economy but also do so much better than it has so far.

In the later stages of industrialisation, both the degree and nature of State intervention in the economy must change to incorporate functional, institutional and strategic roles (Nayyar 1997). Functional intervention is necessary to correct for market failures, both specific and general, as economic decisions are shaped more and more by the market. Institutional intervention is needed to govern the market by setting rules of the game for players in the market, to create frameworks for regulating markets and establish institutions to monitor the functioning of markets, since a market economy requires rules of the game to ensure a level playing field and to pre-empt a free-for-all. Strategic intervention is desirable to guide the market, inter-linked across activities or sectors, to attain broader long-term objectives of development. The pursuit of industrialisation, for example, might not only require a strategic coordination of industrial, trade, and technology policy but also need a strategic use of exchange rates and interest rates. Such interventions have been a crucial factor underlying efficiency and dynamism in the later stages of industrialisation for countries that are success stories in development. The time has come to redefine the economic role of the State in India.

Seventy years later, so much has changed. Market forces matter much more both in the national economy and the world economy. Rethinking on the necessary and desirable role of government must recognise these changed realities. At this juncture, therefore, it is essential to reformulate the questions about the State and the economy. The real question is no longer about the size of the State (how big?) or the degree of State intervention (how much?). The question now is about the nature of State intervention (what sort?) and the quality of the performance of the State (how good?). Those who emphasise the costs of State intervention in the past must also recognise the costs of State inaction in the present and its implications for the future of India's economic development.

At India's present stage of development, the government must continue, and not abandon, its efforts to develop the physical infrastructure, just as it must strengthen, and not dilute, its role in creating a social infrastructure. This is absolutely essential if the economic priorities of the people are to coincide with the development objectives of the nation. At the same time, the government must endeavour to change the nature and the quality of its intervention in the market, consciously differentiating between the functional, the institutional and the strategic aspects. Their impact will be felt over different time horizons. But the government simply cannot afford to abdicate its role in the belief that markets know best and can do everything.

The respective roles of the government or the public sector and the market or the private sector are bound to change over time at different stages of development. Even so, at every stage, there are many things that only markets can and should do. These are best left to markets and the private sector. However, at every stage, there are other things that only governments can and must do. If governments perform these tasks badly, it is not possible to dispense with governments and replace them with markets. Government must be made to perform better. This is easier said than done. Yet, it is feasible, for the government is accountable to people. In India's vibrant democracy, there is a growing political consciousness among citizens. The accountability of governments to their people is clearly visible at election time. Performance is rewarded when incumbent governments are re-elected. Non-performance is penalised when incumbent governments are kicked out. Even if democracy works slowly—and with time lags—the implicit incentives and disincentives for political leaders and political parties do provide checks and balances.

It is clear that, in India, the role of the State in the process of development will continue to be important for some time to come, even as the scope of the market expands through liberalisation in the wider context of globalisation. Most would find this argument persuasive. Yet, many would doubt whether such a redefined economic role for the government is feasible in terms of politics. The willingness and ability of the government to perform such a role depends on the nature of the State, which in turn is shaped by the underlying politics. If we look at the world around us, it is obvious that State in India is not made up of Plato's guardians, so that an idealistic view of the State is not sustainable. However, the nature of the State in India is roughly what one might expect in an economy, polity and society characterised by diverse inequalities, so that a fatalistic view of the State is also not sustainable. In fact, the strength and resilience of political democracy, despite its weaknesses, suggests a realistic view of the State, in which there is a growing consciousness of citizens about their rights and an increasing empowerment of people as voters demanding account ability from governments. There is, then, reason for hope rather than despair.

References

Amsden, Alice H. (1989). *Asia's Next Giant: South Korea and Late Industrialization.* New York: Oxford University Press.

———. (2001). *The Rise of the Rest: Challenges to the West from Late Industrializing Economies.* New York: Oxford University Press.

Amsden, Alice H., Jacek Kochanowicz and Lance Taylor (Eds.) (1994). *The Market Meets its Match: Restructuring the Economies of Eastern Europe.* Cambridge, Mass: Harvard University Press.

Bairoch, Paul (1993). *Economics and World History: Myths and Paradoxes.* Chicago: Chicago University Press.

Bhaduri, Amit and Deepak Nayyar (1996). *The Intelligent Person's Guide to Liberalization.* New Delhi: Penguin Books.

Chang, Ha-Joon (1996). *The Political Economy of Industrial Policy.* London: Macmillan.

———. (2002). *Kicking Away the Ladder: Development Strategy in Historical Perspective.* London: Anthem Press.

Chang, Ha-Joon and Robert Rowthorn (Eds.) (1995). *The Role of the State in Economic Change.* Oxford: Clarendon Press.

Easterly, William (2001). *The Elusive Quest for Growth.* Cambridge, Mass: The MIT Press.

Evans, Peter (1995). *Embedded Autonomy: States and Industrial Transformation.* Princeton: Princeton University Press.

Findlay, Ronald and Kevin H. O'Rourke (2007). *Power and Plenty: Trade, War and the World Economy in the Second Millennium.* Princeton: Princeton University Press.

Helleiner, Gerald K. (ed.) (1992). *Trade Policy, Industrialization and Development.* Oxford: Clarendon Press.

Johnson, Chalmers (1982). *MITI and the Japanese Miracle: The Growth of Industrial Policy, 1925-1975.* Stanford: Stanford University Press.

Lall, Sanjaya (1997). "Imperfect Markets and Fallible Governments: The Role of the State in Industrial Development", in Deepak Nayyar (ed.), *Trade and Industrialization*. Delhi: Oxford University Press.

Nayyar, Deepak (1997). "Themes in Trade and Industrialization", in Deepak Nayyar (ed.), *Trade and Industrialization*. Delhi: Oxford University Press.

———. (2008). "Learning to Unlearn from Development", *Oxford Development Studies* 36: 259-80.

———. (2011). "The Financial Crisis, the Great Recession and the Developing World", *Global Policy* 2: 20-32.

———. (2013). *Catch Up: Developing Countries in the World Economy*. Oxford: Oxford University Press.

Polanyi, Karl (1944). *The Great Transformation: The Political and Economic Origins of Our Times*. Boston: Beacon Press.

Reinert, Erik S. (2007). *How Rich Countries Got Rich and Why Poor Countries Stay Poor*. New York: Carroll and Graf.

Rodrik, Dani (2005). "Rethinking Growth Strategies", *WIDER Annual Lecture* 8. Helsinki: UNU-WIDER.

Shapiro, Helen and Lance Taylor (1990). "The State and Industrial Strategy", *World Development* 18: 861-78.

Stiglitz, Joseph E. (1989). "On the Economic Role of the State", in A. Heertje (ed.), *The Economic Role of the State*. Oxford: Basil Blackwell.

———. (1998). "More Instruments and Broader Goals: Moving Toward the Post-Washington Consensus", *WIDER Annual Lecture* 2, Helsinki: UNU-WIDER.

Taylor, Lance (2007). "Development Questions for 25 Years", in G. Mavrotas and A. Shorrocks (eds.), *Advancing Development: Core Themes in Global Economics*. London: Palgrave.

Wade, Robert (1990). *Governing the Market: Economic Theory and the Role of Government in East Asian Industrialization*. Princeton: Princeton University Press.

2

Y.V. REDDY[1]

Planning and Finance Commissions

It is a great privilege to be invited to contribute to a volume in honour of Mr Abid Hussain. Fifty years ago, I was trained by him for one year at the beginning of my career in the Indian Administrative Service (IAS), when he was Collector and District Magistrate, Vishakapatnam. He initiated me to the science and art of administration with development orientation. He has the rare distinction of being remembered even now in Vishakapatnam by the people with great admiration and affection. He had a dream for Vishakapatnam as a future city, and he shared it as a vision with the people of the district, which in some ways propelled them to move in that direction. When I was Sub-Collector, Gudur, Nellore District, in 1968, Abid *saab* brought a team from Delhi to select Sriharikota for our space programme. Now, it is on the global map. His outstanding contributions to the cause of development encompass multiple levels and are multi-faceted, covering not only public institutions, but private sector and civil society. His commitment to the cause of development and upliftment of the under-privileged was evident from early in his career when he excelled in administering community development programme.

I interacted with Abid *saab* closely on planning and development issues when he was a Member of the Planning Commission in New Delhi, and I was Secretary in Planning and Finance Department of Government of Andhra Pradesh. This presentation on the rise, fall and rebirth of Planning Commission in a new avatar in the context of 14th Finance Commission's recommendations would have prompted him to pull out his pocket book that he always carried with him and

1. Dr Reddy is grateful to Professor M. Govinda Rao and to Professor Pinaki Chakraborty for their valuable comments on an earlier draft.

to start taking notes. This paper in honour of Abid *saab* examines the Planning Commission's roles and functions, the origin of NITI Aayog and the overlapping between the functioning of Planning and Finance Commissions. The paper would also analyse the implications of some of the recommendations of the 14th Finance Commission made on December 15, 2014 on the functioning of NITI Aayog, constituted on January 1, 2015 in place of the erstwhile Planning Commission.

The paper has five sections. In the first section, the origin, structure, functions, evolution and demise of Planning Commission in India, will be briefly recalled. The second section traces the origin of NITI Aayog, outlines its context and structure, and explores the similarities and differences with its previous avatar, Planning Commission. In the third section, the origin, functions and evolution of the Finance Commissions are presented. The fourth section focuses on the functional overlap between the Planning and the Finance Commissions. In particular, the recommendations of the 14th Finance Commission insofar as they impinge on the functions relevant to erstwhile Planning Commission are explained in detail. The concluding section suggests a way forward for the new avatar of the Planning Commission, viz., NITI Aayog to optimise the benefits from the dispensations of the 14th Finance Commission.

Planning Commission

Prompted by the commitment of Prime Minister Jawaharlal Nehru, Government's intention of constituting a Planning Commission was announced in the Finance Minister's budget speech in February 1950. The Commission was established on 15 March 1950 through a Cabinet resolution. While there was a virtual consensus on the idea of planning in India, there was significant opposition to the establishment of Planning Commission, even from within the Cabinet. The then Finance Minister resigned stating that his objection was not merely to the idea of Planning Commission, but also to the method of its working. Following the Finance Minister's resignation, a number of Ministers expressed their opposition to the Commission. Sardar Patel also wrote to Pandit Nehru expressing the disapproval of the Commission's actions. Although there was general consensus in favour of planning as an approach for reconstruction and development of the economy, there was disagreement about the need for an institution like the Planning Commission. There were serious concerns about the role of the Planning Commission in governance.

The Prime Minister has always been ex-officio Chairman of the Planning Commission with a Deputy Chairman in the rank of a full Cabinet Minister nominated by the Prime Minister. Some select Cabinet Ministers acted as ex-officio Members of the Commission. The full time Members nominated by the Prime Minister were subject experts. Thus, the membership of the Planning Commission was virtually co-terminus with that of the Prime Minister. It is very clear that the Planning Commission has been a body of the Union Government and its composition coincided with the political cycles.

The National Development Council (NDC) was established in 1952, also by a resolution of the Cabinet on the basis of a recommendation in the draft outline of the First Five Year Plan. It was composed of the Deputy Chairman and Members of the Commission, the Cabinet Ministers of the Union government and Chief Ministers of all the states and representatives of Union territories and is Chaired by the Prime Minister. As the number of Members exceeded 50, a Standing Committee was established in November 1954 with only 9 Chief Ministers and fewer Union Ministers to improve its effectiveness. The functions of the NDC relate to formulation of the national Plan, reviewing the work of the Plan and considering important questions of social and economic policy affecting the national development. In a way, therefore, the Planning Commission was to be guided by the NDC, but convening of the NDC, its remit and its effectiveness was largely determined by the Prime Minister.

The broad functions of the Planning Commission in practice remained the same since its inception. These were: (a) formulation of medium to long-term plans; (b) advising on the allocation of funds to Ministries in the Union Government through the annual budget; (c) approval of the Plan of each State and allocation of transfers of funds from Union to States, both untied and tied to activities or schemes under Plan; (d) monitoring, evaluation, etc., incidental to Planning;

and (e) assisting the NDC on these matters. While the Five Year Plan had a medium term outlook and strategy, annual Plans focused on the allocation of funds. Planning Commission virtually determined the distribution of Plan funds between the Union Government and the States, and among the States. Plan outlays were generally equated with public investments and capital outlays of budgets. The Annual Plans of the Union were operationalised mainly through the Plan components of the budget.

Planning Commission persuaded the States to establish Planning Boards at the State level. The experience with the State level Planning Boards has been varied both across States and over time. However, they have generally been less central to the process of policy than Planning Commission was at the national level. Annual Plan was expected to be prepared by States within the framework of the Five Year Plan, and the annual Plans of States had to be approved by Planning Commission and operationalised through Plan components of their respective budgets.

A notable function of the Planning Commission that contributed to its importance was dispensing Plan assistance to the States. The matter became clear when the Government of India accepted the note of dissent of the Member-Secretary of the Third Finance Commission that it should confine itself only to the non-Plan revenue expenditure requirements of the States. From the Fourth Finance Commission, the Terms of Reference in the Presidential Order appointing the Commission itself excluded the consideration of the Plan requirements of the States by the Finance Commissions and the Planning Commission became an important parallel channel of transfers. Initially the Plan assistance—its volume as well as grant-loan components to the states was decided on the basis of the projects approved. In 1969 a formula for distribution of central assistance to State plans was adopted by the NDC (called the Gadgil formula after the then Deputy Chairman of the Planning Commission, Dr D.R. Gadgil). According to the formula, the special category states were to receive 90 per cent of the assistance by way of grants and remaining 10 per cent as loans whereas the pattern of assistance to non-special category States was 30 per cent grants and

70 per cent loans. The distribution among the States inter se was done with predominant weight assigned to population, and weights assigned to factors such as backwardness, fiscal performance and special problems faced by the states. Often, when some of the states complained about the adverse impact on them of the norms adopted by the Finance Commission, the Planning Commission stepped in to give some additional assistance to meet their non-Plan revenue expenditure requirements of the States as well.

In the initial years, particularly 1960s, and to some extent 1970s, the State Governments had the benefit of understanding the planning techniques and the associated processes from Planning Commission. Thus, Planning Commission exercised soft power over States, and States also viewed Planning Commission often as a body representing their interests in the Union Government. From 1970s, perceptions started changing as States started feeling that Planning Commission was becoming a political instrument of the party in power in Union Government. The State governments also felt more confident about their capacity to do their own planning. Further, the meetings of the NDC became less frequent, and functioned less as a discussion forum and more of what may be called a posture forum. In recent years, the State Governments expressed resentment about the role of Planning Commission in transfer of funds from the Union Government to the State Governments outside the awards of the Finance Commissions, in particular, through several Centrally Sponsored Schemes (CSS). They also expressed discomfort with the process of approval of State Plans by the Planning Commission.

There was also a perception among analysts that the Planning Commission was encouraging fiscal profligacy in both Union and State Governments through the advocacy of new investments, Plans and schemes, and ever increasing Plan size. There was also a perception that non-Plan expenditure, in particular relating to general services such as police and judiciary were not receiving the attention they deserve. There was also considerable resentment among the Union Ministries about the growing importance of Planning Commission in public investments, including projects involving public-private partnership.

Whether Planning Commission's advice contributed to accelerated growth or not, is a matter on which there have been genuine differences of opinion. However, the actual outcomes of almost every Five Year Plan and almost every Annual Plan generally fell short of the physical targets indicated. The implementation agencies blamed the Planning Commission for wrong design, while the Planning Commission blamed implementation agencies. Both of them blamed the political leadership, which in turn pointed to the role of bureaucracy.

In 2009, the then Prime Minister Prof Manmohan Singh suggested that the Planning Commission should be reformed, but apparently no serious reform really occurred. On 15 August 2014, Prime Minister Narendra Modi announced the decision to wind up the Planning Commission.

NITI Aayog

On 1st January 2015, Government of India announced its decision to set up NITI Aayog (National Institution for Transforming India), in place of the erstwhile Planning Commission, as a means to better serve the needs and aspirations of the people of India. The origins of NITI Aayog could be traced to the disenchantment with the Planning Commission on two important fronts, viz., the perception that it was not able to capture the new realities of macro-economic management at the national level, and that it has not been conducive to sound fiscal relations between the Union and the States. The new realities of macroeconomic management that it failed to relate to were: (a) the increased role of private sector; (b) the allocation of resources being predominantly through financial markets; (c) the nature and process of development being increasingly influenced by independent regulators in a market oriented economy; (d) global factors influencing the national economy; (e) need to allow the states to formulate and implement their plans on functions assigned to them in the Constitution without having to get them 'approved' by the Planning Commission; and (f) in the overall economic management, not only the investment but institutions and incentives, playing a very important role for improving productivity.

Over the years, Planning Commission emerged as an important source of transfer of grants to the State governments for financing of Plan, which was not envisaged in the Constitution. Proliferation of CSS and their one-size fits all approach encouraged by the Planning Commission became a major concern for the States. It needs to be highlighted that over the years, the planning and implementation capabilities of the State Governments have increased. Their critical role in the process of development in terms of economic and social infrastructure has been recognised. There is greater attention paid to what have been described as Kerala model, Bihar model or Gujarat model of development, relative to the macro models considered at the national level. The States resented the increasing role of fiscal transfers at the instance of Planning Commission which in their view was undermining their fiscal space to Plan to suit their varied developmental priorities.

The official notification establishing NITI Aayog concedes that the Planning Commission has served India well, but recognises that India has changed dramatically at multiple levels and across varied scales. It identifies the biggest transformatory forces as demography, in particular, the size, the structure, the settlement pattern and the aspirations of the people. It is explained that these warrant overhauling of the nature of planning process to align with the shifts in the economy. It recognises that the States of the Union of India have evolved from being some appendages of the Centre to being the actual drivers of national development. It is made clear that the new institution will be built on (a) the foundations of an empowered role for States, (b) expertise as a think tank, and (c) becoming a collaborative platform facilitating implementation. In this regard, the role of private enterprise, the impact of globalisation and the criticality of technology are highlighted.

The functions of NITI described under the title "New Role" have been listed in considerable detail under 15 heads: Cooperative and Competitive Federalism; Shared National Agenda; State's Best Friend at the Centre; Decentralised Planning; Vision & Scenario Planning; Domain Strategies; Sounding Board; Network of Expertise; Knowledge and Innovation Hub; Harmonisation; Conflict Resolution;

Coordinating Interface with the World; Internal Consultancy; Capacity Building; and Monitoring and Evaluation. The guiding principles have been described as "Purpose" and listed as: Antyodaya, Inclusion, Village, Demographic Dividend, Peoples Participation, Governance and Sustainability.

NITI Aayog has a governing council, similar to NDC in its composition. It is chaired by the Prime Minister as in the case of Planning Commission with a Vice Chairman corresponding to Deputy Chairman of Planning Commission. A few Cabinet Ministers of Union are ex-officio members of the Commission, while full time members and part time members are appointed by the Union Government. Except for the presence of part time members and fewer full time members, the composition of NITI Aayog is similar to its predecessor.

Though the nomenclature of NITI Aayog is different, the process of setting up is similar to Planning Commission, viz., through a Cabinet Resolution based on the initiative of Prime Minister. The NDC has been replaced with a Governing Council but with a similar composition. However, NITI Aayog has an additional option of creating Regional Councils. NITI Aayog's composition and structure remain similar to Planning Commission in terms of its being co-terminus with political cycles of the Union Government. It remains essentially advisory, but in a departure from the practice of Planning Commission, may not play active role in allocation of funds to States or to Ministries.

It is different from the Planning Commission in terms of articulating the new realities, and expressing intention to change the nature of working of the organisation to capture the new realities. The articulation also emphasises that States have been co-opted as partners and will be consulted in the formulation of policies. Further, its approach goes beyond the limited sphere of the public sector and the Government of India, and it is intended be a catalyst to the developmental process.

The reorganisation of internal set-up is yet to commence and hence it is too early to draw any conclusions about how it will shape up and how the new realities as well as relations with States would be captured in the organisation. Broadly, it can be said that in some ways NITI is more than Planning Commission in terms of the scope and the canvass, but it is less than Planning Commission in terms of its role in allocation of public investments among Ministries and approval of State Plans while being as political and as advisory as the Planning Commission.

The success of NITI Aayog will depend on the manner in which new realities of economic management are captured in the processes of planning being evolved by it. It will also depend on the processes that it institutes to rebalance the fiscal relations between Union and States, mainly relating to transfers from Union and States outside the devolution recommenced by Finance Commission. In fact, it could take up the role of the institution recommended by the 14th Finance Commission in the chapter, "Towards Co-operative Federalism". In this context, NITI Aayog's success will, to some extent, depend on the manner in which it dovetails its strategies and working with that of Finance Commissions.

Finance Commission

Article 280 of the Constitution provides for the constitution of the Finance Commission consisting of a Chairman and four other Members to be appointed by the President. The Commission has to make recommendations on the distribution of net proceeds of the taxes between the Union and the States, and the inter-se allocation between the States, generally described in the literature as vertical balance and horizontal balance. In addition, it is required to recommend the principles that should govern the grant-in-aid of the revenues of the States. Further, through 73rd and 74th amendment, some jurisdiction has been given to the Union Finance Commission to recommend measures to augment the consolidated fund of the States based on the recommendation of the State Finance Commission for flow of resources to the local bodies through States. While these constitute the core Terms of Reference, the Commission was expected to consider any other matter referred to it by the President in the interest of sound finance. The Parliament enacted legislation in 1951, specifying the procedure by which the Commission may be appointed.

In brief, the Finance Commission is a Constitutional body. It is expected to be apolitical. It has to be constituted at least every five years, though making it a continuous body is not ruled out under the law. Its core mandate is restricted to: (a) division of tax proceeds between the Union and among the States, (b) providing grants-in-aid to the States in need of assistance, and (c) transfer of resources from the Union to the local bodies through the States. The recommendations of the Finance Commission insofar as the core mandate is concerned, have been accepted and treated as an award. However, in regard to recommendations made outside the core mandate in the interest of 'sound finance' in deference to the Terms of Reference, a few have been accepted and acted upon by the Union and State Governments.

The Constitution did not specifically envisage transfer of funds by Union Government to the State Governments at its discretion outside the recommendations of the Finance Commissions. However, a provision in the Constitution enables the Union to transfer funds to the States, and the States also to transfer funds to the Union under Article 282 ".....for any public purpose, notwithstanding that the purpose is not one with respect to which the Parliament or the Legislature of the State, as the case may be may make laws." The Union Government could thus justify transfer of funds to the States outside the recommendations of the Finance Commission. Such transfers have been taking place mainly through the advice of the Planning Commission.

There have been five major developments in the functioning of the Finance Commissions in relation to Planning Commission till the 14th Finance Commission. The first and foremost relates to the narrowing of the remit of the Finance Commission restricting to non-Plan revenue expenditure of the States for the purpose of vertical devolution from the Union government as Plan expenditure was largely determined by the Plan size determined by the Planning Commission. Second, the system of sharing of taxes was rationalised by discontinuing the practice of tax specific sharing (of Income Tax and Union Excise Duties) by replacing it with a specific percentage from the total tax pool of the Union government based on the recommendations of the 10th Finance Commission described as the divisible pool of taxes. Third, the Government of India accepted the recommendations of the 12th Finance Commission and discontinued the practice of borrowing from the market and lending it to the State Governments. Fourth, sound fiscal management of the States was insisted upon by Finance Commissions, through implementation of fiscal responsibility legislation at the State level through structured schemes of incentives. In other words, in order to ensure fiscal prudence certain transfers were linked to conditions like enactment of state level fiscal responsibility legislation. It is interesting that while the Planning Commission has generally been criticised for encouraging fiscal profligacy of States by partnering with States for higher Plan-outlays, the Finance Commissions have been using the instrumentality of formula for devolution or grants-in-aid, in the opposite direction. Finally, conditionality governing grants-in-aid to States was extended to policies relating to adoption of a tax regime, viz., Goods and Services Tax (GST), and legislations relating to local bodies. In other words, in the recent past, Finance Commission could have become an instrument of what may be termed as reform policies of Union by prescribing related conditionalities for purposes of grants-in-aid to States, partly on account of additional Terms of Reference.

Overlaps

Recognising that there is some overlap between the work of the Planning Commission and that of Finance Commission, it became customary to appoint a Member of the Planning Commission as a part time Member of the Finance Commission from the 6th Finance Commission onwards. This was expected to enable the Finance Commission to take into account the considerations that govern the transfers from the Union to States on account of Plan. A suggestion to synchronise the time horizon of Planning Commission and Finance Commission to ensure coordination was not implemented.

The Planning Commission advises the Union Government and, to some extent, State Governments in regard to several matters of relevance to federal fiscal relations. The most significant of such advice relates to the transfers affected by the Union Government to the States on the advice of the Planning Commission. These transfers are outside the transfers that take place on account of the recommendations of the Finance Commission. Such transfers could be untied in terms of Central assistance to State Plans, or tied to specific activities or schemes, including CSS. In addition, direct transfers to entities within the State were also taking place for implementation of some schemes and this mode of transfer became the principal component of grants transfers to the States through various flagship CSS. This practice has been given up from 2014-15.

The issue of overlap with the Finance Commission arises entirely in the context of fiscal transfers from the Union to the States. At one stage, a view was taken that all transfers, barring under exceptional circumstances, should take place only on the basis of the recommendations of the Finance Commission. However, as mentioned, the remit of the Finance Commission over a period was restricted to the consideration of non-Plan revenue expenditure requirements of the States, though some grants-in-aid were also recommended for capital works. While the major element of the recommendations of the Finance Commission relates to divisible pool of taxes, some grants-in-aid were recommended for capital works and on specified developmental activities. This, in a way, resulted in the overlap. In the recent past, some transfers on account of grants-in-aid on the basis of the recommendations of the Finance Commission were also treated as Plan schemes. Further, as already mentioned in recent years, the Finance Commissions have also been incorporating considerations relating to policies of the Union Government in their awards, especially grants-in-aid.

It is also note-worthy that recently Finance Commissions took cognizance of categorisation of States as special category in giving award. The categorisation of States as Special Category by Union Government was at the initiative of Planning Commission. Finance Commission was also required to take into account the population of 1971 for purposes of assessing the needs the States in order to reward the States following the practice of Family Planning. The Terms of Reference of Finance Commission, especially the 'non-core' ones often related to areas that were relevant but not central to fiscal relations of Union and States.

As mentioned, a major concern of the States in regard to this overlap was that the increasing share of the transfers from the Union to the States at the instance of the Planning Commission was increasing beyond what was envisaged in the Constitution. In their view, the Planning Commission undermined the role of the Finance Commission and enabled encroachment of legitimate fiscal space of the States by the Union. Some of the States felt that in a way Finance Commissions enabled such transfers by allowing needed excess fiscal space to the Union in their recommendations. At the same time, Finance Commissions were often required to consider non-core items of Union-State fiscal relations with an overlap with the development strategies and policies which were in the legitimate domain of Planning Commission. In brief, both the magnitudes and the nature of transfers from the Union to States in general, and those outside the recommendations of the Finance Commissions on the basis of the recommendation of the Planning Commission in particular, were a subject of major national concern by the time the 14th Finance Commission was appointed.

The 14th Finance Commission took cognizance of concerns relating to Union-State fiscal relations gathered from its interactions with Ministries in the Union, States, political parties and intellectuals. Accordingly, a comprehensive view of Union-State fiscal relations was taken, recognising that there are three channels of fiscal transfers. The first one relates to tax devolution as a share of divisible pool of taxes, which is in the nature of entitlement of the Union and States based on assessment of their resources and needs by the Finance Commission. The second relates to grants-in-aid in the recommendations of Finance Commission, which are in the nature of transfer of funds from Union to States, unlike devolution which is sharing of funds. The third channel is transfer of resources by Union to States outside the award of Finance Commission, essentially by the Union Government on the advice of Planning Commission. Consideration of the contours of the third channel of transfers by the 14th Finance Commission was considered essential for taking a comprehensive view of fiscal relations in making its recommendations mainly on core mandate.

In the Terms of Reference of the 14th Finance Commission, there was no reference to Plan, unlike some of the earlier Commissions. Similarly, unlike some of the Commissions, there was no reference to gross budgetary support to Plan. In a way, this opened the door to the 14th Finance Commission to assess the resources and needs of the States without reference to the distinction between Plan and non-Plan. However, it restricted its consideration to the revenue expenditures only taking the non-Plan expenditure and states' own expenditure under Plan including its matching contribution to various CSS. The Commission was encouraged to adopt this approach in view of the recommendations of an Expert Committee that the distinction between Plan and non-Plan should be dispensed with. The 14th Finance Commission considered all revenue expenditures without reference to a distinction between Plan and non-Plan, leaving the matter of maintaining or not maintaining such distinction to be decided by the Union or the States concerned.

Recognising that the Finance Commissions cannot totally ignore the transfers from the Union to the States outside of Plan account, the 12th and 13th Finance Commissions had suggested an indicative ceiling on overall transfers from the Union to the States. However, the 14th Finance Commission took a view that prescription of such a ceiling was ineffective, but suggested that the Union should consider meeting the expectations of the State Governments that aggregate transfers from the Union to the States out of its total revenues would remain at the same level.

The 14th Finance Commission projected the implicit capital outlay of the Union and the State Governments consistent with the fiscal sustainability. In other words, the five year projections did not make a distinction between Plan and non-Plan, and viewed both revenue and capital expenditures of the Union and the States while recognising a legitimate role for transfer from Union to States outside the Finance Commission. A comprehensive view of fiscal position of Union and States over the five year period was provided.

The 14th Finance Commission did not take cognizance of the categorisation of States into special category, and others on the ground that such categorisation by the Commission is not warranted by the Constitution. Further, it was felt that any categorisation of States by the Finance Commission would have to be by the criteria on revenue and cost disabilities and needs of the States that it develops, and not by automatic adoption of categorisation by Union Government.

The grants-in-aid recommended by the 14th Finance Commission were restricted to revenue-deficit, local bodies and disaster management, strictly warranted by the terms of reference with direct impact on Union-State fiscal relations. This approach was consistent with the view that Finance Commission should avoid duplicating the schemes under implementation by Union Government, especially as CSS. Consequently, the State-specific and sector specific grants-in-aid were not considered.

There were suggestions that the Finance Commission could be made a permanent body and that the working of the Planning Commission should also be entrusted to the Finance Commission. The 14th Finance Commission expressed itself against such a suggestion. However, it suggested that the transfers from the Union to the States outside the recommendations of the Finance Commission should be through a new institutional arrangement that should involve Union, States and domain expertise, ideally under the aegis of inter-state Council. In a way, therefore, the importance of involvement of the States in designing the transfers from the Union to the States outside the Finance Commission was emphasised. There is, thus, a convergence between this approach of the Finance Commission and the objectives of NITI Aayog.

Way Forward

It is clear that NITI Aayog is a replacement of the Planning Commission and, in many ways, a new Avatar basically addressing the observed weaknesses in the functioning of the Planning Commission. The Union-State relations is one aspect, though the most important aspect of the weaknesses, that are sought to be addressed by NITI

Aayog. The recommendations of the 14th Finance Commission do provide an enabling environment for a new approach to Union-State relations in the functioning of NITI Aayog. A full recognition of the far reaching implications of the recommendations of the 14th Finance Commission will help NITI Aayog to design its evolving approach in order to optimise the benefits from the rebirth of Planning Commission as NITI Aayog.

Firstly, the 14th Finance Commission has provided an operational framework to dispense with the distinction between Plan and non-Plan. This should enable NITI Aayog to take a comprehensive and in-depth view of the strategies and policies of each sector in general and public investments in each sector in particular. In a way, therefore, its remit can be expanded and depth increased, where appropriate and desired. The removal of a distinction should also enable reversal of the neglect of non-Plan activities like maintenance and 'general services' often described as non-developmental expenditure and also maintenance of existing public assets created under the Plan.

Secondly, the indicative ceiling on transfers outside the Finance Commission has been removed. At the same time, the rationale for such transfers has been clearly indicated in terms of externalities, minimum standards of services across the country, and inter-state infrastructure in select States. In some ways, the legitimacy and the rationale for transfers through a body such as NITI Aayog has been established by the Finance Commission—a Constitutional body. In this regard, NITI Aayog may consider the experience of mechanisms of fiscal transfers in other federations since almost all of them deal with fiscal transfers as distinct from sharing of divisible pool of taxes which is the remit of Finance Commission.

Thirdly, a new institutional mechanism has been proposed for transfers outside the recommendations of Finance Commission in the interest of sound fiscal federalism. NITI Aayog could take advantage of the underlying logic of such institutional mechanisms and devise its work methods consistent with the spirit of the recommendations. The sectors and activities for which Union transfers to States should take place, the design of such schemes and the distribution of resources among the States will have to be worked out in a forum that has representation of the Union, the States and the domain expertise.

Fourthly, the 14th Finance Commission has eschewed prescribing conditionalities or policies that are considered desirable at a national level. Some of the overlap between the Finance Commission and the Planning Commission has been addressed by the Finance Commission by relinquishing most of the State specific or project specific grants-in-aid and associated conditionalities, in its recommendations. For example, incentives or disincentives or rewards to States for appropriate policies have been left out of the Finance Commission's considerations and, thus, legitimately fall under NITI Aayog. By relinquishing its marginal role as promoter of economic reforms periodically, the Finance Commission has put additional responsibility on NITI Aayog to promote appropriate policies and schemes both in the Union and among States on a continuous basis.

Fifthly, successive Finance Commissions have recognised the fact that budgetary situation of the Union government had direct bearing on state finances, but could not impose any conditions for reform of finances of the Union government nor could evolve a system under which the Union government adhered to its commitment to fiscal responsibility. In the current federal fiscal structure of India, revenue account transfers from the Union to the States constitute more than one-third of the total revenue resources of the States, and hence if Union's revenue performance declines, states also get affected. The creation of incentive fund suggested by the 11th Finance Commission, the conditional transfers and debt relief linked to fiscal responsibilities of States by the 12th Finance Commission and, incentive grants recommended by 13th Finance Commission were instrumental in bringing about prudent management of State finances. Currently, challenges relate to Union finances. The 14th Finance Commission emphasised the importance of establishing fiscal councils with a mandate to make ex-ante assessment of budget proposals. A weak fiscal position of the Union not only has bearing on macroeconomic management and stability, but also impacts State finances. NITI Aayog has an opportunity and, indeed, an obligation to contribute to fiscal responsibility in both Union and State Governments consistent with developmental priorities and sound fiscal-federal relations. NITI Aayog is in a better position to contribute to these objectives since it is a continuing body and plays a critical, though advisory, role in regard to Union finances, State finances and transfers from Union to States on a continuous basis.

Sixthly, the Finance Commission has eschewed categorisation of States, but this does not, in any way, restrict freedom of NITI Aayog for categorisation for specific purposes relating to development. In particular, the States of North-eastern region would require special attention as explained in the report of the 14th Finance Commission itself. In a way, therefore, the responsibility relating to special problems of select Stats would squarely be that of NITI Aayog.

Finally, areas under Schedule VI of the Constitution in North-eastern States remain outside the ambit of the measures recommended by the 14th Finance Commission for *panchayats* and Municipalities. These have been excluded from the consideration of the Finance Commission in the Terms of Reference. This was necessitated by the fact that the Constitution mandates the Union Government to play a direct role in supporting the development of these areas. However, the quantum of assistance given over the years to these regions by Ministries in the Union Government has been very limited. NITI Aayog could consider a larger assistance and more effective intervention for the up-gradation of administration as well as development of these areas to make-up for what the Finance Commission was not permitted to do.

It is quite conceivable that way forward, the constitution of the Finance Commissions could also undergo some changes. Finance Commission is essentially an institution in the nature of an arbitrator giving award in matters relating to sharing of divisible pool of taxes between Union and States, and among the States. However, in this framework, having a serving Member of the Planning Commission, who is a functionary of Union Government associated with political parties, in the Finance Commission as a part time Member, clearly indicates that an interested party is also officiating as an arbitrator—a clear case of conflict of interest. Since the distinction between Plan and non-Plan has been dispensed with by the Finance Commission, and since the overlap between transfers through Finance Commission's recommendations and other transfers have been almost eliminated, this is an appropriate time to discontinue the practice.

The 14th Finance Commission emphasised the role of State Finance Commissions and recognised the critical role of States in regard to local bodies. In this, there is an element of empowering of States in the fiscal management. NITI Aayog could revisit the institutional arrangements for planning at State level to make State level planning institutions more effective. Approach to planning at level of local bodies could be reviewed, taking account of the recommendations of 14th Finance Commission, especially on resource mobilisation, including bond financing.

The Terms of Reference of Finance Commissions other than the core Terms of Reference have been expanding over a period and have also been varying. Many of them had overlap with work of the erstwhile Planning Commission, while a few others related to tax reforms, expenditure reforms, public enterprise reforms, pricing of public-utilities, etc. Further, the recommendations in regard to other Terms of Reference have provisionally been treated as some suggestions and seldom acted upon vigorously. At the same time, the other Terms of Reference reduce the focus and the attention that the Finance Commission could give to its core Terms of Reference. The 14th Finance Commission recognised this and limited its recommendations relating to non-core Terms of Reference essentially to areas that have fiscal implications. NITI Aayog may legitimately address on a continuous basis the undeniably important policy issues often incorporated in other Terms of Reference of the Finance Commissions. NITI Aayog may also contribute to rationalisation of the other Terms of Reference of the 15th Finance Commission by attending to them on its own initiative.

To conclude, Planning Commission has been replaced by NITI Aayog to capture new realities of macroeconomic management and of Union-State relations, particularly to foster the spirit of competitive federalism in a cooperative environment. In regard to the latter, the recommendations of 14th Finance Commission are relevant for NITI Aayog to draw the States into partnership with Union Government for transformation and development. There are several issues of overlap and gaps between the recommendations of the Finance Commission and the aggregate fiscal transfers from the Union to the States, which can be addressed by NITI Aayog at this juncture, when the timing of establishment of NITI Aayog coincided with the recommendations of the 14th Finance Commission. Way forward, such a comprehensive approach by NITI Aayog without distinction between Plan and non-Plan in budgeting and with due regard to the constitutionally assigned role of Finance Commission in fiscal relations between Union and States, will enhance the quality of Planning and fiscal management in India in future.

3

RAJIV KUMAR

India's Triple Transition and the Way Forward

Introduction

India, unlike any other country, has chosen to undertake its social, political and economic transitions simultaneously. In other countries, these transitions have followed each other in a sequential manner, thereby reducing the complexity of the phenomenon and permitting greater degrees of freedom for policy makers. European history is replete with examples of nations completing their transitions from agrarian and feudal societies to industrial societies initially under a monarch or some form of autocracy or dictatorship and subsequently adopting the Magna Carta and similar democratic institutions. It is good to remember Karl Marx's description of early industrialisation in England, where workers without a job were branded with hot irons with a 'V' (to signify Vagrant) and forced into work houses without any guarantee of wages and proper working conditions. Only later, often after prolonged civil wars and social strife, did these societies adopt parliamentary form of liberal democracies.

Even in North America, the transition from slavery to universal franchise and equal rights took centuries and saw bloody conflicts before it was completed. The systematic decimation of native Indians, followed by the extensive use of slave labour, is an integral part of the evolution of US capitalism. In recent history, China completed its social transition out of feudalism, with the installation of the Communist government under Mao in 1949. It has so far held in abeyance its political transition to a liberal democracy. Most East-Asian economies, including Singapore, Korea and Taiwan shelved the adoption of liberal democracy until after their economic transitions, with some persisting with autarchy even after that.

India has had neither the luxury of 'totalitarian regimes' nor the benefits of colonial exploitation to propel its own three-fold transitions. It is the only country trying to build a globally competitive market based capitalist economy, while at the same time affording to its people liberal democratic rights and overcoming the deep-rooted and widespread caste and other social prejudices. The enormous challenge of simultaneously carrying forward this triple transition is exacerbated by India's continental size and diversity. It is effectively a continent masquerading as a country! India's diversity defies description.[1] India's scale, plurality, diversity and the exploding aspirations of its young population, imply that challenges facing the country are beyond the ordinary.

India has travelled a long distance in its economic transition since its independence. Its per capita income in real terms has increased more than seven times since 1960, when it had dipped to its lowest level of $228 per annum. It has firmly put the spectre of famines and hunger behind it and has established one of the most advanced manufacturing capacities and IT (information technology) sector in the emerging world. While its economic achievements are indeed worth noting, it is also rather evident that India has slipped behind in its economic transition relative to other Asian economies. Indian per capita incomes were equal to Korea's at the beginning of the 1960s and equal to China's at the beginning of the 1990s![2] Today, an average Indian earns less than a fifth of his Chinese counterpart and a mere 5 per cent or one-twentieth of an average Korean. India also

1. It has 18 officially recognised languages, boasts of 122 minor languages and 1,600 dialects. All 12 living religions are also represented in India. These differences are magnified many fold by a hyper-competitive and unrestrained media that continues to mushroom, both in print and electronic versions. At the latest count, there were 404 television news channels including 27 in English and Hindi. The rest are in regional languages. 1,05,443 daily newspapers are printed in the country. 900 million mobile phones, about a fifth of them 'smart phones' afford universal access to media for the Indian population irrespective of class, caste, income levels or geography.
2. In 1960 India's and Korea's per capita incomes were US$84 and $155 respectively. In 1990 India's per capita income was US$376 that was higher than China's of US$314 (all in nominal dollars and taken from *World Development Indicators*).

lags behind every Association of Southeast Nations (ASEAN) member country in terms of per capita incomes, except the CLV countries (Cambodia, Laos and Vietnam). Over the last four decades, India has been consigned amongst the 40 poorest countries in the world in terms of average incomes of its citizens.

An extraordinarily young population adds an extra degree of urgency to India's economic transition. India's much-touted demographic dividend arises from 65 per cent of its population being below 35 years of age and 50 per cent below 25 years. Median age in India is one of the lowest in the world. Productively employing this young population can generate a strong growth impulse and push India past the middle-income status over the next three decades.

However, there is also a reverse side. The young population implies that more than 10 million young people will join the workforce every year for the next 10 years and perhaps longer.[3] The number of entrants to the workforce goes up to nearly 12 million a year or one million each month if we take into account the expected migration from agriculture and of people from low productivity jobs to employment with higher productivity and incomes. Thus, the Indian economy has to generate one million new jobs each month for the foreseeable future. This is an extraordinary challenge—the scale and enormity of which are simply unprecedented.

The three simultaneous transitions (economic, political and social) impact each other and make the challenge even bigger and more complex. All three transitions proceed at their own pace. This exacerbates regional inequality and increases India's diversity. This extreme diversity makes democracy an imperative and not a choice. There is no group or class large enough to exercise hegemonic rule over the entire country. Not even the majoritarian Hindutva forces because Hinduism itself exists in myriad forms in the country. Can India's political leadership, irrespective of their party or ideological affiliations, recognise, appreciate and handle this diversity? On this will depend India's future.

3. Chakrabarti (2013).

The most important lesson to be learnt is that given India's complex simultaneous triple transition, it will have to find his own way forward starting from first principles. India cannot succeed by following some weather-beaten development model or economic theology. Neither the Washington nor the Beijing consensus can be adopted wholesale in India. There will inevitably have to be an Indian model that is derived from the ground realities upwards. The model will have to combine the innovative with the pragmatic and the incremental with bold structural reforms.

The Way Forward

Being a mere political economist, I can hardly even attempt to do justice to this vast and complex topic of the nature, direction and prospects of the simultaneously on-going triple transition in India. Also, as an economist, I see considerable merit in vigorously pushing forward all-round economic development in the hope that the rising tide will lift all boats, especially if care is taken against active discrimination against any particular group or community. Successful, economic development would surely facilitate other two transitions.

But I am also acutely aware that economic development cannot provide both the necessary and sufficient conditions for completing India's social transition. That smacks of avoidable Marxist reductionist logic, where by economics explained and determined everything. The Soviet Union splintered into 17 independent countries between 1989 and 1991, principally on ethnic lines. This was despite more than 70 years of sustained economic growth, which was admittedly spluttering during the 1980s. This should suffice to show that conscious efforts are needed to complete the social transition.

An India trapped in the morass of communal conflicts and ethnic violence could not possibly hope to achieve its economic and development goals. The paramount challenge is to ensure that India escapes the catastrophe of prolonged and vicious communal strife whose human costs today could far exceed those in 1947. Such a nasty eventuality must be avoided at all costs. While it is true that law and order and social peace are principally state subjects, correct signals from the Central government will play a major role in preventing this eventuality.[4]

With reference to India's political transition, India was not given much chance of success by global experts when it adopted liberal parliamentary democracy in 1950. There were solid reasons for the scepticism. No other country with comparable levels of poverty, illiteracy, and poor state of other development indicators has survived as a democracy in Asia. India has persisted and succeeded. The hyper-competitive political arena supervised and regulated with reasonable competence by a constitutionally mandated and effectively autonomous Election Commission has seen Indian democracy mature beyond any one's expectation over the last seven decades. This is one unqualified success for which India is justifiably recognised globally. In the last general election, over six weeks in April and May 2014, there were 870 million registered voters, around 9,19,452 polling booths, 8,251 candidates for 543 seats in the Lok Sabha. This was certainly the largest democratic exercise ever undertaken in the world.

Taking Forward the Economic Transition

From the above, it should be evident that the fundamental condition for successfully taking forward the critically needed economic transition is to ensure that both the social and political transitions, specially the former, move forward simultaneously. A failure to adequately address social and political issues have the potential to derail the economic transition and could even see significant retrogression as the country's structural strengths get dissipated and decimated.

There is pressing need for projecting a Long Term Vision for the country.[5] Economic aspirations of India's youth will not be met by focusing only on poverty reduction. That is truly passé despite the mini industry that has emerged around it. The neo-middle class that the current prime minister, Mr Narendra Modi, identified as his key

4. For further detailed treatment of India's major social challenges, see Kumar (2016).

5. It is noteworthy that after failing to publish a Vision document prior to the elections in 2014, as was indeed the original plan, NITI Ayog, the successor body to the Planning Commission announced on May 12th the preparation of a 15 year Vision for the country. This is a good example of 'better late than never.'

support base, aspires for India to be a prosperous economy in their life time. A long term vision that holds out the possibility of India being among the largest three economies at the end of next three decades, will motivate 65 per cent of India's population that is at present below 35 years and which will see this vision being fulfilled before their retirement from active life. That would be in 2046, which also happens to be the centenary of our independence.[6] The vision of a prosperous India within one's lifetime, that is supported by hard quantifiable evidence and analysis, will help harness the immense potential energy of India's young population.

Several forecasts are available for India's long-term economic prospects.[7] Our own estimates reveal that in PPP terms, to reach or exceed current (2014) G-7 per capita incomes by 2046, India will have to achieve double-digit growth rates during 2016-2026 to allow it to taper off over the next two decades (in line with the phenomenon of 'convergence', whereby growth rates become more moderate as economies accumulate capital and approach the frontiers of technology) to yield an average annual growth of 7 per cent in per capita incomes over the coming three decades.[8] This, ambitious but

---

6. At the end of 2014, the IMF ranked India 140th among a total of 186 countries with a per capita income of US$1,688 in constant 2005 dollars. The UN ranked it 150th out of 194 countries in 2014 with a per capita income of $1,586. At $5,870 per capita in PPP terms, India was still among the poorest countries in the world. The population of 1.26 billion converts this poor economy into one of the largest economies with a size of $2.06 trillion at the end of 2015. While size of course does matter in international relations, it should not generate false sense of national well-being and hard power.
7. These are conveniently summarised in Agarwala (2014). Dr Agarwala co-founder with me of Pahle India Foundation and one of the better economists in the country has done some painstaking work on estimating a feasible rate of growth for India over the next 30 years and come up with 6.8 per cent per annum as the most plausible growth rate. He does this by looking at the possible rate of growth of the labour force decomposed by levels of skills, capital stock, skills and total factor productivity.
8. At present (December 2015) India's per capita income and size of GDP in PPP (at constant 2005 dollars) are estimated at US$6,317 and US$7.8 trillion respectively. Mr Modi could set himself an eminently achievable target of an average GDP growth of 8 per cent for the next three decades. This implies an average annual growth in per capita incomes of about 6.7 per cent (assuming an average growth of population of 1.3% over the three decades). This will see Indian per capita incomes US$45,462 and the Indian economy's size will be US$59.32 trillion, well ahead of the US and almost the same as China's. At this rate therefore, India would rank within the top three largest economies but the average Indian will still fall short of current income levels in advanced economies, which are US$39,000 (using the OECD average) or US$46,000 which is the average for the G-7 economies .

not improbable target, will result in an Indian economy with a size of US$82 trillion in PPP terms in 2016, that will be third or fourth in per capita income terms behind the US, China and perhaps Germany.[9]

For achieving the above vision, difficult as it is, India will have to accelerate its rate of economic growth and employment generation. India like China will have to achieve near double digit growth rate for the next three decades. The Vision will have to be backed up with an analytical and policy framework that encourages bold structural reforms that will have to be undertaken along with the focus on better governance and implementation of existing schemes and programmes. The present government's focus on improving governance and execution capacity when combined with a structural reform agenda will yield the desired outcome of putting India on a rapid and inclusive growth trajectory that can be, as it must be, sustained over the next three decades.

Four Preconditions for Accelerated Growth[10]

The first precondition for policy reforms is the rather obvious one of having a reliable and timely set of data. Though this issue has gained more visibility in recent times because of the justified controversy attached to the new GDP series,[11] this is a long festering problem to which sufficient policy attention has not been paid. Should one surmise that this lack of attention reflects policy makers' proclivities to make policies on the basis of either ideological preferences or lobbying by various vested interests. In these two instances, empirical evidence is certainly not required and access to reliable data becomes irrelevant. Let us hope that this is not the case and the statistical system in the country, which provides the

9. For the scenario with 8 per cent rate of growth in per capita incomes, we assume that GDP growth will be 9.2 per cent during the first decade (2016-2026); 8.2 per cent during 2026-2036 and 7.2 per cent during the final ten years (2036-2046).

10. Here we refer only to the precondition for formulating and implementing sound economic policies. Please recall that systemic preconditions for successful economic transition are to push forward the social and political transitions.

11. It is reported that the Central Statistical Office (CSO) will put out a back series using the new methodology that will eliminate the present confusion about the GDP numbers. This is expected in June 2016. While this is welcome step, it may not suffice as the methodology itself is being questioned.

fundamental foundations for rational policy making will receive the necessary resources and attention in future. The present situation in which official agencies publicly express their scepticism about India's GDP (gross domestic product) growth rates is untenable.[12] The government should set up a high-powered task force, with international experts, which should make a thorough assessment of data collection methodology and practices relating to the overall GDP, employment, agriculture and MSME (micro small and medium enterprises) performance.[13]

The second precondition for successfully achieving India's economic transition is to re-establish and regenerate the Development State. Followers of the Washington consensus in India, make the facile assumption that the Indian state is incapable of efficiently delivering its mandated functions including delivery of critically required public services. This assumption is in the nature of a self-fulfilling prophecy. Many foreign observers misunderstood the present prime minister's election slogan of 'minimum government maximum governance' to imply the withdrawal of the State even from its mandated functions under the National Democratic Alliance (NDA) government. Thankfully, Mr Modi has insisted on achieving greater efficiency in the delivery of public services. This implies an attempt at resurrecting the Development State in India. This most welcome step would require a set of four rather difficult reforms, if it has to be sustained and deliver the much needed public services that have an important role in preventing growth from becoming exclusionary and non-inclusive.

First, the system of incentives that drive the behaviour of senior bureaucracy has to be changed. The present administrative system in which mistakes are penalised but inaction is effectively rewarded

12. In a television interview sometime back, the Governor RBI expressed his doubts about the new numbers. More recently, the *Mid-Year Economic Review* brought out by the Economic Division of the Ministry of Finance, has also implied that 7.5 per cent growth rate in terms of new series would be equivalent to between 4.5-5.00 per cent GDP growth rate according to the old series.

13. Availability of reliable and regular data on employment in the organised and unorganised sector is also critical. Such data is not available. For example, the number of workers in the organised sector could be more than 50 million, while Arjun Sengupta committee estimated the number to be only 30 million. The story is similar for aggregate employment.

by allowing time bound promotions, hugely favours 'status quoists' and the noxious practice of passing the buck. The government must move to an outcome-based performance evaluation at all levels of bureaucracy. Attempts so far have been woefully desultory and inevitably produced minimal results. Article 311 of the Constitution that currently offers carte blanche protection to senior bureaucracy would also have to be suitably amended.

Second, a Development State has to be focused on providing the more critical public services and need not be involved in commercial activities that are best left to the private sector. There is hardly any need for the Government of India to continue to own, manage and operate hotels, airlines, textile companies, and even coal and iron ore mines for that matter.

Third, inducting talent from the private sector and civil society into the government on a regular basis will greatly improve domain expertise and implementation capability. This will bring in a semblance of completion within the bureaucracy, which will surely improve performance. In addition, it will reduce the gulf between the government and the governed, and generate some trust that is essential for the emergence of India Inc. in which all vital stakeholders work cooperatively to measure up to global competition.[14]

Fourth, the present system of macroeconomic policy making has to be changed. The existing approach is fragmented and iterative. This often creates avoidable conflicts, often personality specific, that confuses the markets and economic agents. Each ministry or agency very often simply reacts to another ministry in a defensive gesture to either protect ones turf or negate an advantage to the other. This generates unwanted uncertainty and often prevents timely policy response. This reactive or iterative policy making system should be replaced by bringing together all relevant ministries and agencies, including the Reserve Bank of India (RBI), on the same platform, for them to agree on the objectives and modialities for a particular

14. We could emulate and adapt the practice followed by the Japanese Ministry of Trade and Industry (now METI) of establishing tripartite consultative committees in economic ministries comprising officials, industry representatives and academics. This would surely help in designing more effective policies and also their implementation.

programme. This was the mandate of the office of the Cabinet Secretary, which unfortunately has seen an erosion in its role and responsibilities in recent years.

The third precondition is to genuinely create a Team India with the cooperation of all State governments. It is estimated that with successive waves of reform at the centre, the state governments now handle nearly 80 per cent of action required for improving the business climate and raising welfare levels of the common people. The strengthening of the Inter-State Council could be the key step in this regard.

The fourth and final pre-condition for successful economic transition is to bring IT front and centre of governance practices in India. As Nilekani and Shah argue rather forcefully and with sufficient empirical evidence in support of their argument, that with IT in command, India can leap frog development stages traversed by the present advanced economies.[15] To achieve this, the Government will have to jettison its business as usual approach and go for bold and innovative IT-based solutions to India's myriad problems.[16]

Maximising Employment Generation

Maximising employment generation over the immediate, medium and long term must be the principal objective of macroeconomic policy. This is neither synonymous nor co-terminus with maximising the rate of growth of GDP. Adoption of employment maximisation as the exclusive policy goal will have several important implications for formulating macroeconomic policy.

First, policy would have to ensure that economic growth is generated not solely by continuous process industries like oil refining or petrochemicals but by labour and skill-intensive sectors like light engineering, garments, construction, in-bound tourism, etc. This will require putting in place a macroeconomic framework that promotes

15. Nilekeni and Shah, who were together in developing the Aadhar platform provide IT based solutions for 12 sectors in their eminently readable volume. See Nilekeni and Shah (2015).

16. It is worth quoting the final paragraph of the book from Nilekani and Shah (2015) in support of our repeated assertion for the need to jettison the business as usual approach. "We are much better off dreaming and taking risks, and trying to realize a billion aspirations; at best we risk falling flat on our faces. Far more egregious, and most dangerous to our country, is going about 'business as usual', leaving a billion voices unheard and a billion frustrations unresolved".

labour intensive production methods. This will include an active or interventionist exchange rate policy to ensure that Indian firms are assured that they will not have to hedge against an appreciating rupee (in real terms) in the foreseeable future. An active industrial policy might help in identifying and supporting such labour-intensive sectors, provided that the government can enhance its capacity by attracting relevant domain experts.

Second, wage goods price rise will have to be restrained. The Government and the RBI should agree on a joint policy reform package to achieve this rather than adopting aggregate inflation targeting as monetary policy objective. Post facto monetary policy action to control wage good inflation is at best ineffective in preventing distress and at worst causes employment loss by inducing economic downturn through aggregate demand contraction. During the seven years from 2004-2011 average food inflation remained stubbornly in double digits. This was despite a 250 basis points rise in repo rates from 6.0 per cent to 8.5 per cent by the RBI and should be sufficient testimony to the ineffectiveness of monetary policy in controlling food and wage goods inflation.

It is time that the Government recognised that foodgrains are tradable goods and India has sufficient foreign exchange reserves to assure itself of food security in an environment of open economy and globalisation. India would do well to dismantle all tariffs and non-tariff barriers that hamper food imports especially from its neighbouring countries. It should also dispense with all canalising arrangements, including those for fertilisers, as these result in monopolies, distortions and rents. With these barriers removed and as a result of amendments to the Agricultural Produce Market Committee (APMC) Act in 18 states, food importers and domestic traders would have greater freedom to enter wholesale markets and could emerge as more efficient instruments for restraining food prices than any administrative measure. Effective regulation and real time monitoring of food prices are of course the necessary condition for such an open-market policy to work.

Third, an employment-oriented macro policy will necessitate the active promotion of manufactured exports on the basis of creating a world-class export infrastructure that will make our exporters globally competitive. It will be far more effective to replace the entire panoply of fiscal incentives (duty drawbacks, interest rate subventions) for exports by diverting these funds for development of export infrastructure.

Fourth, tourism is an important employment generator and also a foreign exchange earner. India has grossly under utilised its vast tourist potential. It attracts only 7.7 foreign tourist each year (2014) compared to 55.6 million in China and 24.8 million in Thailand. The city of New York itself attracts more than 50 million tourists each year. Creation of adequate tourism focused infrastructure is a necessary condition of increasing tourist arrivals. This is pretty much in shambles today. Indian Tourist Development Corporation (ITDC) would do better by drawing up a time-bound plan to develop a world-class infrastructure at major tourist destinations than to run hotels and motels along major highways.

Fifth, it is well established that MSMEs offer far more employment per unit of capital deployed than large formal sector firms. Some estimates, for example, put labour employed in leather products industry as 1.75 million for MSMEs compared to 0.75 million by their larger, more automated firms. MSMEs also contribute significantly to the country's export effort. Therefore, MSMEs must be more effectively promoted and supported. It may be useful to conduct a 'zero-based budgeting' exercise of the entire paraphernalia of incentives, institutions and policies that is currently in place purportedly for the promotion of MSMEs.

Sixth, hardly any country has industrialised without public provisioning of affordable housing for workers. This effectively lowers wage costs and also serves to improve equity. More importantly, at the present juncture of demand deficiency in the Indian economy, a massive programme of affordable workers housing will provide a much needed economic stimulus.

Seventh, an employment oriented policy will also call for a complete overhaul of fiscal subsidies that are presently directed principally towards reducing capital or technology acquisition costs and supporting middle and rich farmers.[17] These should be phased out. The 2016-17 budget must be commended for making a start in bringing in employment enhancing subsidies.

Substituting labour for capital in labour surplus economies for maximising employment generation has a long analytical pedigree.[18] Malaysia adopted conscious employment-oriented policies after an enquiry into the riots had found that educated unemployment was the principle cause for the race-riots that had rocked the country in mid-1970s. China has also pursued an employment-focused policy since 1982 with remarkably successfully results. It is time that India also gives up all other policy objectives and adopts employment maximisation as its exclusive policy goal that will be used to determine the efficacy of any and every policy measure.

The World Bank estimates labour force growth in India for 2000-2012 to be between 1.3-1.5 per cent per annum.[19] Going forward, labour participation rates are bound to go up and the working age will also go beyond 60, which is the usual assumption underlying these estimates. Therefore, a growth rate of 2.3 per cent per annum in labour force over the next 10 years, declining after that to reach about 1 per cent by 2050 can be realistically assumed. There is also a backlog to be cleared of those who are presently trapped in low productivity jobs in agriculture and self-employed sectors. Therefore, a target of 2.8 per cent annual rate of growth of employment over the next 10 years, (for both, organised and unorganised labour) would suffice to absorb not only the new entrants in the workforce but also to clear the existing backlog. Given the employment elasticity of GDP growth, which will hopefully rise with the adoption of employment enhancing policies, the target of growing employment at 2.8 per

17. We refer here to capital subsidies given under the Textile Technology Upgrade Fund, interest rate subvention for exports even if these are not employment generating and fertiliser subsidies that alone account for as much as ₹72,969 crore and favour only the rich farmers and private fertiliser industry and not the small and marginal farmers. These need to be phased out.

18. For an analytical understanding see, Arrow et al. (1961).

19. World Bank: *World Development Indicators*. This estimate is for the period 2000-2012. The rate of growth for the 10 year period between 2002 to 2012 comes out to be only 1.06 per cent. World Bank gives the definition of labour force as number of people above 15 years of age who meet the ILO definition of economically active population.

cent per annum will yield a GDP growth of 9.4 per cent. Therefore, sustaining a rate of GDP growth between 9 and 10 per cent, over the next 10 years, would be the necessary condition for actualising India's demographic dividend.

The latest survey report from the Labour Bureau for the Ministry of Labour, Delhi, reveals that job growth in the eight most labour intensive sectors during October-Decmber 2016, has been the lowest in any quarter over the last seven years![20] Evidence comes in various forms. Lower admission pressure in private MBA classes; decline for the second year running in the number of applicants for the Joint Entrance Examination for premier engineering institutions like the IITs and NITs;[21] the Jat agitation for reservation in Haryana; and the Patel agitation in Gujarat. The problem is bound to be exacerbated with the unprecedented continuous 17 month (until April 2016) decline in exports and near stagnation in rate of growth of industrial output.

Therefore, the government must focus urgent attention on maximising employment growth. All other goals can be subsumed under that over-arching objective. It will call for a new focus and a different approach to economic policy making that is inherently more suited to India's present needs and for meeting the aspirations of its young population. The biggest advantage of course is that maximising employment generation guarantees that growth is truly inclusive.

Way of Conclusion: The Case of Structural Reforms

The above discussion of the threefold transition, the preconditions for accelerating economic growth and sustaining it over the next three decades and choosing employment maximisation as the principle if not the exclusive and over arching policy goal should provide the necessary analytical framework for policy making in India. With this framework in place, the present government's incremental approach with its emphasis on improving project execution and overall governance can yield significant results in the a number of

20. See Kumar (2016a).

21. *Times of India*, 19 January 2016.

sectors. Policy prescriptions and the road map is already available in these sectors and the key as Mr Modi repeatedly emphasises is in implementing the ideas or statutes already in place. Greater efficiency in the delivery of public services, which is mandated for the government at all levels will contribute to making growth relatively more inclusive as the poor won't just have to wait for the trickle down to percolate to them.

However, there are some sectors in which an incremental approach with its focus on improving governance and delivery will certainly not suffice. In these sectors, structural reforms, some of which may require 'out of the box' thinking have to be implemented in a time bound manner. This will require bringing together a tripartite group of policy makers, academics and actual practitioners to design the package of structural reforms and also prepare a blueprint for implementing them. The five sectors that immediately come to mind are: Agriculture, Manufacturing, Transport, Education and Health. Following a business as usual approach in these sectors will not deliver the desired outcomes. A business as usual approach could actually generate unbearable stresses in an already fragile social and political environment.

We need people like Abid Hussain *sahib* at this juncture. He represented a stream of domestic talent that straddled the two rather unrelated skill sets of 'fresh innovative thinking along with an ability to successfully implement these new ideas within the government. Others that come to mind are L.K. Jha, K.B. Lall, Prakash Tandon and P.N. Haksar. Each one of them made an inimitable contribution to India's development by combining the twin traits of bold thinking and focused implementation. Narendra Modi, the present prime minister must identify people with similar talents from both within and outside the 'system' to achieve his ambitious goals. On this will critically depend his and India's future success.

This is a time of unlimited opportunities for India, seemingly overwhelming challenges and also of sky-high aspirations. India cannot afford to make many mistakes. A lot is riding on India's success. Not only will it bring about the much awaited succour for its poor population but also perhaps provide an exemplar for other emerging economies, themselves trying to complete their own transitions in an increasingly globalising world where open borders and supra-national oversight of even domestic issues is likely to be the norm. Like India, they do not have the luxury and degrees of freedom that were available to those who completed their transitions in the 20th century. There will be significant positive externalities to India successfully completing its complex triple transition. For that, we need a deeper understanding of our challenges and the desire and courage to find solutions rooted in our ground realities.

References

Agarwala, Ramgopal (2014). *India in 2050.* Delhi: Sage Publications.

Arrow, K.J., H.B. Chenery, B.S. Minhas and R.M. Solow (1961). "Capital-Labor Substitution and Economic Efficiency", *The Review of Economics and Statistics* 43(3): 225-50, August. *http://www.jstor.org/stable/1927286?origin=JSTOR-pdf*.

Chakrabarti, K.C. (2013). "Environmental & Social Sustainability: Key Issues & Concerns", Yes Bank–GIZ–UNEP Sustainability Series event on *Environment and Social Risk Management.* Mumbai, April.

Kumar Rajiv, (2016). *Modi and his Challenges.* Delhi: Bloomsbury.

———. (2016a). "The Job Equation", *Times of India*, 28 April.

Nilekeni, N. and Viral Shah (2015). *Rebooting India: Realizing a Billion Aspirations.* New Delhi: Allen Lane.

4

RANA HASAN

Sustaining Growth, Ensuring Inclusion

The starting point of this essay is the notion that India's success in creating productive and well-paying jobs holds the key for meeting its goal of achieving inclusive growth. As the *Economic Survey* has put it: "Productive jobs are vital for growth. And a good job is the best form of inclusion"(Government of India 2013: 26). Where will such jobs—often referred to as 'good' jobs—come from? What types of policies and interventions will spur the creation of good jobs? These are questions that were of much interest to Abid Hussain and which this essay attempts to shed light on. The remainder of this essay is organised as follows.

Section 1 provides an overview of the relationship between economic growth, poverty reduction, and structural transformation, i.e., changes in an economy's structure of output and employment.[1] Treating poverty reduction as a proxy for inclusion, it notes that growth in India has been associated with steady reduction in poverty since the early 1980s, and in this way been inclusive. However, there is certainly scope for making growth more inclusive, and for this to happen, improvements in agricultural productivity and an exit of agricultural workers to more productive employment in other sectors, especially manufacturing, is key.

Section 2 goes on to provide a brief discussion on the policy factors that may have held back agriculture and manufacturing. Section 3 presents a relatively short outline of the policies needed to raise agricultural productivity, while Section 4 provides a more

1. Structural transformation in an economy is usually thought to encompass three processes: (i) changes in sectoral composition of output; (ii) changes in sectoral composition of employment; and (iii) changes in the rural-urban composition of output and employment. The focus here is on the first two processes only.

detailed discussion on the needs of the manufacturing sector—a sector which is the focus of the Government of India's "Make in India" programme launched in 2015, and one that Abid Hussain worked on for many years and believed to be key for India's prosperity. It argues that the Government's emphasis on instilling greater dynamism in Indian manufacturing is much-needed and will be key to India's success in achieving inclusive growth. Section 5 concludes.

It should be noted that omission of services in this essay is not to suggest that the sector cannot serve as an engine of economic growth and job creation. In fact, India services sector has done rather well on both counts and should continue to do so. The focus on agriculture and manufacturing here is simply on account of the fact that for India to sustain growth and ensure inclusion, it is essential that weaknesses in the policy frameworks governing these sectors be addressed urgently.

Growth, Poverty, and Structural Transformation

After three decades of generally low growth, the Indian economy experienced a growth acceleration that started in the 1980s.[2] Growth in GDP (gross domestic product) per capita, only 1.4 per cent annually from the 1950s through 1970s, accelerated steadily—from average annual growth rates of 3.5 per cent in the 1980s, to 3.7 per cent in the 1990s and 5.5 per cent in the first decade of the new millennium. While a slowdown in growth from early 2011 to 2014 has sparked debates about the Indian economy's 'growth potential' and its ability to sustain growth rates of around 6 per cent and higher (in per capita terms) for long stretches of time, India is today among the fastest-growing economies in the world.

A related debate has been about the inclusiveness of India's growth. Determining whether growth has been inclusive or not, is not straightforward. Inclusiveness is a multidimensional concept. Based on the Government's 12th Five-Year Plan documents, inclusive growth is growth that yields broad-based benefits and moves an

---

2. The exact timing of India's growth acceleration and its causes are the subject of debate. Key contributions on this and the Indian growth experience, more generally, can be found in: Rodrik and Subramaniam (2005), Nayyar (2006) and Panagariya (2008).

economy in the direction of more equal opportunities for all. Clearly, one would have to examine data on a broad variety of economic and social indicators to determine whether or not growth has been inclusive. To make the task manageable, one can examine the issue of how inclusive growth has been from the lens of poverty.

Viewed this way, growth in India since the 1980s has been inclusive. From 1951 to 1978, India's poverty rate—the percentage of the population living below a given poverty line—fluctuated between about 45 per cent and 62 per cent with no clear trend (Panagariya, 2008).[3] Beginning in the early 1980s, and broadly coinciding with an acceleration in the rate of economic growth, the poverty rate declined, from 43 per cent in 1983 to 27.6 per cent in 2004-05.[4] An improved methodology for determining the poverty line, introduced in 2009, has led to a larger share of the population being counted as poor. However, poverty rates have declined even according to the new poverty line, from 45.3 per cent in 1993-94 to 21.9 per cent in 2011-2012. The pace of poverty reduction increased in recent years, from an average 0.74 percentage points per year between 1993-94 and 2004-05 to an average 2.18 percentage points per year between 2004-2005 and 2011-12. This has coincided with a significant decline in the absolute number of poor people, from over 400 million in 2004-2005 to about 270 million in 2011-12. In comparison, between 1993-94 and 2004-05, the number of poor remained generally unchanged at about 400 million, even as poverty rates declined.

The pace of poverty reduction has, however, been relatively slow in India in comparison with the high performing economies of East Asia. As Figure 4.1 shows, based on the international poverty line used for comparing the incidence of extreme poverty across countries ($1.25 per day at 2005 purchasing power parities), India's pace of

3. These poverty rates are based on the poverty estimation method developed by the Expert Group 1993, whose method for reporting official poverty statistics has been in use since March 1997. Several methodological concerns with this approach led to the formulation of the Expert Group 2009, which developed a new methodology for updating poverty lines over time.

4. Since 1987, India's poverty estimates have been based on household expenditure surveys conducted over a 12-month period starting in July. Thus, the period 2004-05 covers July 2004 to June 2005.

poverty reduction has been clearly slower than that of the People's Republic of China, Indonesia, and Vietnam. It has been comparable with that of Brazil's. But, with India having much higher levels of poverty to begin with than Brazil, the declines should have been more dramatic.

Figure 4.1

Poverty Reduction in India as Compared to Selected Economies

Percentage of population living below $1.25 a day at 2005 PPP

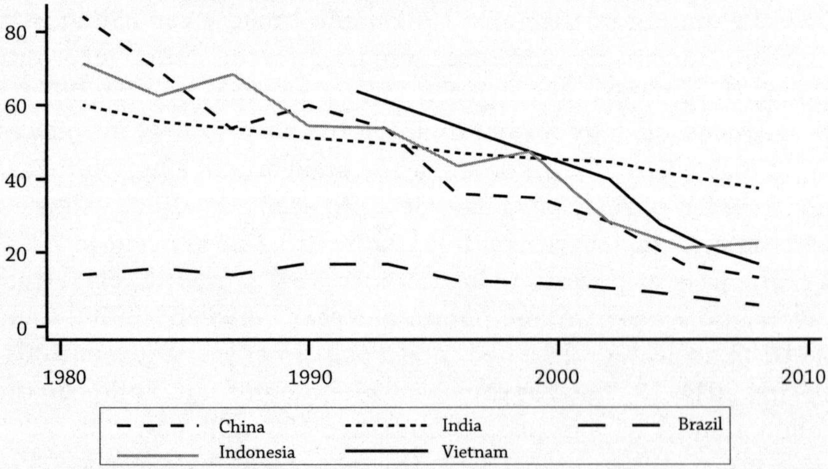

Source: Computed from PovcalNet: the on-line tool for poverty measurement devolopment by the Development Research Group of the World Bank.

Source: PovcalNet, World Bank.

Interestingly, differentials in GDP growth rates do not explain the differential performance in poverty reduction. Consider the following elasticities of poverty reduction to GDP growth reported by Ravallion (2009): -0.8 for China (1981-2005) and -0.3 for India (1993-2005). What these numbers tell us is that for a 1 per cent increase in GDP in China, there was a 0.8 per cent reduction in the poverty rate. In India, on the other hand, the poverty rate declined by only 0.3 per cent for every per cent increase in GDP. Since actual growth in China was also much higher than in India, the net effect of growth on poverty was that much greater.

Why has growth in India not led to faster poverty reduction? The proximate causes for this seem to lie in the unevenness of growth across states and sectors. Regarding the former, rates of economic growth have tended to be lower in some of the Indian states that have accounted for the largest fraction of India's poor.

As Figure 4.2 shows, among Indian states that accounted for more than 3.5 per cent each of India's total poor in 1993, there has been a clear tendency for states with greater numbers of poor (captured by the size of circles representing the states) to grow more slowly from 1993 to 2009.

Figure 4.2

Growth and Poverty Reduction Across Indian States

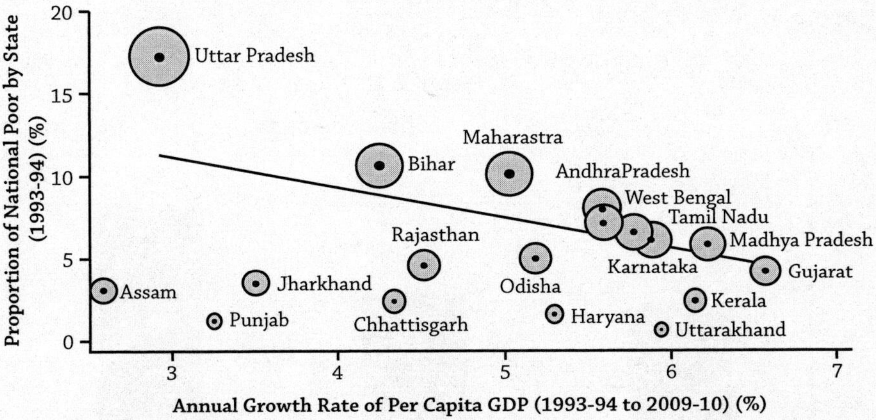

Note: The fitted line is based on states with more than 3.5 per cent of India's total poor in 1993-94.

Source: Hasan et al. 2015.

As regards the unevenness of growth across sectors, Figure 4.3 describes annualised growth rates achieved in each of the three last decades (1980s, 1990s and 2000s) as well as the contribution of five production sectors to growth. The figure reveals that even as each decade has witnessed higher aggregate growth of GDP, agriculture's contribution to this growth has been declining over time, from around 1.5 per cent per annum in the 1980s to around half a per cent in the 2000s. Given that the poor reside overwhelmingly in rural India and continue to depend on agriculture directly or indirectly, growth of agriculture may be expected to translate into poverty reduction more so than, say, the manufacturing sector, especially if the latter is driven by the more capital-intensive formal sector. This is indeed what the analysis of the sectoral composition of growth and poverty reduction by Ravallion and Datt (1996), who use data on Indian poverty and production from 1951 to 1991, indicates. They find that output growth in the primary and tertiary sectors to be poverty reducing but growth in the secondary sector to have no impact on poverty reduction.

It is true that there has been some exit of the workforce from agriculture; however, a majority of the population is still employed in it. Accordingly, weak growth of a sector on which the poor rely is one reason for the effects of growth and poverty reduction to not be stronger.

Figure 4.3

Sectoral Composition of Growth

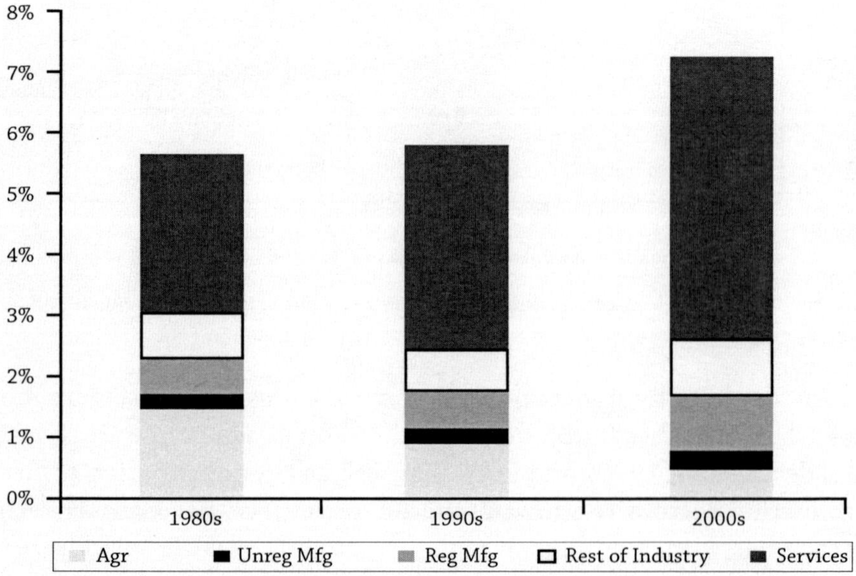

Source: Based on Hasan et al. 2015.

Another reason for the weak growth-poverty linkages is the weak growth performance of labour intensive manufacturing, a sector that did well in many East Asian countries. The manufacturing sector has certainly contributed to growth. But the breakdown of manufacturing into registered (formal) and unregistered (informal) components reveals that it is the former, which tends to be capital-intensive and/or skill intensive, that has contributed more to growth in India. In fact, the contribution of informal manufacturing—which tends to be labour-intensive and has accounted for more than 3/4th of manufacturing employment—to growth has remained fairly similar across the decades.

Figure 4.4

Employment Share and Labour Productivity Differentials Across Sectors, 2009-10

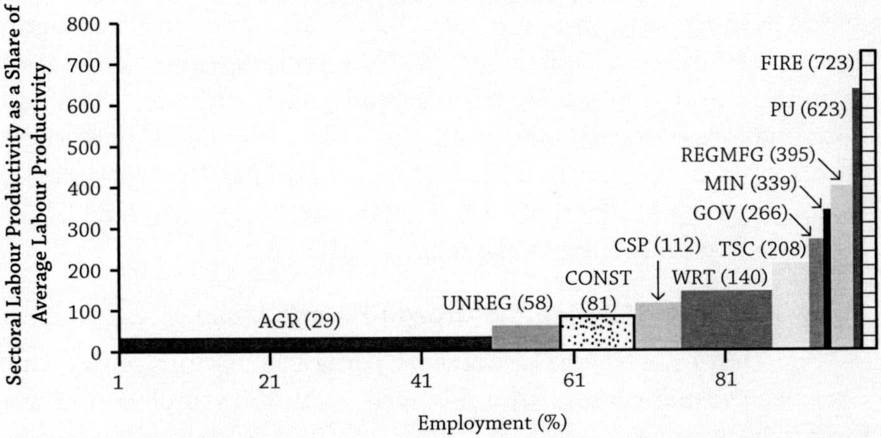

Note: AGR = Agriculture and Allied Activities, CONST = Construction, CSP = Community, Social and Personal Services, FIRE = Finance, Insurance and Real Estate, GOV = Public Administration; Government Services, MIN = Miningand Quarrying, PU = Public Utilities, REGMFG = Registered Manufacturing, TSC = Transport, Storage and Communications, UNREG = Unregistered Manufacturing, and WRT = Wholesale and Retail Trade, Restaurants and Hotels.

Source: Hasan et al. 2015.

The foregoing suggests an urgent need to focus on raising productivity in Indian agriculture and expanding opportunities in the manufacturing sector. This imperative is perhaps best understood by examining Figure 4.4, which describes not only how India's workers are distributed across sectors along the horizontal axis, but also the average levels of labour productivity in the sectors in which they are employed along the vertical axis. For expositional purposes, the labour productivity numbers are reported relative to aggregate productivity. Almost half of India's workers are engaged in the agriculture sector (as may be seen from the horizontal axis). Given the extremely low productivity of the sector—only 29 per cent of the national average (as may be seen from the number reported in parenthesis over the bar for the agriculture sector as well as the vertical axis)—the implication is that almost half of India's workers are trapped in a vicious cycle of low productivity and low earnings.

To sustain growth and ensure inclusiveness, India will have to raise productivity in the agriculture sector on the one hand, and ensure that job opportunities come up in higher productivity sectors elsewhere. Which sectors will these be? There are certainly sectors in which productivity levels are very high as can be seen from Figure 4.4. The difficulty is that many of these sectors—such as finance, insurance, and real estate; mining; and public utilities—have low potential for generating jobs on a large-scale for semi-skilled workers. One sector with considerable untapped potential for generating reasonably high productivity jobs is manufacturing, especially labour intensive manufacturing in the formal sector.

Policy Factors Underlying the Growth-Poverty Links

Are there particular aspects of Indian economic policy that have been responsible for the relatively weak growth of output and productivity of agriculture and labour-intensive manufacturing (as captured by growth of the informal manufacturing sector)? This question is particularly important given that the thrust of India's economic reform efforts since the 1980s were to reduce the role of the state in production and investment decisions and increase India's openness to the global economy.[5] Proponents of reform believed that reforms would not only spur economic growth, they would also significantly expand economic opportunities for India's workers as private investment moved in to labour-intensive tradeable sectors

5. Industrial deregulation and trade liberalisation were key components of reforms. While both had begun in the early- to mid-1980s, dramatic changes in India's industrial and trade policy regimes took place in the early 1990s. Other important elements of reforms included liberalisation of (inward) FDI (foreign direct investment) and portfolio investment, relaxation of entry barriers for private domestic and foreign investment in India's financial sector (including the banking and insurance subsectors) and other services subsectors such as telecommunications and many types of business services.

(i.e., agriculture and manufacturing) in order to exploit India's labour abundance.

But, a closer look at the reforms and the 'initial conditions' that existed at the time of these reforms can go far in explaining why growth in post-reform India has not been as inclusive as expected. In particular, it is important to consider what was not touched by reforms. First, India's agriculture sector not only continued to operate without any significant policy reforms (other than tariff reductions, some of which were negated by continuation of non-tariff barriers such as in cereals),[6] the quantum of public investment in key components of agricultural infrastructure such as irrigation, development of new varieties of seeds, and research extension services also experienced a decline (Figure 4.5).

Figure 4.5

Public Investment and Subsidies in Agriculture (As Per Cent of GDP)

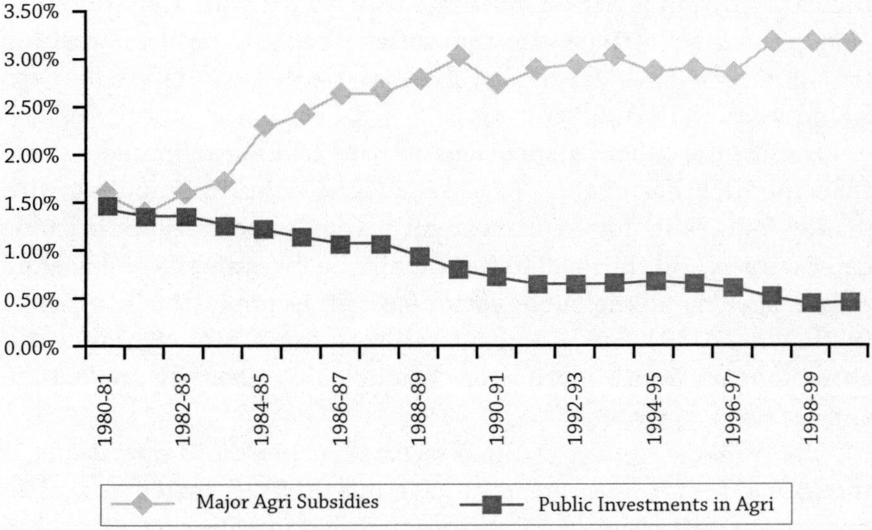

Source: Walton (2010) based on World Bank (2005).

Second, Indian manufacturing continued to operate under difficult circumstances notwithstanding the de-licensing and trade reforms

6. For example, by liberalising the entry of the private sector in marketing, storage, and transport of agricultural products.

of the 1980s and 1990s. First, relative to the high-performing East Asian comparators, India's infrastructure deficits, especially in the power and transport sectors, have constrained Indian manufacturing in terms of its competitiveness. Second, on the regulatory front, as the World Bank's *Doing Business* reports have emphasized, firms in Indian manufacturing have continued to operate under some fairly onerous regulations. For example, in 2016, India ranked 130 out of 189 countries in the ease of doing business. To be sure, there are some areas where India does well, such as in protecting minority interests of shareholders where India is ranked 8th. But, in such key areas as starting a business, resolving insolvency, enforcing contracts and dealing with construction permits, India remains a difficult place to do business. The ranks in these areas are, respectively, 155, 136, 178, and 183. Moreover, it should be noted that the *Doing Business* rankings do not take into account labour regulations. Considering the restrictions on dismissal of workers imposed by Chapter VB of the Industrial Disputes Act on manufacturing plants with 100 workers—among the most stringent in the world—it should not be surprising that domestic and, especially, FDI has tended to bypass modern labour intensive manufacturing.

Finally, the Indian state seems to have had more limited success than the high performing East Asian economies in grappling with market failures that arise from credit market imperfections, learning externalities, and the need to coordinate the investments of disparate private agents and the public sector (see, for example, the discussions in Nayyar 2013). Such market failures can seriously constrain entrepreneurs from adopting new technologies, diversify production, and seek new markets.

The combined effect of these factors has penalised operations in the formal sector and seems to have incentivised entrepreneurs to operate at small scales and in the informal sector. The result has been that India's manufacturing firms remain overwhelmingly of small size (Figure 4.6). Compared with its East Asian neighbours, 84 per cent of India's manufacturing employment in 2005 was estimated to be in firms with fewer than 50 workers; the corresponding shares are 25 per cent-47 per cent for economies such as the PRC, the Republic of Korea, Malaysia, Taiwan, and Thailand (Hasan and Jandoc 2013). The concentration of small firms is a problem because at small scales of operation, firms often get caught in a vicious circle of reliance on traditional, low-productivity technologies with limited earnings and low wages. The lower wages generated by small and informal firms may be seen from Figure 4.7.

Figure 4.6

Size Distribution of Manufacturing Firms

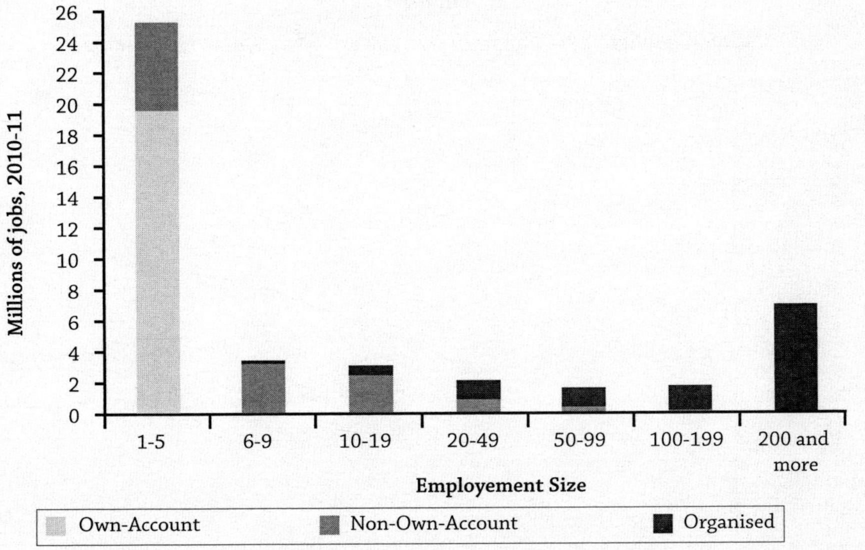

Source: Estimates based on micro-records from Annual Survey of Industry and National Sample Survey Organisation's survey of unregistered manufacturing.

In view of the foregoing discussion, it is not surprising that private investment largely bypassed agriculture and labour-intensive manufacturing, i.e., precisely those subsectors where much of India's workforce earned its living. Instead, the Indian economy experienced a boom in services and growth in non-labour-intensive manufacturing (i.e., either skill-intensive or capital-intensive manufacturing).

Raising Productivity of Indian Agriculture

As noted above, India's agriculture sector has been characterised by a secular decline in public investment since the mid-1990s.

Inadequate irrigation facilities, in particular, have continued to be an important constraint in raising productivity growth. Major concerns in this context include a reduction in real investment, a fall in the water table, wastages and inefficiencies in use of water and low recovery of cost. Currently, only around 70 per cent of the irrigation potential of the country has been exploited. Large scale investment is required to complete several hundred irrigation schemes that have remained unfinished for years due to severe resource constraints.

Figure 4.7

Wages by Size and Formality in Indian Manufacturing Firms

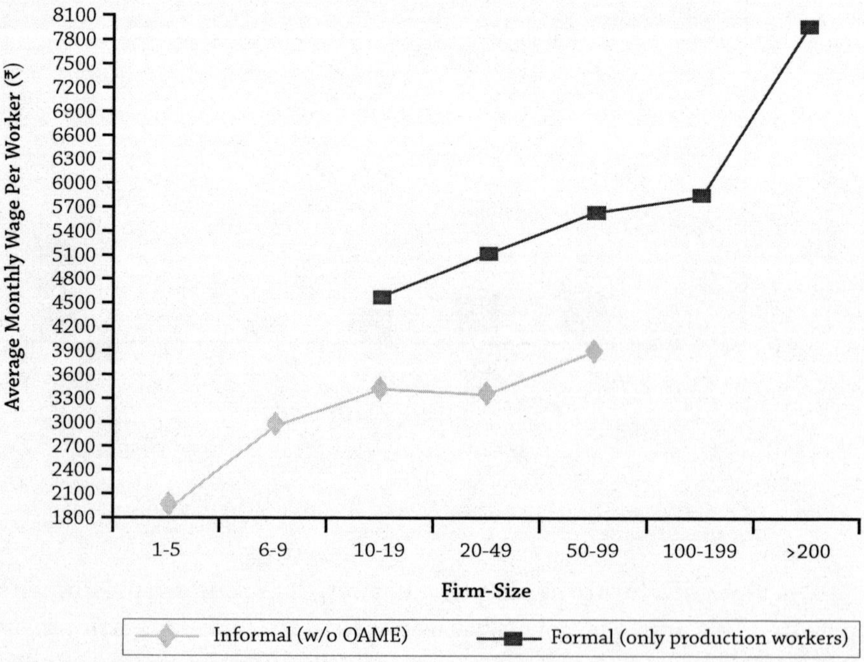

Source: Estimates based on micro-records from Annual Survey of Industry and National Sample Survey Organisation's survey of unregistered manufacturing.

The agriculture sector also suffers from lack of access to formal credit and insurance, which has reduced adoption of improved seeds, fertilisers and modernisation. In recent years there has been a rise in share of indirect credit in total agricultural credit. High dependence on informal source of credit has also resulted in increase in incidence of farm debts and farmer suicides. Indian agriculture has been unable to keep pace with the transformation in the tastes of consumers, which has diversified to high value products like milk & meat products and vegetables & fruits. Indian agriculture also has to deal with an inefficient supply chain as it suffers from uneconomic scales of operation, lack of consistency in supply and quality, and inadequate storage and distribution infrastructure.

While there is no silver bullet for the sector, there is a growing consensus on the agenda for reform in the sector. Key elements of this reform agenda include the following (Gulati and Ganguly 2010):

1. Introduce a 'second green revolution' in the eastern part of India. States such as Odisha, Assam, and Bihar are water abundant but have extremely low production yields. Introducing new varieties of seeds (such as hybrid rice) and developing rural infrastructure and markets will not be easy, but if carried out successfully, would have large payoffs in terms of both growth and inclusion. Moreover, since the eastern region is more suited for cereal or foodgrain production, success in bringing the green revolution to the region will also have the benefit of reducing stress on groundwater reserves and soil health in the northern states where rice cultivation is currently taking place in a big way, but is unlikely to be environmentally sustainable for very long.
2. While raising yields through the development of new technologies appropriate to Indian agro-climatic realities is an important part of the reform agenda for Indian agriculture, there is considerable potential in raising productivity of the sector by bridging the gap between current practice and best practice using existing technologies. Better water resource management lies at the heart of bridging this gap. India accounts for 2.4 per cent of the world's total area and 16 per cent of the world's total population but has only 4 per cent of the total available fresh water. Sustainable management of water resources becomes even more challenging in the context of an agriculture sector which consumes more than

80 per cent of the available water and the alarming increase in the dependence on groundwater for irrigation.[7] Moreover, the gap between irrigation potential created and the irrigation potential utilised has been increasing over time—a reflection among other things of faulty project design, poor quality of lining and silting of canals, inadequate maintenance, and lack of proper coordination between the concerned government departments.

3. The Government has accordingly emphasised the need for conserving water, minimising wastage, increasing efficiency of water use, and ensuring equitable distribution both, across and within states and sectors, through integrated water resources management. In this context, participatory irrigation management will be a critical element of any systemic reform of the irrigation sector and there is an urgent need to increase the involvement of water users' associations in all stages of design, construction, and maintenance of irrigation projects, as well as in planning season-specific crop mixes as per agro-climatic conditions and marketing opportunities.
4. Other elements of institutional change include reforms to the policy regime such as relaxing restrictions under the Essential Commodities Act, so as to create unified agricultural markets in the country; and implementation of the amended Agricultural Produce Marketing Committee Act which would promote private sector participation in agricultural markets. Action is also needed to develop a more vibrant market for agricultural land. Far too many of India's farms are of extremely small size.[8] A better developed land lease market can pave the way towards consolidation of

7. One of the main reasons behind this is subsidised power that is provided to the agriculture sector which leads to overuse of groundwater.
8. Foster and Rosensweig (2011) show that larger farms are more profitable per acre, more mechanised, less constrained in input use after bad shocks, and employ less per-acre labour than small farms. Based on simulations based on key parameters estimated from their empirical analysis, they point out that over 20 per cent of the Indian agricultural labour force would be considered surplus if minimum farm scale is 20 acres.

landholdings and allow agriculture to benefit from economies of scale and new technologies.

5. Finally, improving productivity in agriculture will require diversification of the sector into high value commodities such as fruits, vegetables, and flowers. Agricultural diversification poses special challenges in marketing because the high-value produce of diversified agriculture is much more perishable than foodgrains. Farmers need assured linkages to efficient markets with transparent pricing and also modern logistics and cold chains to ensure transportation with minimum spoilage. The private/cooperative sector has an important role to play in this regard. An important issue in this context is the need to ensure that small and marginal farmers have adequate bargaining strength. An adequate dispute resolution mechanism is also necessary to encourage formation of farmers' groups to avail economies of scale.

Unlocking the Potential of Indian Manufacturing

Indian manufacturing has long performed below its potential. For example, the sector contributes only 16 per cent to India's GDP, vastly below the 40 per cent and 34 per cent that manufacturing in the PRC and Thailand contribute. And as regards employment, in comparison to countries such as PRC and Malaysia where the manufacturing sector accounts for between 20 per cent-35 per cent of total employment, the corresponding share in India has fluctuated between 10 per cent-15 per cent. And while India's employment share is not too different from a country such as Thailand, the quality of employment in Indian manufacturing is significantly lower. This may be seen in terms of the dominance of micro and small (and informal sector) firms in India already noted above.

With the right type of policies and institutional set up, there is little reason why India cannot experience a boom in manufacturing. Notwithstanding the global economic slowdown, a part of the expansion of India's manufacturing sector could come from exports—including in labour-intensive sectors such as apparel where India has natural comparative advantage, but which it has ceded to others due to weak infrastructure and a regulatory environment that has encouraged firms to remain small and in the informal sector. (Market failures on account of coordination and learning externalities are unlikely to be significant contributors to India's under performance in labour-intensive sectors.) More generally, there seems to be no compelling reason why India cannot increase its share in global exports, even in a slow trading environment, given its relatively low share in world merchandise exports (around 1.7% versus 13% for China).

In addition, there is the domestic market where India's growing middle-class presents the country with a unique opportunity. In particular, given the middle classes' demand for more and better quality consumer goods and housing, there is huge scope for India's manufacturing sector to meet this demand by expanding production of a wide range of products, exploiting economies of scope and scale in production, and raising economy wide income levels in the process.

Much of the action, including investment, will have to come from the private sector. But, there are important areas where public policy will have to play a catalytic role. These include public investments in infrastructure, especially transport and energy (and not with standing the scope to expand private investments via public-private partnerships in infrastructure); regulatory reform; and tackling market failures through appropriate elements of industrial policy.

To be sure, this will not be easy. Take the case of regulatory reform. Quite apart from the political capital needed for amending a particular piece of legislation, reform measures often need to be backed by the creation of new institutions. For example, given the legitimate demands of workers for income security, greater flexibility for firms in adjusting employment levels via amendments to the Chapter VB of the Industrial Disputes Act should be introduced alongside credible systems for providing severance pay and retraining, improvements in the functioning of employment exchanges, and steps to ultimately introduce social insurance mechanisms (such as an unemployment insurance system).

Similarly, market failures—such as those on account of coordination failures, learning externalities, and credit market imperfections—may prevent the private sector from entering new product lines and markets, experiment with potentially useful new technologies, and waste the entrepreneurship latent in many small and midsize firms. Tackling such market failures requires implementing well-designed interventions and coordination across a number of different government agencies; by most accounts, there is considerable scope for improvement in India on this front.

Fortunately, the Government recognises the importance of a dynamic manufacturing sector and has launched the "Make in India" programme in 2015. The programme encompasses a number of initiatives including efforts to improve the "ease of doing business" through a simplification of administrative procedures at the central and state levels for both domestic and FDI. At the same time, the Government's agenda on regulatory reforms includes a uniform goods and services tax (through the Constitution (122nd) Amendment Bill) which could do much to make India a unified market for domestic manufacturers; resolve insolvency issues (through a new bankruptcy law), and enforce contracts (though the public contracts dispute resolution bill). An effort by the Government of India at streamling labour regulations is on the backburner; however, it has shown willingness to let states pass reform oriented amendments to key pieces of legislation including the Industrial Disputes Act, Factories Act, and the Contract Labour Act.

The Make in India programme also dovetails with separate initiatives, such as increased public expenditures on infrastructure, the creation of industrial corridors anchored to major metropolitan cities and transport hubs, the Sagarmala initiative to spur port-led development, the Skill India initiative to promote technical and vocational education, and the Smart Cities initiative.

By and large, the programme and the package of initiatives are sensible. For a sector as complex as manufacturing, there can be no simple solution. A dynamic manufacturing sector needs a lot of things including good infrastructure and better regulations, fast, predictable, and coordinated decision-making by central, state, and local government agencies, access to land, skilled workers (from managers to shop floor), affordable housing, and well-functioning cities. Recognition of inter-linkages between the various different initiatives of the Government and the Make in India programme is thus wholly welcome.

Moreover, the programme and package of initiatives also seem to be moving Indian manufacturing in the right direction. For example, efforts to streamline administrative procedures have enabled India to move up 12 places in the World Bank's recent Ease of Doing Business rankings. Perhaps more importantly the efforts at creating unified online portals for the registration of labour identification numbers, streamlining the number of returns that businesses must file, greater use of online portals for their submissions and for various application processes, such as environmental and forest clearances, integrating processes involved in starting businesses, and reduced documentation requirements for exports and imports may have a larger impact on the ecosystem under which Indian manufacturing operates. As various commentators have observed from time to time, businesses operating in India often complain not only about the actual regulations, but also the uncertainties associated with the implementation of those regulations. The efforts at streamlining and improving the administrative systems associated with the regulations may well provide the more transparent and quicker decision-making that businesses have long asked for.

At the same time, it is early days and the ultimate impact of the programme and associated initiatives will likely take years to start paying dividends. In this context, international experience suggests that policymakers must pay careful attention to specific design issues associated with the various initiatives underway. Some key lessons from the international experience are as follows.

First, the financial and political costs associated with providing better infrastructure and better regulations (and better implementation of those regulations) are clearly large. As experience of the last several years has indicated, legislative reform on labour, land, and tax related issues is quite difficult in the context of coalition governments and divided majorities across different branches of Parliament. Moreover, the economic pricing of infrastructure assets is constrained for similar political economy reasons. In such a situation, a geographically focused effort to improve ecosystem for manufacturing is a necessity and the Government's initiatives on industrial corridors provides a logical starting point for focusing efforts to bring dynamism to Indian manufacturing.

Second, in considering the various components of industrial corridors, some lessons from the Chinese experience with its coastal special economic zones are particularly instructive. Chief among these are the importance of recognising the locational advantages associated with being near coasts or major cities with a history or tradition of foreign trading. More generally, easy access to ports, airports, highways and railway are critical if an industrial park or township has to have spillover benefits for a larger geography.

Third, importance of economies of scale in production and marketing, and economies of agglomeration must not be ignored. As noted above, India's manufacturing sector is unique in terms of the heavy concentration of small sized firms. While some of this may be due to the historical importance of traditional craft based industries, its persistence has been on account of a slew of regulations that have dis-incentivised operations at large scale. The bottom line is that a failure to address distortions in land, labour and capital markets that keep Indian firms small will only ensure that reallocation of resources to the most productive firms and sectors will be unnecessarily slow.

Fourth, local governments must take a more proactive role in industrial development. A key reason behind the success of Chinese manufacturing is a strong alignment of local government officials' incentives with local economic development. Manufacturing ultimately takes place in a particular location. If officials in that location do not have the incentives to ensure that firms located there do not grow, or if they do not have decision-making authority over the various inputs that firms need (such as roads, power, skilled workers, and decent housing and educational facilities for workers and their families), the growth prospects of firms and the location in question are bound to be more limited. Admittedly, India has a very different structure of governance for cities and townships than China. But the key take away is that mechanisms for aligning the incentives of local officials with local economic development need to be strengthened.

Finally, there's the question of tackling market failures. Considerations of equity as well as possible market failures have given rise to a lot of policy interventions all over the world, and in this regard India is no different. For example, the Government has for many decades promoted a variety of programmes to assist micro enterprises and small and medium enterprises. They have also utilised a variety of schemes to promote R&D and the adoption of new technologies. An example is the long-running technology upgrading financing scheme of the Government for the textile and apparel industry. A key issue that the Government has to consider is the effectiveness of these programmes.

As a recent study by the Inter-American Development Bank argues, policymakers must be guided by various principles in designing and implementing different elements of industrial policy. Some specific questions to guide policy interventions include: Why is it that the market does not do by itself what appears desirable? Is the policy intervention a proper remedy for the market failure? Are institutions sufficiently strong to adopt the policy effectively? In this context, the study goes on to present a useful typology of interventions based on: (i) a distinction between horizontal, or broad-based interventions versus vertical, or sector specific interventions; and (ii) the provision of public inputs versus market interventions. The least controversial interventions are those involving the delivery of public inputs of a broad-based nature. A one-stop shop for business registration is an example. Diametrically opposite are market-based interventions that apply to a particular sector. A tax exemption for the tourism industry is an example. By and large, the nature of such interventions makes them most prone to abuse or waste. This is not to suggest that policymakers shy away from the more complicated interventions. It does however suggest caution and that a lot of attention be paid to ensuring good design and implementation capacities.

Concluding Remarks

India's favourable demographics, the entrepreneurial dynamism of its private sector, and a small but not inconsequential cadre of well-trained managers, administrators, and science and technology personnel have enabled India to make the most of the reforms of the 1980s-1990s, and grow rapidly over the last two decades. However, this growth needs to be sustained, and it needs to be made more inclusive.

In this context, raising agricultural productivity and enabling workers to move from agriculture to more productive sectors of employment are the key imperatives. Insofar as the move to new sectors is concerned, India has done a reasonably good job in providing new opportunities in services. It must now achieve the same with the manufacturing sector, a sector with much untapped potential for creating productive jobs and powering growth. Toward this end, India has embarked on an ambitious Make in India programme. Now it needs to turn its attention to making this programme a success.

References

Foster, A. and M. Rosenzweig (2011). *Are Indian Farms Too Small? Mechanization, Agency Costs, and Farm Efficiency.*

Government of India (2013). *Economic Survey*. New Delhi: Ministry of Finance.

Gulati, A., and K. Ganguly (2010). "What Ails Indian Agriculture? Policy Reforms for a Second Green Revolution," Paper presented at a conference on *India: Economic Policies and Outcomes.* SIPA and Institute of Social and Economic Research and Policy, Columbia University

Hasan, R., S. Lamba, and A. Sengupta (2015). "Growth, Structural Change, and Poverty Reduction: Evidence from in India", in K.V. Ramaswamy (ed.), *Labour, Employment and Economic Growth: The Indian Experience.* Cambridge University Press.

Hasan, R. and K. Jandoc (2013). "Labour Regulations and Firm-size Distribution in Indian Manufacturing", in J. Bhagwati and A. Panagariya (eds.), *Reforms and Economic Transformation in India*. New York: Oxford University Press.

Inter-American Development Bank (2014). *Rethinking Productive Development: Sound Policies and Institutions for Economic Transformation.*

Nayyar, D. (2006). "Economic Growth in Independent India: Lumbering Elephant or Running Tiger?", *Economic and Political Weekly*, 15 April. Reprinted in P. Balakrishnan (ed.), *Economic Reforms and Growth in India*. Hyderabad: Orient Black Swan.

Nayyar, Deepak (2013). *Catch Up: Developing Countries in the World Economy.* Oxford: Oxford University Press.

Panagariya, A. (2008). *India: The Emerging Giant*. New York: Oxford University Press

Ravallion, M. (2009). "A Comparative Perspective on Poverty Reduction in Brazil, China and India," *Policy Research Working Paper Series* 5080. The World Bank

Ravallion, M. and G. Datt (1996). "How Important to India's Poor is the Sectoral Composition of Economic Growth?", *World Bank Economic Review* 10 (1): 1-25.

Rodrik, D. and A. Subramanian (2005). "From 'Hindu Growth' to Productivity Surge: The Mystery of the Indian Growth Transition", *IMF Staff Papers* 52(2): 193-228.

Walton, M. (2010). *Inequality, Rents, and the Long-Run Transformation of India.* Unpublished manuscript.

World Bank (2005). *India: Re-energizing the Agricultural Sector to Sustain Growth and Reduce Poverty.* New Delhi: Oxford University Press.

———. (2016). *Doing Business 2016: Measuring Regulatory Quality and Efficiency Doing Business.* Washington D.C.

5

RAKESH MOHAN

Transporting India to 2032

What do we Need to do?

I had the privilege of working with Abid Saheb, as he was universally known, when I returned to India from the World Bank in 1986 to work in the Planning Commission. He was then a Member of the Commission. I was one of the three 'Economic Advisers' inducted in the newly formed Development Policy Division, a prescient attempt by then Deputy Chairman, Dr Manmohan Singh, to begin the transformation of the Planning Commission towards a greater and active role in formulating policy. It is ironic that 28 years after that largely failed initiative, the whole Planning Commission has now been transformed into the NITI Aayog, the "Policy Commission"! Those were the days when people like us, returning to India from abroad from suspect institutions such as the World Bank and the International Monetary Fund (IMF), were viewed with suspicion. In fact, the greeting I received from a senior member of the administration on the first day when I arrived went something like this: "Why have you come here? Is there something wrong with you? Or is there some problem in your family? Why would you leave a cushy job in World Bank to come here? You know that we don't treat people like you well here!" India has come a long way since then: the recent Governor of the Reserve Bank of India (RBI), the Vice-chairman of NITI Aayog, and the Chief Economic Adviser, are all members of the Diaspora who have been welcomed back and appointed to such positions. Such openness has come with the overall opening of the economy to the world in all spheres.

That India has changed so much over this period owes much to the vision and foresight of dedicated and open minded people such as Abid Saheb. I would not have survived professionally in the

Planning Commission, and then moved on to other parts of the policy establishment to serve for more than 2 decades after that, if it had not been for the affectionate, warm and almost fatherly support that he gave in my initial years within the Planning Commission, and ever after wherever I was. He was among the first members of the Indian senior policy making establishment who advocated an open Indian economy; who viewed consumerism as a virtue and not a sin; who believed in the great potential of an expanding Indian middle class; who sowed the seeds for development of the Indian capital market; and who saw the dire necessity of completely overhauling the sclerotic Indian regulatory system that had throttled Indian industry. Yet, he was no elitist market fundamentalist: his initial work in community development was path breaking and his human touch with all shades of the community, both rich and poor, could only be seen to be believed.

Despite the fact that I did not report to him, he was the Member who I worked with most closely. My close association with him grew as I assisted him as Member of three Expert Committees that he chaired over the following 10 years: Eighth Plan Group on Industrial Exports, Committee to Review Textile Policy, and Expert Committee on Small Scale Industries. Each of these committees dealt with very controversial issues of the time, and which were concerned with highly conflicting vested interests. What distinguished him was his interest in looking ahead for the country's future, not hesitating in taking controversial positions (e.g. deregulating the textile industry in 1990; immediate abolition of small scale industry reservations in 1998), while striving to do all this in a harmonious consensual atmosphere. He was a great listener and had equal rapport with textile union leaders, textile industry captains, or power loom or handloom weavers. I learned a great deal from him in the art of humane, forward looking and decisive policy making, which served me well as I had the privilege of heading various policy making committees on diverse areas in the subsequent couple of decades.

Transport was among the important portfolios that Abid Saheb was in charge of as Member of the Planning Commission. He continued this interest as founding Chairman of the Asian Institute of Transport Development, a post he held till the time of his death. He therefore had an abiding interest in transport policy for the country, and it is this theme that I have chosen to write this essay on in his honour. Much of the work reported in this paper derives from the report of the National Transport Development Policy Committee (NTDPC, 2014), which I had the privilege of chairing. This was the latest of government policy committees that I have been involved in—a path that Abid Saheb put me on. I wish he had lived to see this report—which I think he would have approved of.

I focus in this paper on the transportation needs of the country over the next couple of decades, and what we need to do to satisfy them. This might seem to be a relatively narrow area of policy to address but, as will become clearer, if we do not make transport investments in the right manner, it will be difficult to achieve the kind of growth rates, around 8-9 per cent per year, that India should aspire to in order to reach middle income level by the early to mid 2030s, and to have any chance of eliminating poverty by then.

We all use transport in our daily lives: for work, for leisure, for school, for fulfilling personal needs and for business requirements. The transport of both passengers and goods is essential for the functioning of any economy. Transport connects producers and consumers. As an economy becomes more complex, the transport needs become correspondingly more demanding. Furthermore, with the emergence of complex supply chains for almost all products—food supplies as well as manufactured goods—the need for sophisticated transport systems has become as important to the farmer as it is for a multinational company. The challenge for India is how we can generate a transport system that is efficient and reliable, but is also affordable, safe and accessible for all. Furthermore, given our energy dependence, energy efficiency is of the utmost importance in designing the Indian transport system, and with transport emissions being key contributors to climate change and urban air pollution, this is another area of concern. As speeds have increased, and poised to increase further, fatalities and injuries have increased exponentially in the transport system, causing extreme levels of human suffering as also high economic costs to the system.

Trends in Growth of Transport

The daily experience of travelling in India, and the time taken for most freight transport, makes it evident that India's transport networks are severely constrained.

Since independence, the growth in freight transport has been broadly consistent with that of overall GDP, and particularly that of industrial growth. The elasticity of demand with respect to GDP has been near unity, if not slightly higher than that. Extrapolation of demand on a similar basis would suggest that if GDP grows at about 7 per cent a year, and freight transport demand grows accordingly, we can expect such demand to quadruple by the mid 2030s. If indeed the economy does grow faster as it did during the 2003-2012 period, such demand could be significantly higher—freight transport might grow by a factor of 6. With railways' capacity expansion having been constrained over the whole period, there has been a consistent loss in the railways' share in freight traffic. It fell from about 90 per cent in 1951 to about 65 per cent by 1980, and further to about 30 per cent by 2010. The share of roads in freight traffic has, therefore, grown correspondingly. The railways have got increasingly specialised over the years in the transportation of bulk commodities like coal, iron ore, fertilisers, cement and foodgrains, though here also roads are beginning to increase their share. Industrial goods are being carried almost entirely by road now, despite increasing containerisation, which can enable much greater use of multimodal freight transportation. Such a pattern is not healthy from both the energy security and environmental point of view. The railways are clearly more energy efficient and less polluting than comparable road traffic.

The fall in passenger traffic share of the railways has been even more dramatic over time. The elasticity of demand of passenger traffic with respect to GDP has varied between 1.4 and 1.8 over the different decades since independence, with the average being around 1.6 to 1.7. Once again, with the railways being capacity constrained, the long term elasticity for road passenger traffic comes out to be about 2.0, and for railways at about 0.9, though there has been some acceleration in recent years. Thus, passenger traffic growth has not even kept up with GDP growth: hence the daily experience of overcrowded trains and non-availability of reservations on a regular basis. The share of railways in passenger traffic was around 70 per cent in 1951; it fell to about half, 35 per cent by 1971, 22 per cent in 1991 and just about 10 per cent by 2011.

With the expectation of passenger traffic growing at almost double the rate of GDP, it may grow in excess of 15 per cent per year over the next couple of decades, which implies that total passenger traffic might increase by a factor of more than 15 over this period. So, even if the railways accelerate their capacity expansion for passenger traffic significantly, they will keep losing their share to roads, and to air traffic for longer distances.

The relative loss of the railways in both passenger and freight traffic is understandable given the relative under investment in recent years in railways infrastructure. It is interesting to note that the share of transport in total public sector investment has been relatively constant at around 13-15 per cent of the total: except that it was increased to about 17 per cent in the Fifth Five Year Plan. Until the mid 1990s, that is, till the Eighth Five Year Plan, the railways share in public investment in transport was consistently between 45 to 50 per cent, with a peak of 56 per cent in the Seventh Plan (when Abid Saheb was in charge of transport in the Planning Commission). However, since the mid 1990s, their share has fallen successively to 38, 36 and 30 per cent in the Ninth, Tenth and Eleventh Plans respectively. The roads share has grown correspondingly from around 20-30 per cent till the mid 1990s to 45-55 per cent since then—consistently and significantly higher than the railways.

The increase in road investment has taken place because of the two transformational initiatives taken by the previous National Democratic Alliance (NDA) government of Prime Minister Atal Bihari Vajpayee: the National Highway Development Project (NHDP) and the Prime Minister's Gram Sadak Yojana (PMGSY). The distinguishing feature of both these initiatives was that they were national in scope with the broad features of both the programmes being outlined ab initio—just as the original design of the US interstate highway system was in the late 1950s under the Eisenhower administration.

Consequently, the acceleration of traffic growth on roads during this period is quite noticeable, as is the growth in motor vehicles—private motor vehicles as well as commercial vehicles. Such growth will continue as the roll out of the road programme continues and, perhaps, intensifies with eventual construction of highways.

This continuous erosion in traffic share of the railways is not healthy from a number of viewpoints. It is energy inefficient, with the railways being far more energy efficient on a like to like basis as compared with road transport. With India being a net energy importer it is also undesirable for energy security considerations. Increasing pollution from motor vehicles is raising environmental and health concerns. The exponential increase in deaths and injuries from road transport is causing immense human hardship, apart from raising economic costs. Finally, increasing emissions from motor vehicles are also a climate change concern. A key transport policy objective for the future must therefore be to reorient traffic from roads to railways.

The lesson for the future is, therefore, clear: there needs to be a transformational initiative, similar in scope to the NHDP and the PMGSY, significantly enhancing public investment for capacity expansion of the railways. The approach has to be much more systematic than has been the experience in transport planning so far, particularly in the railways. The point to point convenience of carrying freight by truck is hard to beat. It is only if there is seamless transfer from truck to rail, or ship, or air, and back to truck can there be any chance of rail freight traffic regaining any share. With increasing containerisation such seamless transfer is now possible, provided there is comprehensive modernisation of the railways infrastructure and rolling stock, and in associated logistical facilities. Thus, future planning for transport has to be long-term, comprehensive and integrated, encompassing rail, road, ports and airports and logistics. The project centric and politically motivated line centric approach must be eschewed.

Passenger traffic by air is beginning to become significant for longer distances and higher fare paying passengers. This trend accelerated in the 2000s with the partial deregulation of airlines, and the introduction of budget carriers. Although the sector is currently undergoing some restructuring, the future potential of large increases in traffic remains high. Domestic passenger traffic increased from about 7.5 million in 1990-91 to about 60 million in 2011-12. Observing the air traffic levels that have already been achieved in China, it is quite likely that domestic passenger traffic could be in excess of 400 million by the early 2030s. Similarly, international traffic could grow in a similar fashion from the current 40 million or so to over 200 million over the same period. With such large increases in the offing, the need for very significant and timely investments in airports, air traffic control, safety, and associated infrastructure is clear. There is also need for modernisation and reorganisation of the regulatory institutions that govern air traffic.

Investment for Growing Transport Needs

I have sketched a broad idea of the kind of growth in transport that can be expected if the country is to achieve sustained annual growth of around 7-9 per cent over the next couple of decades. It is important to understand that, while transport investment is a response to emerging demand, it is also an economic growth driver itself. In fact, in the absence of key transport investments, economic growth at the rate envisaged just cannot fructify: for example, trade growth cannot take place without corresponding investment in ports; coal based power production cannot grow without the availability of rail based transport systems to carry coal from the mines or ports, to the power stations. In other areas, inadequate transport availability hinders the attainment of efficient production capacities that are internationally competitive. In a continental economy such as India's, both inland and international transport costs have to be minimised for its agricultural and manufacturing goods to be competitive in world markets. East Asian manufacturing capacity has become globally competitive on the basis of efficient transport provision and logistics expertise. But it is notable that much of the East Asian production capacity is based in or near the coastal regions. This is an additional challenge for India: its inland manufacturing capacity, which is considerable, would be handicapped if the transport system is not both efficient and cost competitive.

What then would be the broad parameters for investment in transport? In our work in the National Transport Development Policy Committee (NTDPC), we arrived at our estimates from two parallel approaches: a top down model based macroeconomic approach, and bottom up sectoral estimates based on informed projections by domain experts. We found reasonable correspondence between the two approaches for the initial 10 years, but significant divergence as we went further out. Interestingly, it seems that domain experts simply could not imagine the magnitude of demand increase, and hence investment required beyond 10 years or so: thus the top down estimates for the outer years of the 2 decade projection horizon were higher than the bottom up estimates.

India recorded a per capita GDP of about ₹75,000 ($1550) and overall GDP of ₹90 trillion ($1.9 trillion) in 2011-12, the terminal year of 12th Five Year Plan. If per capita income grows on a consistent basis at an annual rate of around 7 per cent (GDP growth in excess of 8 per cent), it would double every 10 years, and grow by a factor of 4 by the early 2030s—to about US$6,000-6,500 (2011-12 prices), and GDP would reach a level of about US$ 9 trillion, levels that have already been reached by China. Thus, achieving such growth should be our minimum level of aspiration. But is it feasible? Annual growth in Indian GDP increased from about 3.0–3.5 per cent during 1950-1980, to about 6.0-6.5 per cent during 1980-2010: we need another phase of acceleration to about 8-9 per cent over the next couple of decades.

What would be the implications for investment in the economy if such growth rates are to be achieved? We have already experienced such growth in the 2003-2012 period. GDCF (gross domestic capital formation) levels were in the range of 35-38 per cent during this period, with corresponding domestic savings rates, supplemented by sustainable modest external savings of about 1-2 per cent of GDP. Enhancement in savings was achieved in all the sectors: households, private corporate sector, public sector and government itself. This was achieved in the presence of broad macroeconomic stability:

falling fiscal deficits, low inflation, financial stability, modest and stable current account deficits. Corporate savings and investments were fuelled by the reduction in crowding out by the public sector, low interest rates and increased profitability. For similar growth to be achieved on a consistent basis over the next couple of decades, similar macroeconomic pre-conditions will have to be maintained on an extended basis: We cannot afford the interregnum experienced during 2012-2014. This is just a necessary condition. Beyond this minimum, investment has to be stepped up again in a purposive fashion in both the public and private sectors, with a certain emphasis on infrastructure broadly and on transport in particular.

The systematic projections made by the NTDPC suggest that the overall GDCF needs to increase from the current level of about 33–35 per cent of GDP to approach 40 per cent by the late 2020s and early 2030s. Correspondingly, total infrastructure investments will need to increase from 5.8 per cent of GDP achieved in the Eleventh Five Year Plan (2007-2012) to about 8.0 per cent over the next three or four quinquennial periods, up to the early to mid 2030s. At this rate, total infrastructure investment would have to rise from about ₹25 trillion (US$425 billion) in the Eleventh Five Year Plan to about ₹70 trillion (US$ 1.25 trillion), ₹100 trillion (US$ 1.9 trillion) and ₹150 trillion (US$ 2.9 trillion) in the following quinquennial periods starting 2017 (all at 2012-13 prices). The corresponding investment in transport is envisaged to be about 3.7 per cent of GDP, 45.0 per cent of total infrastructure investment—up from about 2.7 per cent in the Eleventh Five Year plan (2007-2012). To achieve this, there will be a need to increase both public and private sector investment in transport.

Whereas, the NTDPC projected increasing proportions of private investment in infrastructure—from about 36 per cent of the total in the Eleventh Plan period to around 45 per cent in the late 2020s and early 2030s, there may be need for tempering these expectations with corresponding increases in public investment—which will have corresponding fiscal implications. The private sector share in roads investment was estimated at around 15 per cent in the later years in the Eleventh Plan: this was projected to increase to 25-30 per cent in succeeding quinquennial periods. In view of the various difficulties encountered in implementation of the PPP model, it is likely that these expectations were too high, and certainly much higher than experienced in other countries. Furthermore, as the initial investments are made in the segments with the heaviest traffic, and as the roll out of highways extends to segments with less heavy traffic, there may be reduced opportunities for realistic profitable private investment.

The key departure made by the NTDPC is in its strategy for much enhanced investment in the railways. There has been a very significant step up in public investment in roads from about 0.4 per cent of GDP up to the late 1990s to about 1.0-1.2 per cent in recent years, while investment in the railways has stagnated at around 0.4 per cent. The kind of traffic expansion that is required in freight haulage for a growing economy suggests a similar increase in annual railways investment to about 1.0 to 1.2 per cent of GDP on a sustained basis over the couple of decades. Only then can there be any reversal of the eroding railway share in freight traffic. A beginning has been made in the 2015-16 railways budget, which has proposed a 50 per cent enhancement in railways investment to over ₹100,000 crore, and ₹850,000 crore over 2015-2020. Such levels of investment would be consistent with the kind of investment enhancement needed in the railways, but which will be difficult to achieve without extensive reorganisation of the railways.

The implication of NTDPC's strategy is for total public investment in transport to increase from about 1.8 per cent of GDP in the Eleventh Plan to about 2.0-2.2 per cent over the next couple of decades, while private investment increases from 1.0 per cent in the Eleventh Plan to 1.3-1.6 per cent over the same period. Given the public investment requirements of the railways, and reduced private sector expectations in roads, total public investment in transport may need to be in the range of 2.2 to 2.5 per cent, with corresponding reduction in private investment.

The achievement of such a strategy requires making strategic decisions in terms of relative allocation of resources between rail and road, accompanying pricing and taxation policies, and regulatory and organisational reforms, which can then be used to nudge transport demand toward the desired modal shares.

The detailed examination made by the NTDPC of needed investment in the railways gives primacy to investment in the Dedicated Freight Corridor (DFC) and its continued expansion throughout the next two decades. There will be need for corresponding replacement of the existing antiquated rolling stock with modern wagons for freight as well as passenger coaches, along with significant modernisation of the existing track and signaling infrastructure to enable higher speeds across the system, which will then be exclusively devoted to passenger traffic. These investments are essential if adequate transport facilities are provided for the emerging needs of the growing economy. These investment projections do not include very capital intensive projects such as high speed rail transport that are receiving much current attention: given the other needs it would be a mistake to divert attention to such prestige projects at the present time.

Need for a Coherent Integrated Strategy

Much of transport planning and programming in India has been project centric, and has largely been done in silos, despite the existence of the Planning Commission. There has been little coordination across modes, thus making the system less efficient than it could be. Moreover, with the emerging needs for a modernised integrated logistical system that enables efficient and smooth inter-modal transfers that are the most economical, there is now a clear need for an integrated system based approach.

At present, decisions on investments in highways and expressways on the one hand, and potential DFCs and even possible high speed trains are made in isolation of each other. Similarly, particularly from the freight point of view, investment decisions on ports are also not as closely coordinated with corresponding investments in inland connectivity by rail or road. A specific issue that best illustrates this problem is the transportation of what may be termed as energy commodities. The elasticity of demand for power with respect to GDP growth is around unity. Thus if we expect GDP to grow by a factor of around four over the next couple of decades, so will the demand for power. Given the dominance of coal as fuel for Indian power production, and even accounting for significant substitution by other energy sources, including renewable energy, the power sector demand for coal is likely to increase by a factor of around 2.7-2.8 over this period. It is expected that, at best, domestic coal production could increase about 2.5 times, from about 440 MT in 2011-12 to about 1,110 MT over the next 20 years; imported coal may then have to increase by a factor of five from about 70 MT in 2011-12 to about 350 MT over the same period.

Similarly, just as has been experienced by China, the intensity of steel use can be expected to increase continuously in a growing modernising economy aspiring to middle income status, particularly as industrialisation and urbanisation accelerates. The demand for steel is therefore expected to grow seven fold from around 70 MT in 2011-12 to almost 500 MT over 20 years. Each tonne of finished steel requires three to four tonnes of raw material, thus the transport requirements of the steel industry will be almost double that of coal.

There will also be a corresponding demand growth for petroleum energy resources, most of which will continue to be imported, combining the increasing demand for coal imports, petroleum and petroleum products, and steel related products, along with other containerised goods for export and import, the need for investment in a couple of mega ports on both coasts becomes clear.

The Indian transport system for bulk commodities is already heavily congested. A rail route is generally considered congested when capacity utilisation exceeds 80 per cent. At present, almost all the major trunk routes over which such bulk commodities will be transported are operating at over 100 per cent capacity: hence the frequent build up of coal stocks at pit heads and problems in coal linkages for power stations. Economic growth at the enhanced level envisaged simply cannot take place unless there is the kind of systemic and accelerated investment in railways as emphasised.

This example illustrates the need for coordinated investment programming, encompassing both the public and private sectors, in power capacity, ports, railways, highways and pipelines. In order to avoid emerging bottlenecks it is essential in these areas to have appropriate time sequencing in each of these segments. Moreover, given the long time lays inherent in such large projects: rail tracks, large ports, pipelines, and highways, the need for integrated planning and programming becomes clear.

Governing Transport Development

If this situation is to be addressed, the country will need a greatly enhanced number of transport professionals, researchers and educators in all fields of transport. There is a shortage of expertise in all areas and at all levels, and especially interdisciplinary to take care of pollution and safety concerns, and for integrated planning and implementation. India does not have any institutions in the governmental system, universities, or even standalone ones, which compare favourably with those in peer countries. So the country fares poorly in terms of knowledge production in comparison with peers such as China and Brazil, as it does in terms of engineering quality and execution of transport infrastructure, even though there is no shortage of potential. As an example, even the Research, Designs & Standard Organisation (RDSO), as a dedicated research and standards organisation of the Indian Railways, is staffed with regular railways staff rather than technical experts: it has few, if any, PhDs on its staff. The situation is similar, if not worse, in other sectors.

This situation has to be addressed with some urgency if the challenges outlined in this paper, and in greater detail in NTDPC Report, are to be addressed over the coming years. Institutions take time to get built, as does the production of expertise. The NTDPC has suggested that just one per cent of investment in each sector be earmarked for institution and capacity building and these resources be channeled in a purposive manner for this end.

Where do we go from here? It is clear that, despite the planning apparatus that India has had for 65 years, the institutional framework for formulation of transport policy, planning and coordination is very weak. Now that this system is itself being overhauled with the abolition of the Planning Commission and formation of NITI Aayog, it is an opportune time to set up a technically competent system that is capable of addressing the increasingly complex transport needs of a growing economy that is continental in size and approaching middle income levels.

It is first necessary to recognise that the existing system is simply inadequate at all levels: centre, states and city. Whereas there is a general belief that India has highly technically competent professionals in all spheres, the reality in transport is that the country is bereft of expertise. Although the Planning Commission has had a specific Division responsible for transport for a very long time, it has little expertise and has always been small in size. Consequently, the Planning Commission appointed a "National Transport Policy Committee" at a high level around 1980 to formulate long term policy, and then again the NTDPC 30 years later in 2010. But there is little evidence of the government even having the capacity to process these reports in an integrated manner, let alone implement them. What is needed is a standing technical capacity that is capable dealing with emerging challenges on a continuous basis, rather relying on occasional expert committees.

Integrated transport policy making is rendered that much more difficult with the existence of different ministries for each mode: roads, railways, ports and shipping, civil aviation and urban transport, with none really responsible for logistics and inter modal transport. It might have been expected that the lack of expertise in the Planning Commission could have been compensated by the Ministries, but they also do not have such technical capacity, and are staffed by generalists with short tenures at the leadership level. Given the current Indian administrative governance system, senior officials, while being competent generalists, do not possess domain knowledge of the ministries that they are appointed to. They are essentially birds of passage. The situation at the state and city levels just gets worse.

For these considerations, it is necessary to set up coordinating policy and planning institutions with the requisite technical expertise. The NTDPC has proposed that a high level "Office for Transport Strategy" be set up at both the central level and in each state to formulate integrated transport strategies, policies and programmes. "The OTS must have the resources to build a strong technical team, aggregate, manage and analyse transport data, and be able to assert itself as a compelling advocate of policies that leverage transport for development goals". Such a proposed OTS should be set up as an independent agency, but associated with the NITI Aayog. An institutional structure would have to be organised so that the proposed OTS is enabled to work with existing Ministries and implementing agencies and NITI Aayog. Similar institutions should be set up in each state. At the city level, MUTAs (metropolitan urban transport authorities) need to be formed to plan and implement transport systems for the burgeoning needs of the expanding metropolitan cities in the country.

These institutions should be visibly technocratic, and be of adequate size. The European Commission, for example, has more than 2,000 professional staff in its mobility and transport unit; and the US Department of Transportation has as many as 60,000 professionals. Thus, even the most market oriented advanced economies need in house technical expertise for planning, engineering and execution purposes.

It will then become possible to set up the kind of planning, policy and strategy institution that are necessary for transporting India to 2032. If such an approach is not taken, and if there isn't the kind of step up in transport investment suggested, there is little chance for India to grow sustainably to middle income levels.

Governance and Society

6

DIPANKAR GUPTA

The Master Narrative of Citizenship

From a Nation-State to a Liberal Democratic Nation-State

Like all talented intellectuals, Abid Hussain was a man of many parts and each facet shone spectacularly. But through it all, he had one singular obsession, which he voiced time and again, and more so in recent decades, and that was the ideal of secularism, in both word and deed. What distinguished him from many other mediocre practitioners of secularism, was his unwavering commitment to citizenship. For him, secularism was not a matter of tolerance, but a matter of right; it was not just a wordy public statement but a deliverable that linked material prosperity with fraternity. The essay that follows stays close to Abid Hussain's calling and hopefully does it some justice.

I

The notion of multiple narratives is true not just for India but for other countries as well, including those in Europe. This is where we need to be careful. While many of these accounts usefully contribute to the actual making of a nation-state, we cannot just stop there. The move from being a nation-state to a democratic-state is not an easy task. In this crucial transition it no longer pays to indulgently display one's culture and history, and other like narratives, but to be self-conscious about citizenship. In this process a few cherished histories, heritages, myths, legends, and legacies of great men and women have to be kept pragmatically aside. While some of these articulations may build a sense of community, such as that of belonging to a nation,[1] they are frequently unhelpful if a liberal democratic constitution is to be successfully framed and lived by.

'Nation-state' narratives are about blood, soil, wars, sacrifices, gods, goddesses, religious sites, texts, etc.—all of which are usually a distraction when it comes to crafting a sense of unified and equal citizenship. While these tales of cultural heroics and religious virtues may create ardent nationalists, but nationalists are not always mindful of the ethics of 'citizenship'. If this value is absent, or present only in a lifeless form then all we have is a nation-state, but no democracy. It is necessary to emphasize this for citizenship is hard to imbibe but without it there is no liberal democracy (Marshall 1990). In fact, in the making of a democratic nation-state many pure nation-state narratives may need to be undermined, if not outright erased and denied (Anderson 1983). Post-colonial India did just that with its Republican Constitution when it abolished untouchability, majoritarian privileges and feudal authority. We must also learn to forget many aspects of the past if we have to fashion an actually functioning democratic future. So from a democratic perspective, it is not as if histories, myths and traditions are always positive, though they might help to super-charge a self-righteous nationalism.

There are different versions of what makes for a 'nation-state', and there are also diverse ways of getting there. What they all have in common is that they galvanise their local cultures in one form or another, allowing for some aspects, denying other features and highlighting a select few. So it is not as if in the making of a nation-state, each aspect of the past gets expression: some do and some do not (Anderson 1983). In other words, at the end of the day there is no 'yellow brick road' or a privileged route in becoming a nation-state. We all come to it in our unique and specific manner. For example, when France became France only 18 per cent of the population there spoke French. When Italy became Italy, only 2 per cent of the

1. See Anderson (1983). This work drew a lot of attention because it brought home the fact that nation-state bonds are not self-evident and that in the beginning all nation states began on a bed of cultural and linguistic differences. What brought people in these nation-states together was an 'imagination' which cannot be understood through positive science.

population spoke Italian. In fact, when Massimo d'Azeglio, the 19th century, Turin born Piedmontese artist and statesman, wrote in his autobiography: "Now that we have made Italy, let us make Italians" it immediately became one of the best known quotes of the day (Hobsbawm 1988: 110)

It is, therefore, easier to establish a nation-state than to actually go the distance and create its citizens. Without liberal democracy no nation-state can be said to have fully arrived. In India too we have been wrestling with this project, since Independence, taking a few steps forward and then moving back. There are so many languages, histories and traditions that often work at cross-purposes making the mission of creating Indian citizens quite a challenge. When we began to consider ourselves as 'Indians', we tried to harness our multiple energies in such a manner that it would strengthen the unitary concept of nation-state, but what good would this be if we were not democratic at the same time? Yes, it is true that we had a huge job ahead of us. We had to bring a sense of unity as we were till recently, that is until the anti-colonial struggle bound us, multiple peoples with multiple cultures. Liberal democracy was still far away.

II

But Jawaharlal Nehru, and other nation-builders like him, did a stirring job at this. They looked back into the history of our subcontinent in order to locate unifying factors in our multiple narratives to create a seed bed for democracy to take root. In his *Discovery of India* (Nehru 2008), Nehru found many such features in India. Even at the plane of geography, our high mountains in the north and our deep seas to the south bound the people in this extensive landmass together. He also came across great degrees of similarity between the way rituals and religious practices were performed in different parts of the country. We may add to this mainstream catalogue the many 'little' practices of the people, marginalised communities included, which could be linked in a great chain of unity. Thus, while the harmonious elements in our many practices and beliefs received salience, those that did not had to be put aside. It did not matter how ancient they were, or how many advocates they had; if they came in the way of creating unity, and then citizenship, they were out of the door.

But look at the unifiers? Apart from the very obvious ones such as how gods and goddesses appear under different names in different parts of India; apart from fact that the myths and legends, with little lost in translation, do the rounds in households of the poor and rich, north and south; apart from all these oft quoted references, we also find common themes between the heartland of India and what many of us erroneously consider to be our geographic hinterlands. For instance, Lord Ganesh appears on Tibetan *thangkas*; different version of the third eye of the peacock in North-eastern hill tales resembles Shiva's famous feature; also how the legends of Radha and Krishna, or Ram and Sita, metamorphose in different parts of the country, including the North East, and the list can go on.

These uniform aspects from heterogeneous backgrounds and provenances together help citizenship find a convivial base. We have the *Ramayana* which travels all over India creating a sacralised cartography; different pilgrimage centres; institutes of learning, and sites where Gurus attained their enlightenment, and so on. This search for cultural overlaps across the geography of India is very Nehruvian in its orientation because they were carefully selected to emphasise just one end—the unity of all Indian peoples, where no one culture or history is privileged over others. It is because of this dense imbrication of cultural detail upon detail, practice upon practice, belief upon belief, that our Constitution could definitively assert in its opening line: "We the People of India...." Indeed, our search shows we have common roots that run deep, though on the surface there are so many seeming differences. That we have a recognition of all this is because of adroit acts of leadership without which citizenship would never have been born in this country.

While emphasising unity, care must be taken that this does not violate the ethics of liberal democracy. A nation-state, by itself, could easily be fascist or theocratic, but for it to be democratic, its heart must be cleansed of cultural egotism. In this context, we need to pause and take stock of how religion, indeed religions, can be accommodated within a democratic nation-state. As contemporary history has shown, the many narratives on religion have the capacity to pull us, often with great force and brutality, in different directions—and in that process, not just endanger the unity of the country, but also its democratic credentials. The Congress National Movement was mindful of this possibility, yet the first thing that hit us in the face with Independence was the Partition. And before we knew it there were genocidal wars between Hindus, Sikhs and Muslims, and the wounds of those bloody episodes are the sources of ethnic wars even today. When millions are rendered homeless and thousands of lives are lost, the task of starting anew when your loved ones are gone is about the hardest thing that can be imagined.

In the immediate aftermath of Partition, a few important decisions were taken by our freedom fighters who had now become elected representatives in Independent India. The first was that there would be no talk of any further partitioning of the country. In fact, to advocate it even under the guise of national self-determination would now be considered seditious. Prior to Independence there were a number of statements made by Congress leaders, including Gandhi and Patel, who were quite easy and accepting of regions seceding from India after Independence, should the demand be a popular one. But after India became Independent, especially after the Partition, such ideas were no longer acceptable and became taboo.

From then on, the narrative of the nation-state frequently built on phrases that alluded to the sacral soil of our country that now attained the status of an incontrovertible given. The idea of 'territory' was now uppermost; Partition had seared that into our national consciousness. Before Independence, nationalist leaders had a vague idea of our territorial boundaries, but after Independence, territory became a reality that was non-negotiable. This is why every now and again the symbol of territory acts up in our domestic politics aiming to embarrass religious minorities as if they are somehow 'ethnic' outsiders. If one wants to put any politician in the dog house for good, somehow the charge must be made to stick that this person is out to partition India yet again.

This indeed has happened on a number of occasions in India. When the Punjab problem rose in the 1980s, and more recently in Gujarat in 2002 after Godhra, Hindu activists sought to portray Sikhs and Muslims as 'ethnic' enemies who are bent on slicing up 'our' sacred land. But we were in a sense lucky that we had a counter-narrative going and that is the narrative of 'Gandhi'. This narrative is very important because it is not just a compendium of mudpacks, pacifism, vegetarianism and celibacy, with which Gandhi is usually identified—but about the secular political ideals so central to democracy and liberalism. It is this legacy that the Father of the Nation bequeathed to us and for which he paid for with his life. Without Gandhi we could perhaps have become independent, perhaps even earlier, but India in all probability would not have been a democracy. This is the aspect of Gandhi that we tend to forget: we look at Gandhi as a backward, spiritual, otherworldly ascetic snared by calculating politicians. But Gandhi's most important contribution was that he made India a democratic Nation-State. It is this that Gandhi moulded with non-violence as his sole weapon. This is why he should be understood as an unrelenting and uncompromising liberal democrat for whom debates and discussions were the bedrock of guaranteeing citizenship rights to masses of people of diverse provenances.

It is only after the idea of non-violence is made the centre-piece of democracy that citizenship steps in and majoritarianism is put in its place. If a public space of the kind sought by Habermas (1987: 198) requires a transcendental and epistemological base then it is to be found in Gandhi. If Habermas, by his own admission, was unable to locate an unerring and irrevocable principle which would give the idea of a free public space its conceptual mooring, it is because he did not consider Gandhi's dogged insistence on 'non-violence' in deed and speech. Gandhi did revert, time and again, to religion to further his cause, but always keeping in mind the principle of non-violence. This is what helped us to overcome the many backward narratives of our tradition, and helped us to write a forward-looking Constitution. With a stroke of the pen we abolished untouchablity, a major prejudice laden narrative that we inherited from our backward past. Then we abolished feudalism, and the ground under ancient ties of patron-client relationship slowly began to slip away. With Independence we could not rid ourselves totally of our past, yet we could control its negative influences by giving ourselves a Constitution that guaranteed the principles of liberal democracy. Multiple narratives of different origins, pedigrees and persuasions, were rearticulated to guarantee citizenship.

III

This factor must be kept uppermost even while discussing art, tradition and craft. The best way to give dignity to cultures is not to bottle them in isolated jars, or in insular morphologies, but to see them in terms of connections that citizenship now opens up. We were a major textile power once upon a time. What happened to us? In fact, in 1985 we produced 6 billion square metres of cloth. About 25 years later we are now producing 26 billion square metres of cloth, but mill-made contribution still remains at around 6 billion square metres. The extra amount was produced in power-looms and hand-looms by men and women often working in terrible conditions. The number of *chippas* (workers specialising in hand-printing in Rajasthan and Gujarat) is increasing because migrants from Panipat (in Haryana) as well as from Bihar are keeping that craft alive and thriving. These migrants were never really part of this tradition, but once they picked up the art and expertise they are now virtuosos at it. This is yet another example of how informal workers are being absorbed in the small scale sector allowing old crafts to get a second life and an international market too.

These workers are citizens too, and not just poor artisans. When we discuss the continuation of crafts, we must also keep in mind that the environment of traditional craftsmanship was not always sensitive to the ideas of modern citizenship where rights, working conditions, benefits, insurance, etc., are also important. The worker as a citizen should not be separated from the worker as an artisan. When we see the humble educational background of these unlettered crafts people, their economic vulnerability and their uncertain future, we cannot just rejoice in their production of fine artifacts that represent the material culture of India without paying attention to the harsh conditions under which they work. This takes away a lot of the shine away from their glittering productions. This is why we cannot ignore the narrative of citizenship.

Globalisation, however, is also asserting this fact. It is telling us something qualitatively new is now on the agenda. Citizens want to be served as consumers of state services where the concerns of citizenship are uppermost. It is not anymore about privileges, about patron-client relationship, about simple goodwill, but about citizen rights and what the modern democratic state promises to deliver. Globalisation is not just about international trade, for history is replete with instances of long-distance commerce. So what is new? More speed? More technology? More migrants, internal and cross border? More money being exchanged?

It is all of this and something more. These are quantitative changes, but where is that qualitative factor that makes contemporary globalisation unique? The brand new marker of globalisation today is that people want a life of dignity, where their children will receive a decent education and will be able to visualise a future, where they can live without depending on patrons for help. Globalisation promises a high degree of resemblances between people, especially in terms of accessing institutions that generate social mobility. This is the promise of globalisation, and it can best be served by the narrative of citizenship.

This echoes T.H. Marshall's (1990) view that citizenship confers on all an equality of status on whose foundations structures of inequality can be built. This basically implies that the emphasis is not to make all of us equal in the end, but in the beginning. The ease of access to socially valuable assets should be equal across classes and communities. The distilled point is that all citizens should be able to aspire towards acquiring socially valuable assets and the way to do that is to provide universal health and education. After that levelling takes place, let each person go ahead and be different; let each person get richer or poorer; let each person be successful or a failure. But nobody, at any point should say with any legitimacy that the avenues to achieve were kept away from them. Citizenship is not about 'ends' but about 'means to ends'—that is what needs to be kept 'equal'.

IV

Likewise, when discussing religious traditions the mother narrative of citizenship must be kept firmly in place. When minorities are attacked, it is not hand-holding by bleeding hearts that will give them support, but the laws of the land which guarantee them rights as citizens and protect them against discrimination. Majoritarian politics specialises in minoritising certain populations in the name of the people, soil, history, tradition, etc. Majoitarianism uses these cultural attributes to create fissures that may have continued from the past. But citizenship must combat these attempts and this cannot be done simply by reminding people to be 'good' citizens but by 'enforcing' those laws that guarantee citizenship unambiguously and unequivocally.

Interestingly, minorities that are hurt and victimised nearly always respond in the name of citizens. Their first plea after being attacked is: "We are also citizens. Look after us. We want those people who have maimed and brutalised us to be tried by the law of the land upheld in the Constitution." It is not as if they are asking for simple retribution on the basis of a quick courtyard trial, nor by traditional rules and regulations, but by norms that guarantee citizenship. This is why I have felt for a long time that our Constitution would have done well to replace its opening line, "We the people of India..." with the phrase "We the citizens of India...."

When Partition came with Independence, the fear was that regional assertions might create other 'partitions' too. Therefore, when in the 1950s and 1960s there were demands for unilingual states, such as that of Andhra Pradesh, Maharashtra, Gujarat and Punjab, many leaders thought this was the beginning of the balkanisation of India. That didn't happen. The Samyukta Maharashtra Samiti that fought for Maharashtra did not go on to wave a sovereign flag, but stayed happily within the union of India. They got Maharashtra and Mumbai as its capital, and they were satisfied. Likewise, when other states were formed there was no basic antagonism between their linguistic demands and that of the Indian nation-state. Worldwide, most commentators were unable to grasp this, for in European history, language has always been a dividing factor. This is why one must underline the fact that each nation has a separate set of narratives that guide it to its specific nationhood.

When the demand for linguistic states initially came up, even the leaders of our country were perplexed and unsure. But in spite of the fact that Nehru, Patel and other great and charismatic figures led us into Independence, the demand for linguistic states could not be kept down. Only in hindsight do we realise that our leaders did not fully trust the citizens and did not have full faith in their claims that they only wanted a federal state structure and not independence or sovereignty. Also, there was great opposition from the south Indian states on the question of Hindi being thrust on them as the national language.

But on no occasion did the people of India actually stand up for another Partition, nor did they want princely states to become autonomous or independent. This is why the problems between states should not be seen as threatening to the sovereign nation, but instead must be resolved keeping the legal norms of citizenship in full view. This is why tensions between states in India do not make for a constitutional crisis as they do in Sri Lanka. When differences are respected in terms of the norms of citizenship, even the most loaded cultural markers can be made to turn non-antagonistic.

This is why the early post Independence years were so important in putting the right kinds of narratives in place. These narratives were sifted from among many in our anti-colonial movement as well as in our hoary past to create a present that would help us reach out to a future. Though, during these years, things have often gone wrong, very wrong, yet there is no doubt that we are also able to right ourselves and not slipped into becoming a Hindu state. Nor, for that matter, have our industries stayed idle; they too picked up and started functioning on all cylinders rather quickly, for instance after the Gujarat tragedy of 2002. This is possible because our economy today is an integrated one that functions more or less seamlessly across the country. We are one billion people, but five billion railway tickets are sold each year. This is the number of tickets that are sold, but the actual number of train passengers must be much higher for we all know how many of us travel ticketless. It boggles the mind to visualise the number of people travelling across the length and breadth of this country for economic reasons.

This is indeed remarkable. A century ago, populations rarely moved more than a hundred miles for their necessities. India is no longer an agrarian country with the village as its leitmotif. That was how it was once, but not any more. If you look at India's rural economy today, over 60 per cent of its NDP (net domestic product) is non-agricultural. So where are these people going? What constitutes their work? They are starting tea-stalls, pulling rickshaws, hammering, welding, and working on construction sites and in small-scale industries around us. They are adding to the workforce in the informal sector, though some are also finding jobs in organised industries. Yet we need to note that 93 per cent of our labour works in the informal sector, and this includes a host of enterprises that are run like sweatshops but are contributing heftily to the export earnings of our country. What are we actually doing for the betterment and upward skilling of the worker who toils so hard, most often in degrading and squalid conditions, so that our country can earn foreign exchange? This question comes up again and again. Are we just exporting cheap labour to make huge export profits? What happens to the dignity of the workers; their health, safety and futures? What about them as citizens?

As we celebrate our multiple narratives, let us take a close look at the way the better off sections in our country live and thrive. Different classes meet, intersect, interact, but their respective horizons remain very different. The ambitions, aesthetics, goals and lifestyles of classes are so diverse, that in spite of everyday social connections, there is no bonding or true inclusion at the level of spirit. This is why Ambedkar and Gandhi both argued that it was essential to create a narrative of fraternity which would give substance and body to the legal title of citizenship.

V

What repeatedly queers the pitch in this endeavour are the many advocates of caste politics. There is a veneer of democracy in their attempts to use caste identities to advance social justice, but that can never truly be successful. Caste is, if anything, the ultimate divisive institution that Hindu culture has created, therefore, to use it to right past injustices will only create new ones. To believe that the spirit of fraternity can be advanced by using instruments that deny fraternity is obviously an exercise that is either cynical or unthinking. It is true that caste today is not like what it was in the past as the poor have equal voting rights, but at its core, it is combative, hurtful and antagonistic. The caste order is not just about the 'system', but it also created powerful 'identities' of difference down the line. This latter aspect of caste is often misunderstood or not understood at all. Thus while the old caste system may not have survived, identities are doing quite well. This needs a little clarification.

One of the things that really confuses observers in India, as well as abroad, and what makes the sub-continent beyond the pale of any universal discourse, is caste. The grand puzzle of all is how whole communities accept that their essential bodily substances are polluting and despicable in the extreme? This, atleast, is the pronouncement found in several religious texts, from the *Vedas* to the *Smritis*, that justify the caste system. But how is this possible? This does not happen anywhere else in the world among other subaltern and exploited communities. You may concede that you are not rich, not powerful, not literate, or good looking, but to say that you are essentially despicable because your family is made of despicable substances which runs as much in you as in your forefathers, is an admission of a very different kind. That many intellectuals have certified that it is precisely this trait that sets apart the caste ideology from any other anywhere in the world has legitimised India's uniqueness and exotic value. If this were true, Hindu India truly needs special categories to understand it. How else can one make sense of the fact that the subaltern castes actually participate in their own degradation. (see Dumont 1971)?

It is this popular view of caste that seemingly separates us from the rest of the world. Nowhere else will one find people who actually acquiesce in ideologies that degrade them. This is also why India looks so exotic and hostile to universal categories of analysis and makes Indians the members of a unique species. While such an interpretation of caste is widely acknowledged and has some very persuasive scholars behind it (Dumont 1971 for example; see Gupta 1990 for a fuller treatment), it is still not true. This is an upper-caste view and not one that reflects the narratives of the vast majority of the poorer castes. Such a realisation probably did not come out clearly in the past because in a closed village economy it never pays to argue over relations of superiority and inferiority. This is what allowed the caste system flourish as the landlord's writ was always supreme and it is that which kept the caste hierarchy place. Those that were dominated dared not protest without endangering what little material possessions they had, even their lives. At the same time, to argue that if the system is somehow overturned, caste can become a tool for social justice and fraternity, is still not valid. This is because caste identities that spun out of the system still remain to carry on hostilities that are now no longer subterranean in nature, but out in the open.

VI

To begin with, it is not as if only the Brahmans valorise their sense of identity superiority through the medium of origin tales. The 'Purusasukta' legend in the *Rig Veda* has provided the template for these myths, but it is not the Brahmans alone who indulge in shameless and conceited identity mongering. There are, in fact, thousands of *jati* origin tales, including those of the poorer castes, and they all claim privileged status for their respective communities. What is noteworthy is that not one origin tale of any subjugated caste ever cedes ground by acknowledging its members deserve to be at the bottom because their bodily substances are base and polluting. In fact, an examination of these 'low-caste' tales would show a variety of ways by which poorer and subjugated communities build for themselves an exalted identity. Often they claim to be Brahmans, or warriors, or children of Shiva and Parvati, or belong to the solar or lunar dynasty. Some 'lower-caste' myths even argue that they were cheated by the gods, but a day would come when they would rightfully reclaim their legitimate place in the social hierarchy[2].

If in these origin tales nobody accepts a lowly status in the ritual hierarchy, then it is only correct to refer to 'lower-castes' in inverted commas or prefix the term by using the phrase: 'so called'. The many *jati* myths, regardless of where they are coming from only assert that no caste ever really accepted that their members were inherently polluting and debased. In other words, the very idea that subaltern castes participated in their own subjugation is a complete and comprehensive misreading of reality. The only explanation why this erroneous view has had such a long and unchallenged run is because intellectuals have paid too much attention to textual matters and too little, if any at all, to oral traditions, where so many other *jati* origin tales are to be found.

It is because of this strong sense of caste identity, or caste patriotism, down the order, that compressed packs of symbolic energy were released once the system was disarticulated. All of this fervour that lived in *jati* origin narratives now went into the making of contemporary caste ideologies. If there was just a single narrative where the Brahmans are on top and untouchables at the bottom, there would have been little ideological scope to work up caste politics, which is basically competitive in character. If we believe in a common humanity, we realise that all these myths, whether those of the powerful castes or the poorer ones are all of logically equal status

2. This should not be confused with what the *bhakti* saints had to say. For the *bhakti* preacher it was not as if lower castes were once higher caste, or children of kings and gods, but that the caste hierarchy and sectarian divisions are not godly at all for human beings are all one. The 'low-caste' *julaha/kori* Kabir says this in many of his poems and devotional songs. For instance:

From one drop, a universe.
Who's Brahmin? Who's Shudra?
Brahma rajas, Shiva tamas, Vishnu sattva...
Kabir says, plunge into Ram!
There: No Hindu, no Turk.

See, Hess and Singh 1986: 67.

and when they come out competitively in the open it is because they are propelled by generations of hate and distance. This gulf has to be bridged, but not in the language of caste, because its governing principle is that of incompatibility. Therefore, even when the poor agitate in the name of caste, there is something very divisive in that too. This is what the narrative of citizenship teaches us. If we play into the caste logic, at whatever level, then we have lost the game. Populist politics can hardly be expected to take citizenship forward.

VII

It is never enough then to exult in nation-statehood. It is only liberal democracy, which centralises fraternity, that can give us the true benefits of citizenship. Nation-states reach their highest form when they are governed by a liberal democratic constitution. They sink to their lowest when fired by zealots whose only aim is to recreate the past and delve in culture and tradition. In such cases, it is not at all surprising that these nation-states take a turn to either theocracy or fascism, and elections in such dispensations are a farce that only legitimise the given.

India is clearly different from most other emerging nation-states for it embraced liberal democracy from the start. For this we must be grateful to our founding figures, but we cannot stop there. Liberal democracy is a continuous struggle; it demands relentless vigilance; it cannot rest anywhere but must always strive to higher expressions of citizenship. It is when we drop our guard and are pleased with all that we have and see around us that liberal democracy takes a hit. It is then that insidious tendencies towards identity politics, towards ethnic intolerance, towards a neglect of the economically marginalised, become prominent. To be able to contest these tendencies best one must make sure they never become manifest at all. This is why citizenship must remain the guiding principle of our nation-state even if that occasionally runs foul of popular sentiments. It is not easy to practice democracy because this is one social arrangement that makes no concession to prejudice. A leadership that observes such a mandate alone has the credentials to be called democratic. Others who pander to populist passions do not deserve such an accolade, though they might have won elections by landslide margins.

References

Anderson, Benedict (1983). *Imagined Communities*. London: Verso.

Dumont, Louis (1971). *Homo Hierarchicus: The Caste System and its Implications*. London: Weidenfeld and Nicholson.

Gupta, Dipankar (1990). "Continuous Hierarchies and Discrete Castes," in Dipankar Gupta (ed.), *Social Stratification*. Delhi: Oxford University Press.

Habermas, Jürgen (1987). *Lifeworld and System: A Critique of Functionalist Reason*. Vol. 2 in the series *The Theory of Communicative Action*. Boston: Beacon Press.

Hall, John A. (1993). "Nationalism, Classified and Explained", *Daedelus* 122: 1-28.

Hess, Linda and Sukhdev Singh (trans.) (1986). "Sabda, 30", in *The Bijak of Kabir*. Delhi: Motilal Banarsidass.

Hobsbawm, Eric (1988). *The Age of Capital 1848-1875*. London: Cardinal.

——— (1990). *Nations and Nationalism since 1780*. Cambridge: Cambridge University Press.

Marshall, T.H. (1990) *Citizenship and Social Class and Other Essays*. London: The Syndics of the Cambridge University Press.

Nehru, Jawaharlal (2008). *Discovery of India*. New Delhi: Penguin.

Renan, Ernest (1990). "What is a Nation?" in Homi Bhabha (ed.), *Nations and Narration*. London: Routledge.

7

ABID HUSSAIN

Role of Bureaucracy in India's Development

As the title conveys, this essay is concerned with the role of bureaucracy in a democratic society such as India's. Certain aspects of this theme are discussed with a view to provoking some response to the challenges they pose. To begin with, two sets of preliminary observations are made here—one of a general nature and the other specific to India. These would serve as a backdrop to the presentation.

The first set of observations is as follows: (i) that however strong and determined a people may be, they acquire political attributes of sovereignty only when they belong to a legally constituted state; (ii) that the basic ideas and perceptions which precede the formation of a state usually make their indelible mark on the broad features of the state and permeate its organs of governance; (iii) that however well-conceived and well-crafted the concept of state may be, it must have a body of institutions and functionaries (bureaucracy included) to translate its agenda into administrative reality; (iv) that however efficient and politically neutral a bureaucracy may be, it is bound to reflect the ideology of the state and the passions of its political leaders; (v) that however efficient and meritorious a bureaucracy may be, it cannot deliver public good in a sustainable and fair manner without people' s participation in its activity; (vi) that a state cannot run as a democracy unless it carries with it a deep value of equal moral worth of its citizens, eschewing different forms of privileges and inherited modes of domination/subordination.

This essay was written by Abid Hussain several years before he passed away in June 2012. It was developed over the course of various lectures and discussions with several individuals, especially, Prof C.B. Karki, who provided an excellent sounding board for fleshing out ideas.

The second set of observations, more specific to India, may be stated as follows: (i) that the partition of India in 1947 cast a strong bearing on the features of the country's governance, including relations between its two major religious communities; (ii) that pre-independence political passions, not being primarily focused on democracy, lacked a strong commitment to unshackle the hitherto existing power equations without which democracy cannot function; (iii) that taking over almost intact the entire colonial state apparatus remained contentious and impeded the state from becoming a strong instrument of change; (iv) that induction of democracy on an adult-franchise basis often creates urges and demands which sometimes frustrate the working of the state.

Introduction

The year 1947 was the defining period of India. It marked the birth of India's independence. In the words of Charles Dickens, one would say that it was the best of times and the worst of times.

Nehru in his "Tryst with Destiny" speech said that "at the stroke of midnight hour when the world sleeps, India will awake to life and freedom." He spelt out his vision of independent India and made 'an imaginative bold promise' of making India a modern industrial country. With his words echoing all over the country, there burst a new blaze of light on India. This marked perhaps a most joyous moment in the chequered history of the Indian people.

But it was also the worst of times in the sense that the partition of India brought in its train the ugliest of riots and most ferocious violence that wrecked the lives of millions of men, women and children, and put to flame public and private properties on an unprecedented scale. The vicious fires of communal hatred were spreading and razing the symbols of unity and brotherhood which were the bedrocks of India's true strength and unique identity.

It was also the time when hundreds of rulers of the Princely states of India threatened to disrupt the process of the integration of the country. The lapse of the British paramountcy over these princes had virtually opened a Pandora's Box, complicating the situation for the already harried and harassed nation. Even before the fledgling nation had found its feet, its very existence was in jeopardy.

Faced with such difficult times, the foremost task before Nehru and his colleagues was to stand up with courage and determination to turn the vicious tide of disasters and stop the orgy of murder and madness and also to wean away the princes from their sordid machinations at the balkanisation of India.

It was against the backdrop of such calamities and compulsion of circumstances that Nehru and Patel decided to use the colonial apparatus of state administration, which the Raj had left behind, to control the vandalism and the madness of street terror, and frustrate the designs of the overambitious princes.

In using the very instruments of administration and police that the British had earlier employed to crush the independence movement and arrest the national leaders, Nehru and Patel showed practical wisdom and pragmatism, which did yield good results. Or was it a case of making a virtue of necessity? For it would have been naïve to expect the agitators-turned-government functionaries, who had been till yesterday considered past masters in organising agitations themselves (and some of them had been violent, too, despite the agitators' credo of non-violence), to have the genius for controlling mob violence by initiating and guiding prompt administrative action. Dominique Lapierre and Larry Collins might have stretched the point too far in *Freedom at Midnight* that our top leaders sought Lord Mountbatten's guidance in restoring law and order, but the fact of the inexperience of the Indian leaders in dealing with such crises and contingencies of such magnitude cannot but be factored in. Anyway peace was brought back to the streets and confidence of the people restored in national leadership.

But the consequence of using the erstwhile colonial administrative machinery prepared the ground for the modalities of governance to follow, which to some extent impeded the evolution of democratic institutions and conventions, retarded the pace of change and development, and became a sort of template for our future bureaucrat administrators. Whether this spillover of the colonial institution in the body politic proved to be the bane or a boon for the nascent democracy will remain a debatable point till historical objectivity puts to rest the contentious issue.

It must be admitted that, in the early phase of India's independence, the bureaucracy inherited from the Raj played a useful role in stopping riots, rehabilitating millions of refugees (pouring into India from the newly created state of Pakistan), showing sagacity in apportionments of assets, services and finances between the two states of India and Pakistan. It also provided administrative and legal support to the new task of integrating the Princely states with the rest of India and also furnishing such back-room assistance to the founding fathers of the Constitution as they needed in framing its blueprint.

The colonial bureaucracy, originally created to serve the imperial interests of the Raj, showed unstinting and instant willingness and enthusiasm to commit its loyalty to the new state. It had no reservation in accepting the twin objectives of serving the new national leadership and of working towards operationalisation of India's development programmes. Of the two objectives, they could adjust more easily with the first one than with the second, as the latter called for a radical transformation of their attitudes, behaviours and beliefs, cultivated over a long period.

While Nehru and Patel were quite appreciative of the role most of the erstwhile ICS officers had played in organising the nitty-gritty of the Transfer of Power, and of their meticulousness, discipline and devotion to work, they had lurking doubts about their commitment to the new democratic way of governance. Particularly, Nehru had strong reservations in accepting that, grown and shaped in the image of the British rulers, the colonial bureaucracy would voluntarily give up its inherited ways of officialdom and over-lordship to overnight become servants of people. In fact, the mannerism of some Indian members of the British Raj ICS had so much put off Nehru that he could not help writing thus in the *Discovery of India*: "Indians belonging to the Civil Service, whatever their rank in the official hierarchy, do not belong to the charmed circle (Nehru meant the British members of the ICS). A few of them try to ape the manners of their colleagues without much success; they become rather pompous and ridiculous."

In one of his letters to the Chief Ministers, Nehru wrote that "in their service to the empire, bureaucracy has become an army of pen-pushers to implement a mass of inflexible rules and regulations with little scope for discrimination, much less innovation." More importantly, the strategy of governance formulated by the British had created an administrative style which embodied a culture of distrust. This Nehru knew well. Though himself more attuned to Western ways as he had once described himself as the last Englishman to rule India, he knew that imbibing the spirit of democratic functioning was not easy for the bureaucracy to emulate. The old colonial habits die hard and have an inordinately long 'shelf life'. This mindset was unlikely to go well with the requirements and expectations of a new changing India. Sardar Patel, however, remained convinced, after some initial skepticism, that the bureaucracy could be Indianised and that it was capable of adjustment and could cooperate with the national democratic forces in the country, which in its turn would facilitate change in their methods of thinking and working. Perhaps Nehru believed that the leopard cannot change its spots and Patel believed that lions can be made to eat grass.

Thus, Sardar Vallabhbhai Patel put his complete faith in the capacity of the civil servants to adjust and become Indian in their outlook and performance. He believed that the stimulus of change would come from the political process which was gaining strength in the country and that the Civil Service could not remain immune to it. In 1949 Sardar Patel said that "ICS constituted a ring of service which will keep the country intact." In the Constituent Assembly he went to the extent of saying that these were the people who could become instrumental in creating national unity. "Remove them," he said, "and I think nothing but a picture of chaos will be all over the country." Addressing ICS officers, Patel expressed his trust in them in the following memorable words, "I am going to rely on the 414 of you to help us in the task ahead," the 414 being the number of Indians serving in the ICS cadre at that time.

Pandit Nehru, while admitting the erstwhile ICS officers into his administration, emphasised on them that the administration is meant to achieve concrete objectives for people's welfare and not to exist in "following only rules or procedures. The test after all is the human being, who is the centre of national concern." Laying stress on how to interact with the people, he said, "I might have no time to see secretaries to government or any officials but I never say no to an ordinary man who comes to see me. That individual represents to me the millions of people like him to whom we owe our independence." Administration, he said, had to change its outlook to become more people-oriented. It could not forget that it existed to serve the people. Nehru did not mince words when he said to the civil servants, "I want you to escape the deadly static atmosphere of paper filing, which makes you forget that there are human beings in India." He added for good measure, "Administration is to achieve results and not exist in some kind of ivory tower and the civil servant should stop looking at himself Narcissus like, with complete satisfaction. He has to get over the class-conscious attachment to power and authority." It was imperative that their style of service had to change. The democratic regime called upon its bureaucracy to become more democratic in their attitude of mind and also in appearance. Sir Girija Shanker Vajpai, one of the senior-most ICS officers, said that "we who could work well for the foreigners would do far better for our leaders".

With this begins the story of the reinvention of the bureaucracy in India. But it should also be kept in mind that, the ancestry of the Indian bureaucracy being much older than the Independence Movement, it was, and perhaps still is, apt to occasionally reproduce its atavistic tendencies rather than becoming an innovator and a catalyst for that change which the 60 year old India is still hankering after.

In a way, most other equally important and prestigious organisations, and notably the Indian Army, had also been created and nurtured by the Colonial regime, but their officer cadres have shown a marked change in their attitudes and style of functioning. How come, then, that not only the remnants of the bureaucracy of the Raj days but, to some extent, even the present civil service cadres have managed to preserve their larger-than-life image and persisted with the colonial shibboleth of exclusiveness, class consciousness and intellectual arrogance of a Mr know-all kind. And, surprisingly, they have got away with this snobbery, despite the countervailing demands of democracy for an egalitarian society and the occasional hue and cry of the common people.

It may not be out of place to probe the motives or reasons for Patel the Ironman's implicit confidence in, and Nehru the Visionary's qualified acceptance of, the role of the ICS. Both these trailblazers were actuated by the same ethos of reinventing and restructuring India, but it was manifested in divergent, though complementary, modes. Sardar Patel happened to head the Ministry of Home Affairs, which was charged with the responsibility for internal security and law and order, especially in those highly volatile times. As Minister of States, he had also to deal with five hundred odd Princely states, whose ambitions, fuelled by the lapse of Paramountcy, to become independent kingdoms was posing a grave danger to India's unity and integrity. Conversant as they were with every trick of intimidation and cajolery or whatever in the book of empire-builders, the civil servants were used by the Sardar with conspicuous success for bringing round recalcitrant Princes and integrating their domains with the infant Republic. As experienced guardians of law and order since the British days, their services came handy for Patel in restoring order and peace in the embattled civil society.

Nehru's passion for planning and development and penchant for foreign affairs had been evident even before independence. It was but natural for him to look askance at these status quoists of civil servants' aptitude and ability to deliver in these two crucial areas where the need of the hour was, first, to give nation-building programmes thrust and momentum, and, secondly, to correct the image stereotypes that had been projected abroad by the Imperial rulers to malign and denigrate India. Whether it was the compulsion of circumstances or a dearth of requisite talent in other services or fields, Nehru did appoint a nominated but brilliant ICS officer (V.T. Krishnamachari) as Vice-chairman of the Planning Commission when it was an unquestioned powerhouse for initiating and guiding the economic policies and programmes. By the same token, stalwart civilians like Sir Girija Shankar Vajpai and N.R. Pillai headed the External Affairs Ministry. And it goes to the credit of these civilians and several others of their ilk that they did not let Nehru down. But at the end of the day, the question mark still remains hanging over the wisdom of placing over-reliance on ICS immediately after independence and the years that followed.

Bureaucrats' Relationship with the Political Executive

In the context of democracy, one of the first challenges that the bureaucracy faces is the establishment of a smooth and good working relationship with the political leadership in running the government both at the secretariat and the field level. It was clear from the start that in a democratic set-up such a relationship is central to good governance. Internal consistencies between the political executive and the civil servant remain of vital importance.

In India, the bureaucrats had no hesitation in accepting the primacy of political masters in matters of decision-making and the political executive knew that they needed the expertise, experience and the knowledgeability of rules and regulations of the professional bureaucrat to execute their policies effectively. It has been the country's advantage that such a synergy could be easily evolved.

Fundamental to this relationship was the admiration which the bureaucrats had for their political masters and the regard which the latter had for the former. Perhaps this mutuality of respect was also engendered by the fact that both had been Davids in their own ways and domains and had defied their respective Goliaths—the political leaders standing up to the mightiest ever empire and the Indian element of the ICS measuring up to its highbrow British counterpart, both intellectually and professionally. We should not forget either a common factor shared by them was that a good few of the political leaders and the Indian members of the ICS had had stints in England for studies or training; obviously they would not have remained oblivious to the modalities of parliamentary democracy and government functioning in England which became a template for the fledgling democracy. Then the civil servants respected the politicians for the role they played to influence people's judgement and conduct. The politicians held the civil servants in high esteem for their impartiality, adherence to lawful authority, uprightness, integrity and knowledge of the subject. A minister could rely on the bureaucrats for the right advice he would give and faithfully implement his orders. With the long experience of working for the state, the bureaucrats could handle the day-to-day affairs of administration as if to the manner born, and the political leadership, with its experience of mass mobilisation and close working relationship with the people, could perspicaciously spell out the people's wishes, objectives and programme to be pursued by the government. Since, on many issues, the two had a common approach, no rift would come in the way of harmonious working. Where there was any difference of opinion, the two could sort out things between themselves through dialogue and discussion. Only in rare cases were matters thrashed out and decided at a higher level. The bureaucrats solemnly adhered to their dharma to faithfully implement the final orders of the political executive, which in turn gave them the needed space to act out in a truly professional manner. There are well-documented cases of the differences that arose between Panditji and Lal Bahadur Shastri on the one hand, and their secretaries on the other, which were amicably settled without rancour or ill-will on either side.

It was later that the rhythm of union between the two got disturbed. The happy harmonious relationship between the ministers and their secretaries got distorted. Even the legitimate criticism of a policy by a civil servant, which was earlier welcomed, was interpreted by the ministers as a deliberate attempt, actuated by some ulterior motive, to obstruct their policies. Or, plain and simple, it could be just a clash of personalities if one or both happened to posses massive size egos. Ministers began to prefer officials who would blindly support their line of action without raising any uncomfortable questions. Those who did not say 'yes' to the minister were looked upon as hostile elements and their presence in the ministry detested. The overbearing attitude of officers had also become a cause of cleavage and alienation in the relationship of the two. As said above, the quest or domination of one over the other created an unsavoury politics of self-esteem and one-upmanship, which impeded effective working.

Instances of lack of mutual trust became evident and more frequent. The politicians ignored the usefulness of the bureaucrat and the bureaucrat underrated the functional value of the politician. There was a move to bend the bureaucrat to the wishes of the politician, upsetting the institutional independence of the bureaucracy. There have been cases of political bossism, which prevented the civil and police authorities to act impartially in accordance with rules. This provided backing to the lawbreakers and rendered the lawful authorities dysfunctional. Explaining to cover up such a cleavage in the relationship of a reciprocal recognition, a politician minister said that when he asked the civil servant to bend he crawled, but he also admitted that there were bureaucrats who were upright and honest and defied any unprincipled interference by the politician.

It is time that the respective roles and responsibilities of the two arms of the government were clearly re-defined and punctiliously adhered to. As of yore, the civil servant should be encouraged to give independent advice and to take fearless decisions in accordance with rules. But some ministers have this Tennysonian notion about the bureaucrats under them that 'theirs is not to reply but to act and comply'. What is then an officer to do if a minister asks them to take some action in contravention of law? In such a situation, a bureaucrat, and for that matter any subordinate, has a right to refer the matter to the minister or their superior, as the case may be, noting why the superior political or administrative authority's orders are not tenable. Despite this advice, if these worthies persist, their orders should be carried out if they give them in writing in unambiguous terms. The judges in the Nuremberg trials of the Nazi war criminals refused to accept the plea of the defendants that they had no option but to show unquestioning obedience to the diktats of no less a dictator than Hitler, who had the self-arrogated power and also sadistic inclination to exterminate a person for the slightest dissent. A kowtowing bureaucrat or subordinate is living in a fool's paradise if they think that their unquestioning obedience to an erring minister or superior will wash in a democratic dispensation. Of late, virtually after every change of political guard, whether in states or at the Centre, some bureaucrat or the other had to face disgrace and humiliation for their unquestioning obedience. It is high time officials saw the writing on the wall and showed the moral courage not to abdicate their constitutional and legal responsibilities while implementing the political executive's orders.

Coalition politics at the Centre and in the states as well has added a new dimension to the functioning of the bureaucracy and its relation to the political executive. The most acute problem in a coalition is of coordination among different ministries and departments. Then comes the problem of loyalist bureaucrats and those considered not so loyal to a particular party or minister. Even when a single party government was in place, the problem of coordination would arise from time to time, especially when the high profile ministers with big egos would be at loggerheads with each other. But their differences could be resolved by the intervention of the prime minister or the chief minister or the party high command. Naturally, the problem of confrontation of ministers belonging to different coalition parties has become all the more complex. Each coalition partner has their own constituency to take care of, so they compel the officials of their ministry to adopt and execute policies of their department to serve narrow and self-serving ends, even if they run counter to national or state interests. This problem gets compounded if a minister has very pliant officers who see no disgrace in abdicating their role as advisors and too willingly become the protégés of their political masters.

This problem gets compounded for yet another reason. Of late, ministers have had a great inclination to fill their ministries and departments with officers from their own states. This practice, especially at the Centre, is fraught with a grave danger to the body politic. The all-India character of the Central ministries should not be allowed to be vitiated simply to satisfy an insular-minded politician's ego or some vested interest motivated by partisan or regional considerations.

It is here that the role of the Cabinet Secretary assumes significance. The very raison d'etre of the post of Cabinet Secretary is the need for coordination. Of late, the Cabinet Secretary's position has been eroded, If not downgraded, with the increasing clout of the Prime Minister's Office (PMO), which almost functions as an institution parallel to, or sometimes even higher than, the august office of the Cabinet Secretary. There must have been some strong reasons and imperatives for investing the PMO with special powers. But, at the same time, this fact should not be lost sight of that, when two organisations with parallel powers and responsibilities function independent of each other, sometimes situations arise when the right hand does not know what the left hand is doing. Mutatis mutandis, the same applies to the roles of the Chief Secretaries and the Chief Ministers' Offices in the States.

Then there is the problem of 'committed bureaucracy', which has almost become endemic. Whatever the intention behind the idea of a committed bureaucracy at the time of its conceptualisation, it soon degenerated into 'commitment to the party in power', and further degenerated into 'commitment to a particular political personality or boss'. This is a pernicious doctrine. Surely we need a 'committed bureaucracy' in the sense that they should not spare any effort, even if it goes against their personal ideology, in implementing the mandate of the people as mentioned in the manifesto of the party or alliance in power, provided, of course, their programmes do not transgress the parameters laid down by the laws of the land and the Constitution and the imperatives of democratic institutions as well. Bureaucrats whose commitment is translated into abject loyalty to a particular party or personality have to face indignities, including even imprisonment, and a virtual exile when the regime changes.

Allegiance to an individual or taking sides in partisan politics is the symptom of a feudal mindset, which goes against the core principles and processes of democracy. This is why one of the major exercises consuming the election authorities' time and energy on the eve of elections is to remove biased and partisan officers from sensitive postings. What an irony that, while a sense of commitment is a most desirable quality, the term 'committed bureaucracy' has come to acquire a pejorative connotation! Politicians, and for that matter even bureaucrats, seem to have taken their cue from a Lewis Carroll character Humpty Dumpty, who says, "When I use a word, it means what I choose it to mean, neither more nor less".

To prevent the abuse of political authorities forcing the civil servant to bend, the Constitution provided that a civil servant cannot be dismissed or demoted or have any disciplinary action taken against them except through the due processes of law and after consultation with the Union Public Service Commission (UPSC). But there are other ways by which a minister can use their power arbitrarily to subdue the civil servant. The power of transfer, suspension and promotion could be so used by them as to make civil servants pliable. It is here that the real mettle of a civil servant is tested. But when once trust turns into distrust and mutual respect into incompatible co-existence, governance deteriorates and the pace of development slows down, and sometimes even comes to a grinding halt. B.K. Nehru, in his book *Nice Guys Finish Second* gives an example of the origin of distrust. He refers to the LIC-Mundra case in which the Finance Minister shifted the blame of a certain wrong-doing on his Secretary, the natural fallout of which was that the civil servants stopped taking fearless decisions as they had hitherto done. Once the civil servant became unsure of the minister's support, they started slowing down proceedings lest they be hauled up for acts of omission and commission. This again emphasises the need for establishing a harmonious relationship between the civil servant and the political masters. They should reassure and restrengthen each other to discharge public duties. This symbiotic relationship is what a good administration requires. A good administration is possible when the two arms of government are in consonance with each other and work with a common commitment to serve the nation.

With innumerable changes taking place in the sphere of information sharing, public criticism and PIL (public interest litigations), an atmosphere is getting created for avoiding high-handed arbitrary action and recasting relationships of mutual respect. This is a good augury for relations to improve. Democracy helps to consolidate a healthy nexus between the administrator and the politician, which would fulfil people's aspirations and redeem India's pledge of democracy.

Security and Law and Order

One of the prime obligations of the state is to ensure security and maintain law and order. The state machinery has to ensure that the daily life of a citizen is free of street conflicts of violence, arson and vandalism, so that people could pursue their legitimate interests freely and make the best of the opportunities that exist to make their lives productive and enjoyable.

The impetus towards provision of security is largely possible by creating and nurturing a close and harmonious relationship among people, state officials, local politicians and civic activists. But there are situations where local chieftains and politicians do not offer full assistance to the state authorities in preserving law and order for reasons of their narrow immediate gains or even some sinister intent and nexus with anti-social elements. It is on such occasions that the integrity of officials and their adherence to the rule of law has been tested. They are required to assert their administrative authority to prevent transgression of law. This has at times exposed officials to harassment by local politicians. And in cases where bureaucrats, under such circumstances, could not stand up to their bullying tactics, they lost their esteem in public eye and, ironically also, over time fell in the eyes of the very politicians who had wanted them to ignore concerns of law and order.

Some of the breaches of law and order take place due to the short-sighted populist aspirations of politicians. Claiming to help people, they encourage certain pressure groups to squat on public land, travel ticketless on public transport, pilfer water and electricity, and indulge with impunity in like anti-social activities. Politicians do this to garner votes from the poor and also to oblige the constituents of their vote banks. Thus, law is suspended and illegality encouraged. Abuse of authority also caused vendors to pay protection money, and small shopkeepers to pay *mamuls* to petty police, and municipal officials. Builders and contractors get away with grabbing of lands and even heinous crimes like kidnapping and murders. This has brought discredit both to the politician and the police, and hurt those who are law-abiding and needed to be protected. It is these acts and failures of administration, which increasingly pushes the society into extra-legal arrangements, mostly in collusion with professional musclemen, when law is not respected and indiscipline thrives. Crime syndicates, mob rule, hoodlum outfits and mafia spring up as a substitute to legal authorities. They become a parallel government whose writ overrides even that of a legal authority and nullifies all the advantages of a democratic polity and leads to the breakdown of law and order on a vast scale.

At times, on some controversial issues, even the legislators, always on the lookout for fishing in troubled waters, bypass legal processes and organise rallies and counter-rallies by hiring local unemployed and lumpen elements. Such acts, perpetrated or inspired by our very law-makers, bring normal life to a grinding halt and provide an opportunity to anti-social elements to indulge in violence and wanton destruction of private and public properties.

There is a growing feeling, and not without some genuine reasons, that during communal and caste riots, administration has mostly failed to be impartial, fair and firm. In the face of such accusation, the administration's pet excuse is that, due to local political pressure under stressed circumstances, they deviate from performing their duty firmly.

In a pluralistic and multi-religious country like India, occasional communal tension and sporadic violence cannot be ruled out. But these cannot be treated as merely problems of law and order. These are manifestations of collective religious and behavioural disorders. Though timely police and administrative action does control them from exploding into anti-social and violent mob fury and rampaging and major upheavals, their real solution lies in a political process guided by an enlightened and vigilant leadership, which could remove insecurity felt by the various sections of society and bring them into the mainstream of the national fabric and make them stakeholders in the common wealth. But there are politicians who gain political advantage by fanning religious, caste, class and gender differences. There are some among bureaucrats also who succumb to such tendencies, forgetting that thereby they are guilty of gross dereliction of duty they are pledged to perform.

The impetus towards preservation of law and order is largely possible by creating and nurturing a close and harmonious working relationship between state officials, local politicians and civil activists. In the states where law and order has prevailed, one has witnessed substantial gains made by citizens in their businesses, occupations and vocations. Dividends of peace were thus shared by larger sections of society. It is this that the officials and politicians should try to ensure in all states. Admittedly, there is greater realisation by politicians and administrators to cooperate and maintain stability and peace in society. But the road to hell is paved with good intentions. Unless the realisation of a serious problem is translated into quick remedial action, it soon goes into oblivion. The spurt in militancy and terrorist activity has added to the responsibilities and woes of administration.

If we go by the daily grim reports in the print media and the kaleidoscope of visuals in the electronic media, crime in the country seems to be on the up and up, what with crime syndicates ruling the roost, even stray criminals are operating with greater ease than ever before, kidnapping and extortion in some states are flourishing like a legitimate industry, and, on the pretext of lack of action by law-enforcing agencies to book criminals, rampaging mobs are lynching suspected criminals. There are a variety of reasons for the rising crime graph, like fast population growth, increasing urbanisation, swelling ranks of the unemployed and underemployed, proliferating consumerism, youths' increased addition to drugs, and tensions fuelled by religious, ethnical and sub-national aspirations. All these factors, barring the demographic one, have more or less contributed to the high incidence of crime in most countries—developed or developing, not to mention the developing ones. But what has compounded the problem in India is that the bureaucrats, whose forte is enforcement of law and order, have either lost their professional touch, finesse and also perhaps interest in preventing or curbing crime, or they themselves stand in mortal fear of, or are in cahoots with, the arch enemies of the civil society. The reigns of lawlessness and the consequent spurt in crime during the twilight years of the Mughal Empire was a vital contributory factor in letting the British gain an easy foothold in India and establish their own empire.

A country has to constantly guard against two dangers to its integrity, namely, the foreign aggressor and the internal transgressor. The internal transgressor is more dangerous of the two, as like termites, they work insidiously and destroy the body politic from within. It is ironical that, while our borders, barring some cases of infiltration and skirmishes with foreign intruders, are being vigilantly looked after by the Indian Army and the paramilitary forces, the enemy within is proving too strong for our law-enforcers, who find even small-time crooks difficult to contain, let alone daring even to raise an accusing finger against notorious and powerful dons and gangsters. Adding to the law-abiding citizens' woes is the criminalisation of politics and the horrendous politician-bureaucrat-criminal nexus. Lawlessness in society has very wide ramifications and, sooner than later, adversely affects the economy of a country and other vital sectors. Crime syndicates run a parallel economy and gain entry into every area of economic activity to gain legitimacy for their ill-gotten wealth. This poses a grave danger to the national economy as well as the social fabric. The life-style of criminals wallowing in wealth and lording it over law-abiding citizens is a sure invitation to adventurous youth to take to crime as a career.

The main culprit for this sorry state of affairs is undoubtedly the ubiquitous politician, but administrative officials cannot wash their hands of the responsibility of preventing and curbing crime. Bureaucrats have a twofold task in addressing this problem. Backed with inputs from sociologists and economists and under the direction of the political executive, they have to find widely-acceptable lasting political solutions. But the immediate task of deterrence and control of crime calls for initiative, bold but imaginative handling, innovative measures and even use of sophisticated equipment, and, above all, personal courage to frustrate the designs of these enemies of civilised society and humanity. The restoration of normalcy in Punjab after a long-drawn period of turmoil and bloody violence shows how a determined political leadership and a bold but imaginative bureaucracy can handle a hyper-critical and sensitive situation. There have been instances when bureaucrats, including senior police officers, have shied away from postings in areas affected by terrorists and militant outfits, while the need of the hour is for our guardians of law to answer the call of duty fearlessly in these hazardous regions. Let us hope our bureaucracy will rise to the occasion and give primacy to the maintenance of law and order which is the primary need of civil society.

Rule of Law

Democracy is the government of principles and not of persons. Some of these principles serve as broad guidelines and their primary purpose is to give a sense of direction to the state. The Directive Principles of State Policy in the Indian Constitution belong to this category. The state has to take due note of them while laying down policies and enacting laws, but they are not justiciable. But most other principles have to be enshrined in the statute book to ensure that all men and women in a democracy are treated equally and arbitrary acts of habitual lawbreakers and men of power, pelf and position are held in check. This can happen when the rule of law prevails. The rule of law thus becomes the prime concern of the state executive and bureaucrats have to see that the rule of law is not violated by any individual or any section of society.

But in the given socio-political environment things as they stand today, officials have on several occasions been found guilty of compromising wantonly and not letting law take its due course. The abdication of the rule of law jeopardises the functioning of democracy. Officials close their eyes to infringement of laws, especially by the rich and politically influential. The criminal offenders are let off instead of being punished with due process of law. The politicisation of crime and politics makes administration indifferent to arresting crime and is prone to skip over enforcement of law. Token compliance of the rule of law, therefore, brings little comfort not only to the weaker sections of society but also to the law-abiding citizens belonging to all other sections of society.

There is a growing tendency noticeable among officers where decisions are made not by the application of principles of law, but in a manner suiting the interest of the lawbreakers and mischief-makers. One of the charges against bureaucracy is that it has let go the sanctity of the rule of law which is the operating instrument of justice in a democratic society. Exercise of public acts should find its source in legal rule and the relation between state and individual should be regulated only by law. But if the government itself is seen as a compulsive habitual violator of law, it would be unrealistic to expect a voluntary adherence to law by the citizens. 'Government is a potent teacher, it teaches its people by its own example'. The basis of law is that it is equal for all and with no exceptions. However rich and powerful a person may be, they could not be exempted from the operation of law. It is noted that when landlords and employers deny equal rights and cause physical or mental harm to their employees, the state authorities remain mute or take side of those who violated the laws. Bureaucracy palpably fails to live up to its duty to be the defenders of the rights of individuals. Daily routines of office should not remain their main concern while vital tasks are ignored. Of late, the print media, electronic media and civil society organisations have exposed the failings of politicians and civil executives in this regard. They are creating a public opinion at the instant. But these would still remain muted unless top political leaders of the ruling party and the opposition exert to press the rule of law as an effective instrument.

Judicial process is also under criticism. Thousands and thousands of cases remain undecided. The resourceful rich find easy access to lawyers and sometimes to judges. They get the judgement bent to condone their mischief. Moreover, some of the criminal elements get elected to legislative bodies and they neutralise the police and the judicial authority. The politicisation of crime and politics has been responsible for the failure of the state.

It is not just empty rhetoric that it is in the exercise and prevalence of the rule of law that democracy can survive and the country would progress. What is India's record in observing the rule of law? The rule of law is the keystone of the arch of democracy. Remove the keystone and the whole edifice comes falling down. Though presently, India's record in the observance of the rule of law is not something to cheer about, it does have some positive features.

The higher judiciary has been reasonably fair in the administration of justice. But the judiciary should also have frequent introspection, so that justice is available to every citizen which is unbiased, affordable and not unduly delayed. It is regrettable that inordinate delays in trying cases are causing irreparable harm to the social fabric.

Delayed justice has two ramifications. First, the cost of litigation escalates, and as a German proverb says, go to law for a sheep and lose your cow. Secondly, delayed justice is not only virtually but actually denial of justice.

A fair election process is nothing but an extension of the rule of law, for a government changes hands in a democracy under a due legal process. Any change of government or its prolongation outside the jurisdiction of law will mean the very negation of democracy. The elections in India have been reasonably fair, free and also, to a certain extent, peaceful. If the Election Commission of India can make the elections fairer, freer and more peaceful, they will be strengthening the rule of law and striking a blow for democracy.

Theodore Roosevelt said that nobody should be above law and nobody should be below law. In simple language it meant that, first, everyone, irrespective of their status, is equal before law and, secondly, there should be no oppressive law. An oppressive law is mostly used in a selective way by the powers that be, and thus violates the very spirit of the rule of law. Even in applying normal laws, Indian enforcing agencies have had a dismal record. When armed with draconian laws, they have used them indiscriminately and tyrannically. It can be said that in India the laws are not oppressive, but the law-enforcing agencies make them so.

Some two hundred years ago, poet William Blake of "Tiger, Tiger, burning bright" fame said, "One law for the lion and the ox is an oppression." Such a notion might have been welcomed in the non-democratic regimes of the past as well as the present. But nothing can be a greater anathema to a democracy than this perverted and pernicious doctrine. In a theoretical sense, India may not be following this doctrine, but some special safeguards to bureaucrats and politicians in high position, granting them some legal immunity not available to common man, and the requirement of presidential or gubernatorial permission to prosecute them, confirms the notion that there is some sort of discrimination in the application of laws. Such a discriminatory provision goes against the spirit of the rule of law. The only way to uphold the rule of law and thereby the institutions of democracy is to have the same law for the lion and the ox.

The Indian society defaults on two other counts, namely, (1) in the interpretation of laws, and (2) in the non-compliance of laws. The first default arises when rules or laws are interpreted differently for different people. One of the most frequent charges against the executive officers is that they are not averse to practicing this perverse notion: 'show me the man and I will show you the rule'. Such a twisting of rules makes nonsense of the rule of law. Happily judicial officers do not share this perverse tendency but mostly interpret laws on their merits. Of course there can be black sheep in their ranks too.

As regards the second default, we are reminded of the words of Thomas Jefferson that "the execution of the laws is more important than the making them." The citizenry also compounds the problem of non-execution by willful non-compliance of some very crucial and beneficial laws. The classic examples are the daily violations of traffic laws by hundreds of thousands of vehicle owners and the high incidence of fatalities and crippling injuries throughout the country. Similarly, civil laws pertaining to health and hygiene, construction of buildings, etc. and so vital for the safety of life and property, are given the go by with impunity, while the concerned authorities do not appear to be too keen to insure their observance, either for some monetary consideration or owing to an attitude of 'anything goes'. This negates one of the cardinal principles of the rule of law that, if a law exists, it must be complied with.

While concluding, it may be said that the existing laws, most of them framed by the alien rulers to suit their colonial ambitions and to meet different situations and contingencies of a different era, must be reviewed without avoidable delay. The benign and necessary laws should be retained in the statute book, duly revised and updated in conformity with the present societal needs, while the laws that have outlived their utility or are misfits in a democracy should be done away with.

Role of Bureaucracy in Economic Development

With independence, economic development has emerged as a big plank of Indian democracy's commitment to its people. State's role is no longer confined to management of land revenue. Significant sectors of new economic activities have become the concern of the state. What was hitherto a police state has assumed the role of a development agency. Under the aspiring guidance of Prime Minister Nehru, selected men from bureaucracy were drafted to work side by side with the political representatives of people, economists and other professionals to draw up road maps of India's economic development and execute them together with other experts. In the context of Five Year Plans, names of officials like V.T. Krishnamachari, Tarlok Singh and others cannot be forgotten.

A host of Indian administrators spearheaded the plans of economic development. They worked from village level to national level to trigger of economic projects. At the grass roots-level a number of young bureaucrats worked in community development and extension programmes. They took active part in matters of loan distribution, sinking of tube wells, supply of seeds and fertilisers etc. They also worked to promote small scale industry in small towns and social education among the illiterate. Thus, they were involved in the texture of everyday village and urban life in myriad ways. Later a sort of statism provided the bureaucracy a slews of opportunities to initiate work and intervene in national economic projects. With the charisma that the state functionary acquired from the state as such, they got started well. River valley projects, steel plants, hydro-electric projects, national transport and road works, etc. were executed and managed by selected men from bureaucracy and other allied technical services. While these works attracted the attention and appreciation of people the world over, the basic programmes to lift the poor remained unsatisfactory. Ruling politicians who relied on the support of landlord and the rich made the bureaucrats play down land reforms. Bureaucracy also found the internal group structure of society more convenient to support the rich against the poor. There were innumerable cases where resources and public goods meant to reduce poverty were diverted away from areas that would benefit the poor. The better off sections benefited from such diversion of resources. They gained at the expense of many. Provision of funds earmarked for executing social development programmes also provided opportunities to make money. Funds were diverted to feed the greed of corrupt officials and their political counterparts. Capture of the levers of implementing agencies by the rich accounted for this. It is believed that such diversion of funds was made to benefit the non-targeted few. This would not have taken place had the civil service not been a party to it.

There are indeed glowing accounts of good work by several bureaucrats in this regard. But their number has started dwindling. It is to overcome this that the Panchayati Raj Institutions (PRIs) were later conceived and put in place. Since eradication of rural poverty is the fundamental responsibility of administration, the worth of bureaucracy is tested in its performance in this area. It is not merely the allocation of funds which is more important, but the real issue is to prevent the transfer of funds to benefit the non-targeted few. Since the levers of power have already been captured by the rich and the politically powerful, nothing much can be done unless the members of the disadvantaged community get empowered. The government officials and the political executive have to make it happen. Bureaucracy has to show much enthusiasm in this regard. But it is ultimately the political will that would determine the rate and pace of success. Many of the legislative directions meant to transfer economic assets to the poor and landless have remained ineffective for want of implementation. Bureaucracy could have done more by way of greater concerted action to meet this challenge. In fact in some of the southern states, the local administrators succeeded in implementing tenancy reforms and ensure land rights. But there are limits to what bureaucratic action could do in this regard. It is clearly the failure of politics which is responsible for the status quo to continue.

Some of the failures of bureaucracy had been due to the fact that it had been asked to do jobs which, rightly speaking, did not belong to them, nor for the state to undertake. As the saying goes, elephants are poor flyers than swallows because being elephants they cannot fly. All hopes are now placed in reforming the administration to provide access to people to opportunities for development on a far and widespread scale. The achievements of Indian bureaucracy have to be considered in the context of the economic system in which it is placed. Reforms are an essential part of economic development in state policy. The role of bureaucracy in this has over time started to wane. Political elements often resist their role if it is contrary to their vested interest. This has got to be corrected but this cannot be left to bureaucracy alone to devise an administrative mechanism to handle the situation.

The pressure of collecting money for elections, which are always round the corner, has also provided an excuse to politicians to collect money from the businesses and industries. Bureaucracy's role in curbing this has remained limited; all the same it cannot be exonerated fully for this gross malpractice, which is causing incalculable public harm. When a politician takes a hefty amount from a corporate or business house, it is not a largesse from a generous friend but an inverted give-and-take business proposition. The politician, if returned to power, more than compensates the donor by awarding contracts, exempting duties, relaxing rules and conditions for the use of important services and utilities, and so on. In most cases the process of 'return gift' is possible only by circumventing rules and norms, which is not possible without the knowledge and acquiescence of the concerned bureaucrat. Whether it is the concerned bureaucrat's discreet silence, half-hearted acquiescence or willing connivance, it is inexcusable.

With greater economic liberalisation and the end of licence raj, the scope for making money by politicians and officers has shrunk. It is for the free market to decide the various contours of economic development, which earlier was the preserve of the bureaucracy, but here again the regulations to check proper working of the market forces has become a source of official interventions, opening up possibilities of harassing and extracting money.

There was a time when the government officials were not to be seen close to the private sector and profit was a dirty word. There existed a divergence between the state and the private sector. Of late, this divergence has been reduced and the private and public officials are seen working together in the general interest of economy. Public and private partnership is no longer a suspect. However, there would always be a risk that the public officials may be purchased and the public departments working as monitoring agencies could still make money. Government cannot make do without some sort of regulating authorities in some area or the other. At least there has been some change for the better and we should be grateful for small mercies, hoping that the future has brighter prospects.

A discussion on the role of bureaucracy in economic development will not be complete without mentioning their role in the working of the PSUs (public sector undertakings). Nehru saw industrialisation as the key to the amelioration of the weaker sections of society and state ownership of industry, especially in the core sector, as a means of having a commanding position in the industrial sector. Some PSUs did achieve appreciable success, but, by and large, PSUs were low on profitability, and the return was not commensurate with the massive investments. The expectation that public enterprise would be an important agent of country's development was only partially fulfilled, as quite a few needed very long gestation periods and failed to give the projected returns. The reason was not far to seek, as industrial enterprises need an entrepreneurial approach instead of bureaucratic control where compliance with procedures takes precedence over fulfillment of objectives and production targets. Moreover, a government department is not a happening place and a copybook approach fits the bill. On the other hand, a PSU, though an 'offspring' of government, has to contend with the dynamics of market and happens to be a place where there is no end of happenings. So, in place of controlling, a PSU needs managing. While a controller is guided by his bible of set rules and time-tested sacrosanct procedures and has very little space to use discretion and function independently, a manager has to be innovative, enterprising and forward-looking. That is why there are now persistent public demands and the occasional outcry also for better mechanisms of public administration by borrowing some ideas from the modern concepts of managerialism, and even government departments, unable to deliver with obsolete practices, are not averse to change with the changing times and shed off stark statism by adopting some features of management.

Discontent at Social Transformation

Much of the discontent with the bureaucracy has been in the area of social transformation. The Indian Constitution was committed to create a society of equals by eradication of those elements of social fabric which kept the people backward and unsure of their role in a democratic set-up. Laws to that effect were legislated by the Parliament and State Legislative Assemblies, but the administration could not evolve a proper mechanism to translate them on ground. The political and administrative arms of executives have to own up responsibility for this failure.

In a democratic set-up it is imperative that political parties and their cadres should create public consciousness through political education and spearhead a people's movement against the social evils which vitiate the life of people at large.

Political parties cannot abdicate their responsibility in this regard. They have to be instruments of social transformation. So also the bureaucracy has to be, both at the ground and at the national levels. The authority that the state has conferred on bureaucracy and the high position assigned to it have to be used to advance social causes across the different groups. The state has not succeeded in preventing these rights being violated and the blame has, therefore, to be shared both by the bureaucracy and the politicians.

One of the reasons for the tardy implementation of laws in this regard is that most of the officers and their political chiefs were themselves not keen to implement them. Perhaps their class origin accounted for that. Those of the officers who tried to implement laws met with silent and vocal opposition. If, however, things have not happened as foreseen, the entire blame cannot be placed on the bureaucracy alone. Social taboos are strongly embedded in the Indian social customs and traditions, and breaking them requires wider societal acceptance and greater ideological force than the bureaucracy could unleash. The upper caste opposition to social transformation proved much stronger in the north than in the south. The later appears to have fared better, since it had a long history of social movement against the exclusion of lower castes from the public sphere. To get things changing in social mores is more a matter of social movement, yet there are a number of officers who used their administrative authority to bring about social change. Their example has to be followed, which would catch the public imagination and serve as an inspiration to others. It must be a constant endeavour of good administration to bolster up and build such institutional support groups which would spearhead a movement in favour of social transformation. Thus their efforts could be made to gain greater support in mitigating the distress of oppressed classes. Strong action taken against social evils like bride burning, demand for dowry, *sati*, instant divorce, and such other reprehensible practices has been highly appreciated when the officials stood firm and determined to prevent them from happening. Administration cannot remain indifferent to prejudices and crimes against Dalits, who are excluded from upward mobility. One can explain their backwardness, but the task is to lift them out of their poverty, backwardness and sub-human plight they have suffered for centuries and still continue to suffer. Democracy means not only giving them just the right to vote but also giving them a sense of dignity and freedom and equality of opportunities. The state has to deepen and broaden its activities to transform their lives. The governments have to pass enabling legislation, but it is for the executives to see that the laws are implemented and don't just adorn the statute book as showpieces. Bureaucrats who fail to do this bring neither credit to service nor fulfil their obligation to the Constitution. There are certain social and political movements which spread disharmony and create divisions among people and subvert the very values of democracy. It is the raison d'etre of democracy as an instrument of state to create new social norms and reorder relations to make people free of fears and to enable them to exercise the rights given to them by the Constitution. Administration must have the moral worth of the downtrodden acknowledged and become the instrument of social transformation.

Administration has also remained negligent in protecting the individual's civil rights. Being more attentive to group rights, any slight of a group, albeit unintended, is taken up more seriously than the individual's rights when crushed by the group in senseless retaliation. Both the politician and bureaucrats turn Nelson's eye to the group's encroachment on the rights of the individual. There are again some outstanding examples of administrators who, in such moments of clash between the group and the individual's, have not hesitated to stand by the individual.

Economic liberalisation has brought in its wake the necessity for curtailing government size and role, but there are still some areas where government indifference or apathy will do more harm than good. The following advice by Amartya Sen and Jean Dréze has a prophetic ring to it:

> While the case for economic reforms may take a good note of the diagnosis that India has too much government interference in some fields, it ignores the fact that India also has insufficient and ineffective government activity in many other fields; including basic education, healthcare, social security, land reform and the promotion of social change. This inertia, too, contributes to the persistence of widespread deprivation, economic stagnation and social inequality.

The Scourge of Corruption

Another phenomenon for which politicians and bureaucrats are severely criticised is corruption. There is a damaging accusation that corruption in administration has become so rampant that nothing else gets done until money is paid.

Corruption has many dimensions. It is defined as the abuse of public office for personal gains. It is perceived as a high-gain and low-risk activity. Corruption involves misuse of power. It makes application of law arbitrary. Men in office use their authority to permit illicit gains in return for bribes and any other forms of allurement. People are made to pay money under the table to get even those things done to which they are otherwise rightfully entitled.

Artificial shortages are created which become lucrative opportunities for making tainted money. But one of the most blatant acts of corruption has been the exposures, leading to the arrest of the top government functionaries including bureaucrats and high military officers and heads and members of some public service commissions and other agencies. These exposures are just the tip of the iceberg, and it is difficult to quantify the magnitude of corruption. In short, discretionary powers are abused and with that the standards of service have fallen and the democratic constraints muted.

Corruption remains a conflict phenomenon so long as the pie to be shared is small and politicians and bureaucrats compete with each other to grab the lion's share of the booty. But with governmental mega-spending the pie has grown so that there is enough for everybody to share and to spare. And when the administrative and political arms collude, its operation cuts deep into the vitals of the state. People lose faith in the functionaries and in the system of governance. The state becomes a market and decision-making resembles an auction performance, favouring that bidder who offers the highest money under the table. The networking of brokers makes law-abiding citizens helpless. Corruption at higher levels creates conditions which encourage functionaries at the lower levels to become corrupt also. The poor are the worst hit by corruption. Street vendors pay protection money to local inspectors, small shop-keepers and rickshaw drivers pay to the policeman and slum dwellers to the municipal inspector. The private contractors and builders get away with unlawful deals and activities by paying money to the higher ups. Not only the weaker sections of society, but also the better-off people have to suffer owing to corrupt practice.

For some time now, yet one more source of corruption has been budgetary subsidies, development grants and loans. These have provided opportunities to political and administrative officials and also bank officials to make money without fear of being hauled up. The recipients of these loans and largesses have also been willing partners in this loot. Only a very small percentage of these grants and loans is utilised for genuine purposes while the major portion is diverted to non-productive and non-developmental channels. Recovery of loans is tardy and lending institutions unabashedly call these defaults as 'non-performing assets', which run into billions of rupees. Rajiv Gandhi had remarked that only 15 per cent of the government money intended for the poor ever reaches them. Most of it leaks out to fatten the wallets of corrupt officials and those who are already well-to-do. Since it is all in the knowledge of people, it has brought a bad name to the state and its functionaries, both political and administrative.

While there are worthy examples of those who were not tempted to stoop down to making illicit money, there are many others who succumbed to the lure of the filthy lucre and acquired assets beyond their means. There was a time when venal officers in higher echelons of government could be counted on one's fingertips. But, today in the face of stark materialism and consumerism, most official functionaries, high or low, have come to believe in Oscar Wilde's dictum that the "best way to resist a temptation is to yield to it." To cut the above abuse of authority and power, vigilance organisations were set up. But a weak accountability in the system could not let the administration be cleaned up. Nor could corruption be restrained through sporadic raids. Attempts to counter corruption have also failed because of a nexus between bureaucrats and politicians, which proved stronger and nullified counter corruption measures.

Further, when the state assumes too big an interventionist role, corrupt officers find more and larger scopes to harass people. Of late the magnitude of corruption has gone up in the face of governmental mega-spending on government projects, especially relating to infrastructure and defence. Without a proper mechanism of accountability the larger the money allotted, the greater the opportunities for the corrupt to make money. In each transaction where money is committed to be spent, corrupt administrators, both political and from the bureaucracy, find room for securing cuts. This enriches their private coffers at the expense of public exchequer and interests. People are short-changed and state deprived of full benefits of the projects which were meant to serve the people. Most of the public goods have become a most lucrative source for making money. Lack of transparency and accountability lets the corrupt operate with impurity. Politicians explain corruption as a necessary evil since it is linked with political funding of elections. Some justify it under the pretext of providing money to the political party to which they belong.

With economic liberalisation and emergence of free market, corruption at the ministerial and official levels has declined. But there are other avenues to compensate for that. Discretionary powers which are still there are abused and become a source for making money. It is hoped that with greater visibility, accountability and competition in the market, some dent could be made on the evil of corruption.

How one wishes the cost that the country has to incur because of this malaise of corruption could be quantified, both in monetary and non-monetary terms! The following list is merely indicative and can be easily extended:

Financial and Fiscal Cost: (i) manipulated high cost of projects, goods and services, so as to include the amount to be given to government functionaries by contractors and suppliers; (ii) expenditure on frequent maintenance or replacement of the above on account of inferior quality of construction or supplies; (iii) low collection of taxes, customs and excise duties, royalty, etc.; and (iv) misuse of government transport, manpower and other facilities by ministers and officials.

Social Costs: (i) citizens made to pay heavily to government functionaries as illegal gratification to get even their legitimate work done in government offices and judicial courts; (ii) adulterated or sub-standard food stuffs, drugs, petroleum products, equipment and various other necessities, affecting the health of men, machines, buildings, etc. (iii) bribes to functionaries—high and low—of recruitment agencies (including high profile public service commissions); (iv) manipulated high fees for admission to professional colleges and even high profile schools; spurt in crime due to collusion of government functionaries with criminal elements; (v) low standard of health and other civic services and utilities.

Economic Cost: (i) parallel economy with its attendant evils; (ii) manipulating prices of necessities (including vegetables, edible oils, etc.) by hoarders.

Political Cost: (i) social discontent leading to tensions and even violence; (ii) frequent elections; (iii) corrupt image of politicians, officials and businessmen damaging economic and political relations with foreign countries.

The above can be said to be the tip of the proverbial iceberg. The bottom line is that corruption is holding the whole body politic in its vicious tentacles. Not only politicians, government functionaries and those manning banks and other PSUs but also the members of the public are to blame for this grim situation. But those in power have to share major part of the blame. First and foremost, officials and citizens alike have to retrieve their moral fibre from the abysmal depths it has sunk. Incorruptible ombudsmen and vigilance commissioners should be empowered to book corrupt functionaries, irrespective of their status. Even persons holding the highest political, executive and judicial offices should be answerable for their acts of omission and commission.

Corruption is a canker which is not only affecting the political, economic and social health of the country internally but is also projecting a negative image of India abroad, ironically at a time when the world is taking notice of India for the second time (the first time it was when the Nehruvian ideas had caught the imagination of the world). All this talk that India is one of the fastest growing economies and that it is emerging as a regional power and such other rhetoric will end up as '*Mungerilal ke sapne*', if immediate sincere efforts are not made to control corruption in governmental functioning.

Monarchies and dictatorships do not survive long if corruption is rampant. So a clean administration is needed in any system of government and in a democracy it is its very essence and lifeline. It is hoped that with more of media attention, fair elections and larger participation of the civil society in administration, together with new rules and regulations pertaining to the expenditure incurred on public works and the right to information, corruption could be curtailed significantly. There are innumerable instances where clean and uncorrupt officials and politicians have made a difference. They have not stooped down to make money. The human capacity to live up to one's social responsibility has to be made the order of service. There are worthy examples of officers who remained above corruption. Their acts of honesty should be acclaimed so that their examples would motivate others to follow them. At the moment, it looks like wishful thinking!

Imperative that Bureaucracy Reinvent Itself

There is a general disenchantment with bureaucracy. It is not seen as people friendly; nor is it looked upon as an effective guardian of law and order. It is perceived as an instrument of coercion in the service of political bosses and too willing to subvert rules and regulations to serve the interests of more fortunate and better off sections of society. Serving the common man by taking care of their interests does not figure high on its agenda. This is severally explained. In some instances it is attributed to its class-related origin and its self-centric obsession. It is difficult to refute S.R. Maheshwari's observation that "civil service is not a mere technical instrument; it has an inherent tendency to exceed its instrumental function and emerge as a separate force within society".

What is most galling is that in the name of misconceived neutrality, officials have remained disinclined to implement reforms which were meant to undo various forms of injustice and inequality. They have remained passive observers of practices which hurt the poor and the dispossessed. Officers forego efforts to implement reforms due to an assortment of motives. These motives may also be related to prospects in their careers by siding with the better offs and the elite or they may be influenced by their personal ideological aversion to the projected reforms. If at all, they will only go through the motion of implementing the reforms, as their outlook and lifestyle being markedly different from that of the common man also hinders their relationship with the people. They treat people as subjects rather than citizens with some inalienable rights. They favour status quo as defined by the upper classes. This contributes to maladministration and sullies the good name of the service.

This is basically an attitudinal problem, which is a legacy of the past. Bureaucracies were particularly important in developing countries and India was no exception. But the nation had to pay a certain price. The bureaucracy inherited from the British administration, though serving the independent India's interests with zeal and sincerity, often operated at a remove from its own society and constituted an elite group more in common with their British counterpart, and also made conscious, and as Nehru had put it, 'ludicrous' efforts to be their spitting image. This attitudinal problem, handed down from one generation of bureaucrats to another, continues to haunt us even today and constitutes a main hindrance to people-oriented governance, which is a prime requirement of democracy. When our youngsters join the exclusive club of bureaucrats after some grueling tests and interview, they get imbued with a disproportionate sense of self-importance, which in most cases goes on growing with their progressive elevation to higher posts. As a wit has so tersely put it, half of the harm that is done in this world is due to people who want to feel important. Unless the present crop of administrators reorient their attitude towards the mode and goals of administration, they would become impediments rather than instruments for the realisation of democratic governance in the true sense of the word.

Bureaucracy must become more effective and efficient in its core area of enforcing law and order and assume a prominent and active role as a provider of public goods and services to common man. It must recreate the sense of pragmatic idealism which was once its hallmark and should become more mission-oriented with a sense of pride in doing service to the people. It should integrate itself with a concern to reduce socio-economic inequalities, work harder to see people enjoy human rights and get easy access to better education, health and other welfare programmes. It cannot any more remain indifferent to the needs of people who suffer indignities in the society. These hapless people are to be taken care of and not abandoned as scum of society. Of late, bureaucracy has helped things to happen to some extent, but this token effort of theirs is too little to give significant momentum to the amelioration and transformation programmes. Bureaucrats must also let their conscience, as Adam Smith said, raise the voice of moral reasonableness without which a man becomes thoughtless and has no qualms in perpetrating injustice.

The moral stature of the Indian bureaucrat must rise. Today it is accused of certain moral decadence and not without some cogent reasons. The following shocking statement occurring in the Report of the Fifth Central Pay Commission is either a true indictment or a point stretched too far:

> Integrity has never been a strong point of the bureaucracy in India and the situation has definitely worsened in recent times. There are accounts of some of their activities which are not worthy of the service to which they belong. There is a damaging suspicion that, under the cover of this elite service, they indulge in certain unethical activities. This may not be true in all cases, not even of a sizeable section, but public perception being what it is does harm the image of impartiality and fairness of the whole service. It is a classic case of one rotten apple sullying its fellows.

Here it is worth mentioning a practice in Uttar Pradesh where bureaucrats go though a periodical ritual of naming the most corrupt member/members in their cadre. This ritual can be commended or condemned, depending on one's perception. One implication of this nature of indictment is that corruption is permissible only up to a certain limit and not beyond. Corruption is thieving of the worst kind. By the same logic of letting off less corrupt bureaucrats, common thieves should also be let off if they steal within certain limits. Corruption is corruption, and a corrupt officer or politician or even a private person, whatever the degree or kind of their moral turpitude, should get their just deserts.

There are many ongoing efforts to improve and lift up the moral credentials of service but these seldom achieve their aim. While these efforts should not be given up, it would be fair to assume that the watch-dog role of the civil society and social activists would have beneficial impact on officials. Similarly, the new laws relating to accountability and transparence could also help to constrain the unethical and unlawful acts of the officialdom.

No social institution can survive long in a moral vacuum. So democracy, too, requires more than its share of moral anchorage. India's cultural heritage is strong enough to provide norms and values, which could constrain unethical behaviour that societies can no longer bear. Democratic societies cannot do without a commitment to higher values. The gap between the exercise of power and the norms of morality should be narrowed and bridged.

There are several externalities relating to society's economic and cultural shortcomings which generate inducement to injustices to thrive. These diverse combinations of concerns should be encountered in collaboration with civic and political forces. Good politics is needed to provide good governance within the framework of democracy.

There was a time when access to civil service was mostly confined to youngsters hailing from well-educated and dominant classes. Access to civil service gave them a sense of power and status that was not normally available to others in the society. Quite a number of those who joined the service worked with a sense of dedication, but, not being socially identified with, or related to the harsh realities of, the common man's life, they could not be sensitive to their concerns. That situation should change with increasing recruitment of candidates from the marginal sections of society. Their direct experience with the realities of common man's miseries and discomforts should motivate them to serve the people better and give administration a direction to lift the marginalised section of society out of poverty, misery and disease. But it is also imperative that this new class of bureaucrats should be exhorted to insulate themselves from any feeling of vindictiveness they might be harbouring against the upper classes. Let us hope the principle of noblesse oblige guides their thoughts and actions. This fear is not unfounded, as some politicians belonging to this class have not shied away from expressing their vindictiveness and occasionally carrying it out too.

The dharma of good bureaucrats should be to empower the people to do what the people themselves could not do in terms of bringing about a socio-economic transformation. The commanding position that the civil service occupies in the executive machinery could help them to bring about a more decent life within reach of the common man. They could create in a substantial way a social space that would enable people to energise their socio-economic development. This calls for an extraordinary effort to be put in by politicians and bureaucrats in unison within the framework of democracy. This would bring good governance to the people and not only sustain but also enhance the credibility of a vibrant democracy. Happily, there are now increasing cases of individual officers working towards this objective. May their tribe thrive!

Administration and Politics

Disenchanted with politicians, one might be tempted to believe that politics is a rival to a just, open and fair administration; that administration, once cut off from politicians, would enable the bureaucrats to serve the people better; and that it is the interference of politicians in administrative matters which deviates and distracts bureaucrats from performing their duties in accordance with time-honoured norms. But it would be naïve to believe that in a democracy politics would not be a factor in administration. Rather it is the very spirit and indispensable condition of democracy that bureaucrats cannot and should not function in isolation from politicians. The parliamentary form of government is essentially a party government and politicians cannot be excluded from governmental functioning. The party in power lays down the basic policies and politicians have a role to see that those policies are implemented. They lend support to the bureaucracy in doing so. Further, when the lot of common man finds its meaning in political terms, politics and administration cannot be kept hierarchically separate.

In several cases, administrative action would amount to an infraction if it is not underpinned by political approval and action. In several situations politicians play an important part in solving substantive problems. What is needed is that a bureaucrat should not abdicate his constitutional responsibility to administer by rules and not to bend to accommodate such demands of politicians which are not in conformity with the laws which the politicians themselves have legislated. Failure to do so would be against the spirit of democracy and would amount to the bureaucrats' dereliction of duty.

Politicians have a right to be people's watch-dogs to prevent officials' high handedness and to see that bureaucrats, who are generally wedded to status quoism, do not hinder the working of reforms which will ensure growth in all sectors and justice to larger sections of society, and do not become an obstacle to the emancipatory aspirations of the people. Administrative actions have inescapably to be within the context of given policies. But that should not mean that politicians can take the law into their hands. Flaunting political influence, which is a negative feature of majoritiism, they should not deflect the law and order authorities to deviate from their path of duty. This causes an estrangement between the politician and the bureaucrat and hurts the cause of good governance.

Such of those bureaucrats who understand the 'historico-political matrix' into which they have to work are intellectually better-equipped to use the avenues of politics for the betterment of people. They can see politics as the essential and unavoidable principle fundamental to administration. It is this source of understanding that makes bureaucrats handle politics effectively and lend support and direction to improve governance. On the other hand, when party leaders become endlessly critical of the executive machinery, it takes away legitimacy from the bureaucrats to be effective.

Abuse of political power by politicians can erode the principles of good governance. Remedial measures have to be taken by parties themselves to correct the ways of the party men who are tempted to abuse power arising from the charisma of office. Imaginative and stern steps have to be taken to improve the working of both the party functionaries and the bureaucracy. Administrative reforms and reorientation of politicians through party democracy could go a long way in improving matters. The roles of both are well defined in the Constitution and in the initial period they were well maintained. The same should be restored by greater discipline of politicians both within and outside the party and by depoliticisation of bureaucracy. Both have to work in harmony to become effective tools for economic and political development of the country, which is a necessary condition for transformation of society through democratic means for democratic ends. It is nice to note that, of late, politicians and bureaucrats are no longer treating each other as rivals. Each has to do the task allotted to them in the Constitution. This current prevailing thought is good for ensuring good governance. The potential that the two represent can generate a tremendous force in the service of the country.

Conclusion

The challenge for democracy is to make political leadership and bureaucracy work together to create an egalitarian society. The combined task of bureaucracy and political leadership is to inculcate capacities, create institutions and conventions, enthuse moral behaviour, which would empower people to become effective citizens as visualised in the Constitution. They should channelize the state power to stop corruption, coercion and violence in the society. It is a shared public role of the politician and the bureaucrat to create conditions that would ultimately bring peace and happiness to all Indians, irrespective of caste, creed or religion, which remains one of the main objectives of democracy. This path is indeed arduous, hard and long. But it is the only way to reach the destination which Nehru had promised us in his "Tryst with Destiny" speech in 1947. Let the politicians and the bureaucrats dedicate themselves to this task. There could be no better way for concluding the above thoughts than by reciting some lines from Cardinal Newman's Hymn, which Bapu loved to recite:

Lead, kindly light, amid the encircling gloom,
Lead thou me on!
The night is dark, and I am far from home–
Lead thou me on!
Keep thou my feet; I do not ask to see
The distant scene—one step is enough for me.

8

PRATAP BHANU MEHTA

Being Free to be Free

Introduction

Dr Abid Hussain was one of the pioneers of freedom in India. My intellectual life was greatly enriched by his weekly call to me after he had read my column. In his inimitable way, he would challenge and admonish me to think harder about what I had written. Invariably these conversations turned to matters dear to him: the future of diversity and secularism in India. I once joked that he had been an economic liberaliser by conviction much before it became fashionable to espouse the cause. He immediately retorted that economic freedom was a politically hard battle to win, but it is was psychologically easy; but social and cultural freedom, though politically easy to espouse, was likely to be psychologically harder to live with. This insight has struck me as deeply important and profound. It is also broadly right. The resistance to freedom in Indian democracy needs a fuller diagnosis. This short essay is offered in the spirit of a dialogue with Abid Saheb, one of the last of the true liberals, who combined a commitment to economic freedom, with an insistence on cultural freedom. But most of all he knew that neither could be sustained without the cultivation of virtue. Freedom requires more self discipline. It also is sustained by the ability to enjoy the world in it own right, to accord individuality its rightful place. I know of no other liberal in India who has embodied this virtue as much as Abid Saheb did. This champion of freedom left us at a moment where genuine defenders of freedom are few and far between; and even fewer are those eleveated souls who understand that freedom rests on a presumption of trust and generosity. This short essay is a continuation of my dialogue with Abid Saheb.

The experience of freedom in India has always uneasily hovered between hope and fear. The Independence of India was a watershed event in Indian history. Its constitutional articulation promised a great deal: protection of individual freedom, instantiation of equality, creation of a new form of fraternity, and the unbounded possibility of a new future. Yet, even in the moment of its enactment, independence was overshadowed by fear. We feared individual freedoms like free speech enough to encumber its protection with so many qualifications. State intervention in the cause of equality was justified. Deprivation and extreme inequality would make a mockery of freedom. But we soon found that what we often got was not equality, but a massive increase in state power. We hoped for a new fraternity. But the very tyranny of compulsory identities that had cast a violent shadow on Independence in the form of partition, continued to give our politics the colour of fear. And the sense of unbounded possibility was always hampered by the deadweight of the past: the openness of democracy often constrained by social hierarchies and continuities in administrative cultures inherited from the colonial state. As Ambedkar phrased it well, to enter into independent India was to enter a life of contradictions, and the dialectic between those contradictions is still playing out.

Independence was a complex experience. In the dominant narrative, India acquired the power to author her own destiny after experiencing colonial subordination, finally able to take care of her own material power and prosperity. But for most of the nationalist movement India's independence was meant to be something more than simply a quest to protect India's interests, as vital as that consideration was. India could itself be an example of a pluralist society, eschewing domination, and even more ambitiously a helper of the human race, in achieving the unity of mankind. Independence was supposed to have a meaning larger than what the ideology of the nation state allows. But this quixotic dream, shared by figures as diverse as Tagore, Nehru and Aurobindo, soon ran into the grim realities of world politics. Indeed, nothing signifies our distance more from the highest aspirations of Independent India than the contempt with which we currently think of this project. For Gandhi, who was a forlorn and unhoused figure on the day of independence, the form in which independence came was itself a sign of failure. We gained sovereignty and independence, but only to subordinate it to a new form of collective tribalism that led to the partition of India.

But Independent India could not afford to let the weight of a higher morality get in the way of securing India's interests, and it embarked upon its journey as a nation state. But while independence was a break with the past in one crucial respect—Indians could hold their own government to account—it was not by any means a revolution. In fact India's relationship with the legacy of colonialism it was trying to overcome was far more complex. At the risk of being provocative one can say that what distinguished India's colonial experience was that India's ruling classes did rather well out of it, for the most part. British rule was, let us not forget, welcomed as a form of liberation by many sections of society. For many Dalits, it was exactly the shock a stifling and oppressive social system needed. In the early years, many Hindus had seen it as liberation from Muslim rule and an opportunity to acquire power in a different form. But even for India's privileged, the British Raj offered opportunities for the consolidation of their own power. And India's privileged opted for democracy as an antidote to revolution since they realised very shrewdly, that democracy could be made to serve the interests of power. The new social contract was written in a way that guaranteed that any change would be incremental and ameliorative, not radical and revolutionary. One can debate the human costs of revolutionary versus incremental change. But it did ensure that while Independent India was new, it was not radical.

It also has to be said, that as much as India's ruling classes may have experienced colonialism as subjugation, they never internalised a deep sense of humiliation, because they benefitted from it. In this sense it is interesting to speculate that Chinese intellectual history experiences Western victory with a much deeper sense of humiliation. Therefore, the Chinese state has had more single minded ideological pursuit of the wealth and power to seek parity. In India linguistically, culturally and socially, colonialism sunk deep roots to the point that it defined India's elites, in some ways even their identity. For

China, therefore the discourse on Westernisation was largely an instrumental one: about its use for knowledge and power. In India the debate over Westernisation was immediately more cultural, but therefore also more sentimental. India became independent, but it also remained a Western power, as it were.

The imagination of freedom that emerged was, predictably, a melange of compromises. Its beauty was that it allowed for the negotiation of many complex demands on the state: it gave all the classes some hope; but its workings equally ensured that privilege would not also be seriously challenged. That is the dilatory compromise which has given the independent India an amazing stability. But the question for India is: will the weight of accumulated disappointments with India's prospects ever surpass the narrative of India as a site for hope? And can this turn into a politics that is angry and resentful? This is a large historical question that will turn on how just and secure India's developmental trajectory turns out.

But there are two other compromises in our imagining of freedom that need a relook. The Indian state has always tempered its grant of freedoms with a discourse of fear that has infantilised, inhibited and restricted our freedoms. Second, there is a tension in the Indian Constitution between individual liberty and community rights. Of course, some community rights are sometimes necessary to prevent injustice. But the dominant imagination has turned India from a zone of freedom into a federation of communities. Both of these aspects of the way we imagined freedom need to be rethought. The rest of the essay reflects on this need to liberate freedom from fear, and liberate freedom from the traps of identity.

The Fear of Expression

A sense of fear has always inscribed itself, in our experience of freedom. It has inscribed itself in law. The number of laws restricting freedom of expression in India for example that are premised on fear is a scandal for a liberal democracy. These were legitimised under the shadow of partition, under the pretext that the Indian state needed to protect its citizens from their own worse passions. In addition to these traditional restrictions, the state has, in the name of security, acquired overweening and near unchallenged powers of surveillance and detention. These powers operate, in their most draconian form, in areas like Kashmir and the North East, where the subjective experience of political freedom, is still something of a mirage. The effective correlate of freedom, the idea of privacy, an inherently protected zone I can call my own, where I am accountable to no one, so long as I am not inflicting harm on others is increasingly vanishing. And there is a vicious circle: as the power of entities outside the state, small terrorist groups, social media, movements of capital, make the state's ability to exercise control harder, the state demands even more control as a countervailing force. To be fair, almost all liberal democracies have let fear triumph over their traditional solicitude for rights and privacy. But the net result is a freedom embedded in an ever present sentiment of fear.

The new government, more than any other in recent memory, likes to project the idea of setting India on a new path, almost making new tryst with destiny. It wants to replace pessimism with hope, defeatism with action, and low expectations with high ambition. But there is one area where the Republic really does need a cleaning of the cobwebs that the Nehruvian consensus has bequeathed to us: the domain of liberty. Mr Modi made "Minimum government. Maximum governance", the centrepiece his campaign. He has said that he reposes trust in crores of ordinary Indians. And he has reiterated that he wants an Indian state where every individual feels secure. But it has to be said, that on basic freedom, Mr Modi's pronouncements seems like an exercise in monumental irony. Not only has his government not lifted the pall of fear, it has at every turn exacerbated it. The one great failing of the Nehruvian consensus, beginning with its advocacy of laws of sedition, through the first amendment, and now through regulation of social media, was this. It crafted a whole series of laws that are handy tools for suppressing civil liberties. They may have used them sporadically, but their very existence damaged our freedom. They may have been products of the fear partition and a precarious nationhood generated. But like all fears, they proved to be self fulfilling prophecies, instruments to curb freedom.

Many laws restricting freedom were premised on imagining the Indian citizens in a certain way. Indian citizens were not capable of handling liberty, they were prone to violent excess that required their speech be restricted, they were thin skinned and would take offence at almost anything. India's citizens could not be trusted to handle liberty, so the paternalistic state needed to step in. These powers in turn, created a whole train of abuses in our system that all political parties have connived in. The Nehruvian consensus was this: The state is virtuous, the citizen infirm. Therefore empower the state at the expense of the citizen. If Mr Modi is serious about "minimum government" in the sense of the term that matters most, he would do well to concentrate on the state of our civil liberties. The Nehruvian state, in this domain, had become, "Maximum arbitrariness, Minimum freedom." Can creating the republic anew reverse this presumption and go for "Maximum freedom and Minimum arbitrariness?"

Just think of the appalling number of bad laws that abridge liberty that Congress has bequeathed to us. If Bharatiya Janata Party (BJP) misuses them, Congress will have set the precedent. Why do we have sedition laws still on the books, which have been routinely used to suppress social protest and dissent? Why have the restrictions on speech enacted by the First Amendment been so widely used? Ironically, on these two issues, the BJP actually has an intellectual inheritance to claim: K.M. Munshi and Shyama Prasad Mukherjee were the two most articulate critics of some of these draconian provisions. It is a pity that the BJP forgot its own inheritance.

The list can go on. The Armed Forces Special Powers Act needs a thorough review and needs to be withdrawn from areas like Kashmir and the North East. What might minimum government mean for Indian citizens in an area subject to such draconian restrictions? Then there is the list of archaic laws: Section 295A of the Indian Penal Code is unlikely to repealed. But it does need to be amended, because the way it is functioning in practice, and the interpretations the Court has given to this law, has a chilling effect, almost equivalent to a blasphemy law. It is now an obstacle even to works of scholarship. Section 66A of the IT Act was struck down by the Supreme Court. But the clamour for replacing it is growing. But any attempt to replace the struck down act will be dangerous; it is open to the interpretive whims of officials. The colonial law makers, and the assemblies under them, at least had the good sense, to more clearly articulate what terms like offensive might mean. This law is so vaguely drafted that it will have far reaching effects on social media, and will be abused by Chief Ministers of all parties. There are other laws that need reform. Our law of criminal defamation is woefully out of date and makes questioning of companies and states that much harder. The government has a reactionary position on Section 377 of the IPC. What will minimum government mean, if it intrudes in the most intimate aspects of our lives? Hopefully, the Supreme Court will correct its own howlers, since this is a fundamental rights and discrimination case. But BJP should not stand in the way. The government has rather ominously opposed a right to privacy.

All these laws abridge an important aspect of our liberty. They say government should be trusted more than citizens. They are enacted in the name of making us more secure. But they have the opposite effect of making us more insecure. Many of these laws, like laws protecting offences against religion generate more offence by their very existence. A state that routinises the use of sedition or special powers, or seeks to intimidate the press, is not likely to elicit allegiance from its citizens. And a state that does not give its citizens the private space they require for their dignity breeds the worst kind of psychological fears. These laws, more than almost any other are open to partisan manipulation and selective outrage. Each government wants them, and uses them against their favourite targets. We often object to them, not on the principle that these are bad laws, but on basis of who they target. These laws inherently discriminate in their operation. In some cases fixing the judicial system is the answer. But the opposite is also true: when the laws themselves signal arbitrariness and disregard for individual dignity, it will generate judicial pathology.

These laws have extracted price. In a country where due process itself can be the punishment, these laws increase the asymmetry of power between state and citizen. A genuinely new tryst with destiny would require a new tryst with freedom. If Mr Modi is serious, this is the place to start. If he truly wants to overcome Congress' legacy he needs to start by making a new tryst with freedom. But all the signs are that he fears freedom more than he fears fear. This will not be healthy for India's quest for a deeper freedom.

The Freedom of Identity

The sentiment of fear is inscribed in social relations in more ways than one can list. In a traditional caste hierarchy marked by inequality, fear pervades the social order. For many the core promise of freedom was the liberation from one of most egregiously hierarchical social orders known to mankind. And there have been massive changes in this social order. Migration and urbanisation can mitigate some of the most coercive aspects of caste. Political empowerment has in many cases overcome historical subordination. The language of purity and pollution is increasingly a pale shadow of its past. But this social change in turn has produced new fears, and new curbs on freedom. In many areas of the country Dalits still remain at the receiving end of brutality, now prompted as much by fear of their independence, as by considerations of purity. And there is the often unarticulated fear and anxiety that grips the privileged when previously oppressed classes begin to find a voice. This psychological undercurrent of fear still acts as a profound barrier in creating the kind of fraternity that the Constitution envisaged.

India's self presentation is that of a tolerant society, capable of managing extraordinary diversity. To be fair, India has been remarkably successful at providing a home for all kinds of groups and cultures. It has celebrated diversity. While diversity is to be cherished, the form of group diversity we have promoted has also become a barrier in two ways. First, it is compatible with a segmentation and distance between groups that is a barrier to a spirit of freedom. In traditional society, each group could find a place because each group had its fixed place. To put it very schematically, it was a form of toleration compatible with walls between communities. Indeed, one the major challenges for Indian society is that we have internalised forms of toleration that are suited to segmented societies. It is compatible with the idea that boundaries should not be crossed, populations should not mix, and that to view the world as a competition between groups is fine. There is no country in the world that talks so much of diversity. Yet no other country also produces such a suffocating discourse of identity; where who you are seems to matter at every turn: what job you can get, what government scheme you are eligible for, how much institutional autonomy you can get, what schools you can run what house you can rent. Conceptually, there is no incompatibility between celebrating diversity of the nation and refusing to rent housing to a Muslim just because they are Muslim. Such a conception of toleration does not work where the need is for boundaries to be crossed: people will inhabit same spaces, compete for same jobs, intermarry and so forth. Our moral discourse is so centred on diversity and pluralism that it forgets the more basic ideas of freedom and dignity. The dream of freedom in our Constitution was to imagine a form of citizenship, where citizenship does not have to carry the burden of identities. These identities may be important to individuals. They are private facts about them, which they can do with as they please.

The most virulent form in which freedom is curbed is the freedom of women. On the one hand there is massive social change underway: female enrolment in post school education is now equal to that of men. Yet their low labour force participation, the increasing and brutal violence against women, is probably the single biggest curb on freedom. Yes in comparative statistical terms, India's story on violence does not look horrendous. But this is a small consolation in a culture that women find deeply oppressive and unsafe. It is a familiar fact that often the only site on which the politics of tradition and modernity is played out, is gender; social conservatism simply acts as a garb for repressing women.

None of these pathologies will be addressed if we do not reconceptualise India as a Zone of Individual Freedom (ZOF) rather than a Federation of Communities (FOC). The basic moral intuition is simple, and involves no cultural baggage or "western values." Every group in this country has at sometime claimed that something—a cultural practice, or a state project, not be imposed upon them if they do not consent to it. Minorities use this argument, rightly, against majoritarianism. The simple intuition is that this privilege extend all the way down to individuals. So the claim that India should give primacy to individual freedom entails a moral individualism; in that individual is the unit of moral justification. But it takes no stand on what kinds of lives individuals might want to lead, whether these are ones of deracination or thick cultural belonging. All it says is that these should be freely chosen. And it applies the same argument that is used to see India as a federation of communities: nothing must be imposed upon communities that they would not accept.

The real battle in India is not between secularism and communalism as conventionally understood. It is between forces of community repression and individual freedom. It is a battle between two different ideas of India: Is India a FOC or a ZIF? In our political culture the idea that India is a federation of communities has become almost inescapable commonsense, in a way that poses a great threat to liberty and distorts our intellectual culture. Both ideas rest on variants of the idea of toleration, but their underlying logic is different. We often confuse the two. Here is the core contrast in the 'two ideas of India'.

On values, the FOC places primacy on group diversity. ZIF places primacy on individual freedom. ZIF values diversity, but as an outcome of free individuals exercising their choices. It rests on the intuition that the groups claim the same moral rights, namely that nothing should be imposed on them that they could reasonably object to, should be applied to all individuals within group as well.

On toleration, FOC is compatible with segmented toleration: each group has its rightful place, so long as it stays in its rightful place. This has been the traditional Indian conception of toleration, peculiarly ill fitted to an age of mobility and competition in the same spaces: different groups will inhabit the same workplace, intermarry and so forth. ZIF recognises that the challenge is not protecting community identities; it is protecting those who breach them.

On citizenship FOC is premised on differentiated citizenship. What rights you have in particular areas depend upon your identity. This applies not just to areas of personal law, which are out of the purview of common deliberation. But these extend to matters like right to administer institutions. The degree of autonomy an institution is allowed in education for example depends on its identity, not functionality or financial relation to the state. ZIF is premised on common citizenship as much as possible, and on the idea that rights and identity must not be as closely aligned as in FOC.

Both differ in approach to identity. FOC is enamoured identities. Our legal identities are in part mediated by compulsory group identities. Our social and political interactions are premised on inescapably slotting people into identities; individuals are this caste, that religion and so forth. There is no escaping this identity. ZIF acknowledges that people should not be targeted for being who they are; occasionally an axis of deprivation structured around identity may need to be addressed. But it finds suffocating the constant need to slot individuals into compulsory identities.

Both have a different approach to justice. In FOC, the primary metaphor for justice is representation and balancing. The distribution of power should match the distribution of identities. No matter what representatives do, they count as representatives of a particular community by virtue of ethnicity. The primary mode of politics is balancing; if one community is given something, another community must be given something in recompense. For ZIF the primary metaphor for justice is equal opportunity of individuals. ZIF is suspicious of claims to represent, because it is suspicious that they are unified community claims that can be represented; what individuals do is more important than what group they stand for. In FOC the emphasis is on a politics of overt symbolism that can serve the needs of balancing and representation. For ZIF, the emphasis is on institutions that can protect individual rights.

With these rough contrasts, the intellectual history of modern India looks quite different. Our Constitution's ambition was to convert India into a zone of freedom, to liberate individuals from the burden of compulsory identities, to create a common citizenship and to give primacy to individual rights. But it made few compromises that allowed identity to become central to thinking about citizenship. But what the Constitution left as a tension, our political culture transformed into a full scale advocacy of India as a federation of communities. For example, its conception of Indian citizenship was to think in terms of Hindu plus Muslim, not to think beyond Hindu and Muslim; it was to think in terms of a collection of castes, not beyond caste. And our existing social practice has deep affinity with this way of thinking. ZIF does not argue that these identities will vanish, only that they will be largely private matters.

Only if India is imagined as a zone of freedom can the forces of social repression be challenged. But the working of this depends upon the credibility and justice of state institutions. India's biggest tragedy is that a discourse on individual freedom is an object of suspicion for two reasons. First oppressed or marginalised communities think that a focus on individuals is a ruse to disguise the oppression that comes from their membership in a community; it throws a veil over oppression and injustice. Second, there is an inherent paternalism that constructs this as an elite project. But the first worry can be addressed only if institutions do not discriminate on account of people's identities, and actual opportunities are not determined by accidents of community identity. The second worry is misplaced: the core idea is simply that individuals have the right to author their own lives; this ability to challenge the dictates of community is valuable at all levels of society. The prerogatives of community do not licence assaults on freedom.

Conclusion

The deepening of freedom requires that we do not let the state use fear to usurp freedom, and we do not let community piety usurp our freedom to author our own lives. Some might say that in India the big battle is over economic freedom. The sentiment of fear is inscribed in the economy. It goes without saying that any just and sustainable economy will, not only unleash private productive energies, it will also have to provide substantial public goods and welfare, and a complicated array of administrative regulations. A modern society is, for good reason, called a 'risk' society, and a vast system of administrative law has to regulate these risks. This will require, to a great extent, state intervention in the economy. It is hoped that these interventions will be backed by democratic legitimacy, so that there is a sense in which we can call these regulations our own. Rather than being curbs on our freedom, these interventions are instruments of our good that we have consented to in some fashion. But there has always been the sense that so much of state intervention in India is not about enhancing our capabilities, expanding our effective enjoyment of freedom, it is about distrusting citizens to the point where the state becomes the source of fear. To adapt the hyperbolic language of the 19th century anarchist Proudhon, the state's protocols of registering, taxing, enroling, licensing, measuring, authorising even the most ordinary business or transaction, leaves most economic agents reeling. But it is not only state distrust that restricts economic freedom: community narratives are hostile to migrants. India's middle class is imagining cities not as free spaces of civic reciprocity and a shared public sphere but as gated communities and barbed wired fences. The more a state distrusts its citizens the more it will seek control. In India reasonable economic and institutional liberty, is always precarious, and there is still no consensus on the degree of economic liberty we are comfortable with, free of fear.

Freedom is many things: it is expressed in legal rights. It has a psychological connotation, a sense of being free. It signifies not just protections against the state, but horizontal protections against being dominated by others in society. It has an individualist aspect: one is truly free, as the great poet Pushkin once suggested when one is accountable to no one but one's own self. But it has a collective dimension: freedom can be enjoyed only in concert with the freedom of others: it created and nurtured through partnership. Freedom is a social experience: the ability to access spaces of a city, unfettered. Freedom has to be reconciled with other values: primarily the need for social cooperation. Freedom requires a range of background conditions to operate without conflict: reciprocity, a sense of judgement, and even justice. But this Independence day, there is a sense of foreboding that instead of deepening the experience of freedom, we are rendering it more precarious. We need a conversation about what Independence should mean—for every citizen.

9

SUDIPTO MUNDLE[1]

Two Aspects of Governance

Public Service Delivery and Corruption

Introduction

An exceptionally sociable, kind and gentle person, and a loving family man, Abid Hussain was an outstanding civil servant, a diplomat and an adviser to several Prime Minister's in his public life. He was also a person with a deep commitment to India and to high moral values. Sliding standards of governance, the rising incidence of corruption, adulteration of the idea of inclusive India and the erosion of moral values that he witnessed in the later years of his life seemed to cast a shadow over his otherwise cheerful demeanour.

I had the good fortune of knowing 'Abid Bhai', his charming wife Karki and their whole family over several decades. Fairly early in our relationship, Abid Bhai once asked me what price India paid for its endemic corruption. Could we say, for instance, that India lost x percent of growth because of corruption. This was long before a whole literature emerged on the relationship between corruption and growth. I had no answer for him, not to suggest that lost growth is the only possible price of corruption. However, the thought stayed with me as I progressed through my career of over four decades in the field of development, sometimes as practitioner and sometimes as researcher.

Placing corruption within the larger context of governance failure, I came to recognise that the question of more or less

1. I would like to thank Rana Hasan and Deepak Nayyar for inviting me to contribute this paper as my small tribute to Abid Hussain in this festschrift volume in his memory. I would also like to gratefully acknowledge the assistance of Satadru Sikdar in writing this paper.

successful development depends quite crucially, though of course not exclusively, on successes or failures of governance. I would maintain that this proposition is robust to varying contexts across different geographies and for countries in different stages of development.

This essay discusses some issues relating to two aspects of governance: a positive aspect, service delivery, and a negative aspect, corruption. In section 2 we develop the concept of governance as service delivery and a metric for measuring the quality of governance, so defined, particularly in the context of competitive sub-national governments in India. Section 3 presents the case for dealing with the supply side of corruption in the interface between business and government, and spells out an approach towards the establishment of an ethical business institution to curb the incidence of corruption. Section 4 concludes.

Governance as Service Delivery

Conceptions of governance have ranged from a narrow definition that governance is what governments do to a much wider definition that governance is the way in which individuals, groups, and institutions, both public and private, manage their affairs and resolve conflicts of interest in an orderly manner (Weiss 2000, DARPP 2009). The narrow definition, what governments do, is obviously the most appropriate if our purpose is to assess the performance of governments, national or subnational.

Given that definition of governance, what is the criterion that enables us to distinguish between good and bad governance or to establish a metric for assessing the quality of governance? In a recent paper Fukuyama (2013) has described the quality of governance as "a government's ability to make and enforce rules and to deliver services." The authority-service duality embedded in this concept of good governance can be traced back at least two and a half millennia. Kautilya's *Arthashahstra*, the authoritative treatise on India's traditional concept of good governance dating back to the 4th century BCE, states that the king must have coercive authority, *danda*, but also outlines the principles for its fair application to serve the common good, *Dharma*.[2] Around the same period of history we find in different parts of the world remarkably similar conceptions of good governance as the need for authority and an order preserving government to ensure peace, security and prosperity of the people. It is a view shared by the Shang emperor of China in the East and Plato, with his concept of the ideal Athenian state in Greece, then the centre of civilisation in the West (Spengler 1969, Shome 2012).

This core concept of good governance as the duality of authority and service, adapted to changing times and conditions, has survived over the centuries through Machiavelli (1515),[3] Hobbes (1651), Adam Smith (1776) among other philosophers. In our own times, the duality in Fukuyama's definition resonates with many similar formulations (Arrow 1974; La Porta et al. 1999; Besley and Persson 2011, Acemoglu and Robinson 2012). It is important to note that in this historically robust concept of good governance authority, the ability to make and enforce rules, is not an end in itself but a means to an end, i.e., the delivery of services. This distinction is key in developing a metric for rating the quality of governance.

Fukuyama lists four possible approaches for assessing the quality of governance: procedural measures, capacity or input measures, output measures and measures of bureaucratic autonomy. Stating that as bureaucratic capacity increases bureaucratic autonomy should also increase, he goes on to define an optimal path of good governance. It is a path that moves from a combination of low levels of bureaucratic capacity and autonomy to high levels of bureaucratic capacity and autonomy.

While this specification of a good governance path is interesting, it has little operational value. Fukuyama does not provide any metric for measuring either bureaucratic capacity or bureaucratic autonomy, nor does he provide any functional rule relating capacity to autonomy, i.e., the so-called optimal good governance path. He also does not specify how the two variables, bureaucratic capacity

---

2. See the translation by L.N. Rangarajan. (Kautiliya 1992)
3. See the introduction by George Bull to the Penguin edition of Machiavelli's treatise on statecraft (1969). The original Italian version was probably completed in 1515.

and autonomy relate to his own core concept of good governance, i.e., authority and service delivery.

Of the four measures that Fukuyama lists, only the output measure of service delivery is compatible with the concept of good governance discussed above. As explained earlier, in the authority-service delivery duality, authority is not an end in itself but only a means to an end. We are thus left with an unambiguous measure of good governance, namely, the quality of service delivery.

However, governments deliver not just a service but a multiplicity of services. These can range from infrastructure services such as transport, connectivity, water, and power to social services like education and health, to fiscal performance, to maintenance of law and order, to justice delivery, etc. So the first challenge that arises in empirically assessing the quality of governance, defined as service delivery, is to develop a credible metric that can aggregate indicators of the quality of all these services into a comprehensive index of the overall quality of governance.

Before turning to this empirical question it is necessary to address two prior issues. The first issue is that service delivery outputs such as the quality of infrastructure, education etc., may depend on factors other than public action. This concern has led Fukuyama and others to reject service delivery output as a measure of the quality of governance.

This view is based on a misconception that outputs of service delivery are functions of governance along with other determinants. In the definition adopted above, service delivery outputs are not functions of governance and other determinants. They are themselves the constitutive elements of governance, whatever their determinants. As such, the fact that these outputs are functions of multiple determinants is quite irrelevant.

Further more, let us grant for the sake of argument that these outputs are not in themselves constitutive elements of governance but only a function of some undefined element called governance, along with other determinants. Multiple determinants are not a problem for isolating the impact of governance on these outcomes. Econometric techniques enable us to do that decomposition.

Governance quality can then be estimated as the residual-analogous to the measure of technical progress in the Solow (1957) aggregate production function.

The second issue is the close correlation between service delivery outputs and the level of development, represented by per capita income, that has been widely observed over time and across geographies (Besley and Persson 2011; Evans and Rauch 1999; La Porta et al. 1999; Rodrik et al. 2004). In an earlier paper Mundle and associates also reported such correlation at the sub-national level in India (Mundle et al. 2012). Wilson (2016) has recently reported similar correlation at the sub-national level in China.

These 'development clusters', as Besley and Persson have called them, may appear partly because of underlying determinants that drive both development and public service delivery, and partly because of mutual inter-dependence between service delivery and development. Thus two countries, or subnational jurisdictions, with the same level of governance inputs such as capacity, process efficiency, autonomy, and transparency may have different levels of service delivery if they are at different levels of per capita income. So we need to control for the differences in per capita income if we are interested in assessing the pure impact of governance inputs on service delivery outputs.

Turning to empirical assessments of the quality of governance, most of these have been undertaken at the national level. Broadly, two approaches have been adopted. Some follow the 'big data' route. All available data on a wide range of indicators, bearing on one or another aspect of governance, are processed and aggregated into five or six major dimensions of governance.

These may include but are not limited to service delivery outputs. They could include data from official as well as private sources, secondary data as well as survey data, objective data as well as perception data, data from large random surveys as well as the opinions of some individual observers, and so on. The best known exercise in this genre is the World Bank's *World Governance Indicators*, a series that is regularly revised and updated (Kauffman et al. 2007, Kauffman and Kray 2015). Another similar exercise is the Mo Ibrahim

Foundation's *Index of African Governance* (Rottberg and Gisselqucst 2009, Rottberg et al. 2014).

The other, parsimonious, approach is to assess governance on the basis of a few carefully selected key indicators that best capture different dimensions of the quality of governance, or some aspect of it. Thus, Transparency International focuses on the corruption aspect and produces the annual *Corruption Perception Index* (Transparency International 2014), UNDP produces the *Human Development Index* (UNDP 2014), Freedom House assesses governance from a libertarian perspective (Freedom House 2015) and so on.

The study by La Porta and associates (1999) and Besley and Persson (2011) are probably methodologically the most rigourous in this genre. Both assess the overall quality of governance based on aggregating a small set of key indicators, mainly objective data drawn from official sources, not perception surveys and individual observer opinions.

Assessments of governance at the sub-national level are rare.[4] India is an exception with half a dozen studies now available.[5] While some assess the overall quality of governance (Mundle et al. 2012; 2016), others focus on specific aspects such as infrastructure and social service delivery (Bhandari 2012) or economic freedom (Debroy et al. 2013).

All these studies adopt the parsimonious approach, basing their assessments on aggregating a selected list of variables. The study by Mundle and associates, for example, chose 14 indicators that capture service delivery across 5 broad classes: infrastructure, social services, fiscal performance, delivery of justice, law & order, and quality of the legislature. Most of these studies, though not all, are also based on objective data drawn from official sources. The studies also vary in their choice of indicators and in their methods of aggregation.

---

4. See however the earlier cited paper by Wilson (2016) which analyses the relationship between the quality of governance and growth at the sub-national level in China,
5. Mundle et al. (2012; 2016), Bhandari (2012), Debroy et al. (2013), Malhotra (2014), Tan and Rao (2015), World Bank (2015), Mathew et al. (2016).

A comparison across six of these studies of the rankings of states[6] shows there is a remarkably high degree of consistency. This is particularly so in their assessment of the best and worst performers clustered at the top and bottom of the rankings.

Thus, Gujarat, Tamil Nadu and Andhra Pradesh are the three best performers in both the Mundle et. al (2016) study and the Debroy et al. (2013) study. In fact Gujarat and Tamil Nadu are among the top six performers in five of the six studies, while Andhra Pradesh and Karnataka appear among the top six in four studies (Table 9.1).

Table 9.1

Six Best Performing States Comparison of Different States' Performance Estimates

Public Service Delivery	*Economic Freedom*	*Competitiveness*	*Ease of Doing Business*	*Policy Effectiveness Index*	*Public Affairs Index*
Mundle et al. 2016	*Debroy et al. 2013*	*Tan & Rao 2015*	*World Bank 2015*	*Malhotra 2014*	*PAC 2016*
Gujarat	Gujarat	Maharashtra	Gujarat	Punjab	Kerala
Tamil Nadu	Tamil Nadu	Tamil Nadu	Andhra Pradesh	Himachal Pradesh	Tamil Nadu
Andhra Pradesh	Andhra Pradesh	Karnataka	Jharkhand	Karnataka	Karnataka
Kerala	Haryana	Gujarat	Chhattisgarh	Haryana	Maharashtra
Punjab	Himachal Pradesh	Andhra Pradesh	Madhya Pradesh	Maharashtra	Gujarat
Karnataka	Madhya Pradesh	Uttar Pradesh	Rajasthan	Tamil Nadu	Punjab

Source: Mundle et al. (2016)

At the lower end, Assam and Bihar appear among the six worst performers in all six studies. Odisha and Jharkhand appear among the bottom six in four of the six studies, with Uttar Pradesh, Madhya Pradesh and West Bengal also appearing among the bottom six in three studies (Table 9.2).

6. Only those states that are common to all six studies are compared

Table 9.2

Six Worst Performing States: Comparison of Different States' Performance Estimates

Public Service Delivery	*Economic Freedom*	*Competitiveness*	*Ease of Doing Business*	*Policy Effectiveness Index*	*Public Affairs Index*
Mundle et al. 2015	*Debroy et al. 2013*	*Tan & Rao 2015*	*World Bank 2015*	*Malhotra 2014*	*PAC 2016*
Assam	Odisha	Himachal Pradesh	Punjab	Kerala	Uttar Pradesh
West Bengal	Uttar Pradesh	Bihar	Himachal Pradesh	West Bengal	Madhya Pradesh
Odisha	West Bengal	Assam	Kerala	Assam	Assam
Jharkhand	Jharkhand	Uttarakhand	Bihar	Madhya Pradesh (+Chhattisgarh)	Odisha
Bihar	Assam	Chhattisgarh	Assam	Bihar (+Jharkhand)	Jharkhand
Uttar Pradesh	Bihar	Jharkhand	Uttarakhand	Odisha	Bihar

Source: Mundle et al. (2016)

In the absence of a rigorous theory of governance, and constraints of available data, a great deal of judgement is involved in the preparation of these empirical assessments of governance. Moreover, these studies also differ in their objectives, their consequent choice of indicators, and their methods of aggregation. Hence, the robustness of clusters of good and bad governance performers identified in these studies is very important. It points to the objective reality underlying the identification of these clusters.

This is a good point at which to return to the question of development clusters raised earlier. It was mentioned that governance quality and the level of development are closely correlated. Therefore, to estimate the pure impact of governance inputs on governance outputs, it is necessary to control for the level of development. Mundle et al. (2016) have done this in their earlier cited study, and compared the Governance Performance Index (GPI) of Indian states with their Development Adjusted Governance Index (DAGI).

It turns out that some of the states in the middle or lower end of the GPI rankings such as Madhya Pradesh, Chhattisgarh, Bihar and Uttar Pradesh move up significantly in their DAGI ranks, implying that in service delivery per se they are performing much better than would be expected at their level of development. Others like Assam unfortunately slip down further. Some states at the upper end of the GPI ranking such as Gujarat and Kerala also slip down significantly in the DAGI ranking, suggesting that the high quality of service delivery in these states is partly a legacy effect arising from their high level of development.

After adjusting for the impact of development, the functional relationship between DAGI scores and governance inputs such as bureaucratic capacity, autonomy, transparency and processes can be estimated once suitable metrics are developed for quantifying these inputs. This function will in turn point to the interventions required to strengthen the quality of governance. Such interventions will have resource costs. This is obvious in the case of improving bureaucratic capacity. But changing processes or bureaucratic autonomy will also require resources since all such changes will entail initial adjustment costs. The DAGI function should enable us to calculate the trade-offs between these alternative interventions, thereby identifying the cost effective combination of interventions for strengthening the quality of governance.

A Business Institution Against Corruption

From a positive aspect of governance as service delivery, we now turn to a negative aspect, corruption. Media reports and assessments produced by institutions like the World Bank (*Ease of Doing Business*) and Transparency International indicate that corruption is endemic in many countries around the world.

A large number of studies on corruption have been published, especially since the 1980s, when multilateral agencies like the International Monetary Fund (IMF) and World Bank started focusing on corruption as a major factor adversely affecting growth in developing and transitional economies. Some of these studies are empirical and some theoretical.[7] Among other issues, they have addressed the question why corruption has remained endemic despite the fact that governments in many countries have set up institutions to investigate and prosecute those involved in corruption.

In this context Avinash Dixit (2015) has explained in a recent theoretical paper why this is not surprising. There is a major problem of incentive compatibility in leaving it to governments to deal with corruption since, typically, it is politicians in power and bureaucrats who are among the main beneficiaries of corruption. They constitute the demand side of the market for corruption (bribery). He has suggested it could be more effective to address the supply of corruption, i.e., the individuals or businesses who pay the bribes.

A distinction needs to be made here between big corruption and petty corruption where officials demand bribes to perform tasks that they are supposed to perform in the normal course of their duties, e.g., make pension payments. This kind of petty corruption is really extortion by public officials, who can exercise power by not performing their duties in a proper and timely manner. Basu (2011) has suggested that in such cases punishment should be handed out only to those seeking the bribe. Not those who are forced to pay it to get a service which is there's to receive as a right. Those paying the bribes will then have no disincentive to blow the whistle, and knowing this should dissuade many potential bribe seekers from seeking a bribe.

Big corruption consist of cases where officials bend the rules or procedures to favour an individual or business entity in return for a bribe. In all such cases, the entity paying the bribe obviously benefits, but other stakeholders lose, e.g., competing businesses, consumers, or government and society at large as in cases of tax evasion or padding up the price in government contracts. Analysing the phenomenon of corruption in a game theoretic framework, Dixit has shown that it should be possible through collective action, in which businesses cooperate, to ostracise their corrupt peers. And the threat of such ostracism and sanctions could help deter businesses from pursuing corrupt practices.

7. See among others Mauro 1997, Aidt 2003, Rose-Ackerman and Palifka 2016.

This theoretical insight is confirmed by many real world cases of businesses regulating themselves and monitoring their own compliance with an agreed code of behaviour, without recourse to formal courts of law, official law enforcement agencies or the police. The earliest recorded case of such self-regulation is among the Maghrebi traders who operated in the Mediterranean trading area in the 11th century (Greif 1993).

In more recent times such self-regulation is noted among the Jewish, Indian and Arab diamond traders operating between New York, Antwerp, Amsterdam, Ramat Gan and Dubai, among other places (Siegel 2009). Self-regulation to enforce their internal ethics, along with sanctions for violation, have also been noted among trading communities operating in global markets for products other than diamonds.

Further, such self-regulation is not limited only to communities engaged in global trade. Until recently, the local Mafia or Cosa Nostra had a vice like grip in Sicily, extorting protection money from some 80 per cent of the island's businesses. It now finds its business crumbling. This is all thanks to Addio Pizzo, a civil society movement that was started in 2004 by an intrepid group of young volunteers. The name literally means 'Goodbye to Pizzo', Pizzo being the protection money hitherto extorted by the Cosa Rostra. Today some 800 businesses in Italy, including corporates like Benetton, supermarket chains, nightclubs, travel agents, architects and others have signed up on a code against paying the pizzo. These members of the movement enjoy widening support from consumers, clients, civil society, the media and others while the Sicilian Mafia is in retreat.

These real world illustrations of the feasibility of businesses self-regulating their compliance with a code of behaviour is encouraging. At the same time, the incidence of such self-regulation seems to be limited to close knit business communities operating under challenging conditions. The Maghrebi traders operated across markets in different jurisdictions, under conditions of information asymmetry, and limited means of enforcing contracts. This is also true of the global diamond traders today. The Sicilian businesses were totally at the mercy of the Cosa Nostra, and individually could do little to resist the extortion.

What is common to these experiences is the essential dependence of individual businesses on the material and moral support of the relevant community, and the development of relationships of trust based on a shared culture within the community. This is backed by the implicit threat of a high penalty, sanctions and loss of all support, in case the trust is betrayed. Replicating such conditions, or creating conditions that substitute for them, to establish a broad based business community institution against corruption, cutting across different industries, trades and ethnic communities may be quite challenging.

One of the key conditions of success for a self regulating business community institution seems to be a relationship of trust embedded in shared ethnic or cultural bonds of an ethnic/religious group such as the Jews, Arabs, Gujarati or Sindhi Indians, Chinese, etc. Absent that, a broad based institution would have to be built around a different model, e.g., an institution led by eminent citizens respected by all in a given society.

A second key condition seems to be the urgent need of an individual business for the support of other members of the institution, by way of financing, contracts, and preferential treatment in business transactions. The corollary is the heavy penalty of losing such support in case the ethics code is violated. The design of any such institution would have to address this question of benefits, why would a business want to be a member of such an institution?

The core elements of such a broad based business community institution are briefly discussed below, i.e., an ethics code, a 'good and clean' business rating system, a code compliance assessment office (back office), a communications and external relations office (front office) that serves as the interface between the institution and other stakeholders, especially businesses, and a governing council that leads the institution.[8]

8. The following section draws on the author's presentation at the conference "Towards a Business Community Institution Against Corruption" organised by the World Bank in Mumbai, 30-31 March 2016.

The foundation for such an institution, it's raison de'tre, would be an ethics code for good and clean business. Business associations the world over and many corporations have such ethics codes. The specific feature of this code would be a list of do's and don'ts for doing business without corruption.

Based on this code, the institution would have to develop a rigorous 'good and clean business' rating system. This system would start with a scrutiny of audited accounts available in the public domain in the case of publicly quoted companies. Other companies that want to be rated would have to make their accounts available. Established techniques of corporate forensic analysis would provide the first layer of assessment, drawing attention to oddities and outliers where they appear. Successive rounds of further scrutiny, and more detailed investigation where warranted, e.g., for firms that seem to be politically connected, would lead to a rating.

The rating system would be somewhat analogous to a credit rating system. All quoted companies, and others which wish to be rated, would be rated annually. However, only the names of firms with high ratings would be made public. Naming and shaming of those with poor ratings can be left implicit to avoid a hostile pushback, especially during the formative phase of the institution. To undertake this forensic analysis, along with monitoring, investigation and detection of bribery complaints, the institution would have to have a Code Compliance Assessment Office (the Back Office) staffed with appropriately skilled personnel.

The other major arm of this institution would be the Communications and External Relations Office (Front Office). The main task of this office would be to develop and implement an effective strategy to communicate the mission, activities and benefits of this institution to all stakeholders; build the institution brand, its influence and voice; and grow the membership of the institution. The larger the membership of the institution, the more effective it will be.

The larger and more prestigious the membership, the greater would be the demand for membership of the institution. However, there are many concrete benefits of membership which the front office can also leverage to grow the membership. Thus, business to business transaction benefits would include improved standing in debt and equity markets, lowering the cost of capital to the firm. Well rated members of the institution would constitute a safe, hygienic, platform in which to do business and strike deals with other members. The members could also agree on a system of preferential treatment in business dealings with other members. There would also be the collective security of the institution in whistle-blowing against corrupt practices, cartels, etc.

Benefits in business to consumer transactions would include enhanced brand value. It would also include media and civil society driven consumer preference for products of well rated firms and greater competitiveness. Business to Government transaction benefits would include the enhanced reputation of well rated firms in dealing with government, stronger collective lobbying power vis-á-vis government in matters of corporate law, regulation, governance, etc.

Among its other activities, the front office would organise the publicity campaign, including the announcement event, for the best rated companies each year. It would liase and build relationships with all stakeholders including businesses, consumers, media, government, education institutions and civil society organisations to build up societal movement against corruption. These will be critical but challenging tasks for the success of the institution. The front office would have to have staff who are appropriately skilled to undertake these tasks.

To lead the organisation and coordinate its activities, the institution would have to be headed by a governing council, supported by a secretariat. To ensure the credibility and reputation of the institution, the council should consist of eminent persons widely known for their standards of probity. Business leaders themselves should not become members of the council, no matter how committed they may be to the institution, to protect the institution from becoming, or perceived as becoming, a cartel of insiders. In some sense, the institution would be a referee of competing businesses, so there would be an obvious conflict of interest if the heads of one or more of these businesses were to become members of the council.

Concluding Remarks

This paper has discussed some issues relating to two very different aspects of governance. On the positive side of governance, it has discussed the concept of governance as service delivery, and proposed a metric for rating governance performance based on this concept in the specific context of sub-national governments. On the negative side, the paper has addressed the issue of corruption, and proposed that effective action to contain corruption might actually have to be initiated outside government, by a business institution against corruption. The paper has discussed what might be the core elements of such an institution.

In both aspects, the success or failure of the proposals contained here will depend very much on the prevailing sociopolitical context and prevailing values. Performance rating of governments, national or sub-national, can be a powerful tool in promoting better governance. However, that can only happen in democratic societies ruled by elected governments, where parties compete on the basis of their governance performance rather than identity. Similarly, the 'good and clean business' rating of businesses can be an important tool to curb the 'supply' of corruption provided market conditions, consumer preferences, and prevailing social values enable such ratings to be translated into better bottom lines for business.

It is encouraging that of late political parties in India, particularly at the sub-national level, have started competing on the basis of performance in addition to traditional identity politics. This has also been facilitated by the greater fiscal autonomy of states, following the award of the 14th Finance Commission, since the state governments are now primarily responsible for the selection, design and delivery of social and economic programmes in addition to justice, law and order.

It is possible to take the view that such changes notwithstanding, identity politics based on caste, religion and ethnicity will continue to trump performance. Similarly, with regard to corruption, one can take the view that when corruption is endemic, initiatives to curb it whether by government, business or civil society are bound to fail. However, against that cynical view we also have the heartening experience of tipping points, of how small initiatives have sometimes culminated in dramatic change (Gladwell 2000).

References

Acemoglu, D. and James A. Robinson (2012). *Why Nation Fail: The Origins of Power, Prosperity, and Poverty.* New York: Crown Publishers.

Aidt, Toke S. (2003). "Economic Analysis of Corruption: A Survey", *The Economic Journal* 113(491): F632-F652, November.

Arrow, K. (1974). *The Limits of Organisation.* New York: W.N. Norton & Co.

Basu, K. (2011). "Why, for a Class of Bribes, the Act of Giving a Bribe should be Treated as Legal", *Working Paper.* New Delhi: Ministry of Finance Government of India. March.

Besley, T. and T. Persson (2011). *Pillars of Prosperity.* Princeton: Princeton University Press.

Bhandari, P. (2012). "Refining State Level Comparisons in India", *Planning Commission Working Paper Series.* New Delhi: Planning Commission, Government of India.

D.A.R.P.P. (2009). *State of Governance: A Framework of Assessment.* New Delhi: Department of Administrative Reforms, Public Grievances & Pensions, Govt. of India.

Debroy, B., L. Bhandari and S.S.A. Aiyar (2013). *Economic Freedom of the States of India 2011.* New Delhi: Academic Foundation.

Dixit, Avinash (2015). "How Business Community Institutions can Help Fight Corruption", *The World Bank Economic Review* 29(Supplement): S25- S47. World Bank.

Evans, P. and J.E. Rauch (1999). "Bureaucracy and Growth: A Cross-national Analysis of the Effects of 'Weberian' State Structures on Economic Growth", *American Sociological Review* 64: 748-65.

Freedom House (2015). *Freedom in the World 2015: The Annual Survey of Political Rights and Civil Liberties.* Rowman& Littlefield Publishing Group.

Fukuyama, Francis (2013). "What is Governance?", *Governance* 26(3): 347-68, July.

Gladwell, M. (2000). *Tipping Point: How Small Things Can Make a Big Difference.Little.* New York: Brown & Co.

Greif, A (1993). "Contract Enforceability and Economic Indebtedness in Early Trade: The Maghrebi Traders' Coalition", *American Economic Review* 83(3): 525-48, June.

Hobbes, T. (1651, 1981). *Leviathan.* London: Penguin Books.

Jacobson, P. (2014). *AddioPizzoNewsweek.* 17 September.

Kauffman, D. and A. Kraay (2015). *The Worldwide Governance Indicators (WGI).* The World Bank Group.

Kaufman, D., A. Kraay and M. Mastruzzi (2007). "Governance Matters VI: Aggregate & Individual Governance 1996-2006", *World Bank Policy Research Paper* 4780. Washington.

La Porta, R., F. Lopez-de-Silanes, A. Shleifer and R. Vishny (1999). "The Quality of Government", *Journal of Law, Economics, and Organization* 15(1).

Machiavelli, N. (1640, 1961). *The Prince.* Penguin editions.

Malhotra, Rajeev (2014). *India Public Policy Report 2014 (IPPR).* New Delhi: Oxford.

Mathew, C.K., A. Mukunthan and V. Divekar (2016). *Public Affairs Index: Governance in the States of India, 2016.* Bangalore: Public Affairs Centre.

Mauro, P. (1997). *Why Worry About Corruption*. Washington: International Monetary Fund.

Mundle, S, S. Chowdhury and S. Sikdar (2016). "Governance Performance of Indian States 2001-02 and 2011-12", *NIPFP Working Paper* No. 164, March.

Mundle S, P. Chakraborty, S. Chowdhury and S. Sikdar (2012). "The Quality of Governance: How have Indian States Performed?", *Economic and Political Weekly* 47(49): 41-52, 8 December.

Kautilya, V. (1992). *The Arthashastra*. English translation by L.N. Rangarajan. New Delhi: Penguin Edition.

Rodrik, D., A. Subramanian and F. Trebbi (2004). "Institutions Rule: The Primacy of Institutions Over Geography and Integration in Economic Development", *Journal of Economic Growth* 9: 131-65.

Rose-Ackerman S. and Bonnie J. Palifka (2016). *Corruption and Government: Causes, Consequences, and Reform*. Cambridge University Press. March.

Rotberg, R.I., A. Bhushan, and R.M. Gisselquist (2014). "The Indexes of Governance", in Robert I. Rotberg (ed.), *Measuring Governance*. Waterloo, Canada: CIGI.

Rotberg R.I. and R.M. Gisselquist (2009). *Strengthening African Governance: Index of African Governance*. Cambridge, MA: World Peace Foundation

Tan, KheeGiap and Kartik Rao (2015). "Sub-national Competitiveness Analysis and Simulation Studies for 35 States and Union Territories of India", *International Journal of Indian Culture and Business Management* 10(4): 476-93.

Shome, P. (2012). "Governance: History, Contemporary Debate & Practice", in S. Kochhar (ed.), *Policy Making for Indian Planning: Essay on Contemporary Issues in Honour of Montek S. Ahluwalia*. New Delhi: Academic Foundation.

Siegel, D. (2009). *Culture, Custom and Crime in the Diamond Trade*. New York: Springer.

Smith, A, (1776, 1970). *The Wealth of Nations*. Books I-III. London: Penguin.

Solow, R. (1957). "Technical Change and the Aggregate Production Function", *The Review of Economics and Statistics* 39(3): 312-330, August.

Spengler, J.J. (1969). "Kautilya, Plato, Lord Shang: Comparative Political. Economy," *Proceedings of the American Philosophical Society* 113(6): 450-57.

Transparency International (2014). *Corruption Perceptions Index, 2014*. Berlin: Transparency International.

UNDP (2014). *Millennium Development Goals: India Country Report 2014*. UNDP and Social Statistics Division, Ministry of Statistics and Programme Implementation, Government of India.

Weiss T.G. (2000). "Governance, Good Governance and Global Governance: Conceptual and Actual Challenges", *Third World Quarterly* 2(5): 795-814.

Wilson, Ross (2016). "Does Governance Cause Growth? Evidence from China", *World Development* 79: 138-151.

World Bank (2015). *Assessment of State Implementation of Business Reforms*. September.

Weblink:

http://dipp.nic.in/English/Investor/Ease_DoingBusiness/StateAssessmentReport_14September2015.pdf

Part 2

Tributes

1

JAGDISH BHAGWATI

Shaping India's Future

The sudden death of Abid Hussain by a massive heart attack last Thursday, was a tragedy for his family. He was in London with his wife Karki (a woman of great charm and intellectual achievement) on way to Washington to be with his daughter Vishaka and died in his sleep, in keeping with the generosity of spirit that marked his life: he would not impose a long illness on his beloved family.

Many have written already about the prominent role he played as a public servant and as a public intellectual. There was little that he had not touched and transformed into success and there were few important positions which had not come his way, including membership of the Planning Commission at a time when the Commission was relevant to our economic policymaking, and secretaryship in the commerce ministry. He had even been our ambassador to Washington during 1990-1992, and left an indelible impact on the two countries' relations at a critical time when they were on the cusp of change.

But, none of these enumerations do him justice. He must be remembered for the most compelling of his achievements; and these are twofold: his pioneering work on community development and his unwavering support for our economic reforms.

When I and current Prime Minister Manmohan Singh were together at St John's College in Cambridge in the mid-1950s, we had shared aspirations to fulfil Jawaharlal Nehru's call for a "tryst with destiny" by taking the Indian economy to dramatic improvement over the dismal record of nearly a quarter of a century of bad policies. As it happens, in a parallel which is remarkable, my friendship with

Abid Hussain went back to over 50 years as well; and it remained very close also.

But it began differently; and here, I can also point to a unique achievement of Abid which has no parallel at all. I went as an OECD consultant to Ankara in 1962, to the Devlet Planlama Teskilati (the Turkish Planning Commission), to "advise" on economic policy. Wherever I went, I was asked if I was Abid Hussain. I naturally said: No. But then I discovered that Abid was an icon in Turkey. So, I started saying: Yes. I began to be treated much better!

Why was he an icon? The reason was that he was helping Turkey with setting up its community development programme, seeking to lift up the rural communities. Abid had been a pioneer in our own community development programmes. It is a sad commentary that today we make much of "new kids on the block" like my colleague Jeffrey Sachs with his village projects which are mostly hype, even ignoring his dramatic failures as with shock therapy in Russia. Instead we need to honour our hero Abid.

But Abid's other principal achievement, for which the nation must honour him, is that, along with the prime minister, he was the one, unwavering proponent of our reforms. He was resolutely, but politely, against the extensive proliferation of senseless regulations and controls: he had seen it at first hand in the commerce assignment. He loved the witticism that the problem in India was that Adam Smith's Invisible Hand was nowhere to be seen. He matched it with his own wit as when, told by an American friend that immigrant Indians were of great benefit to America, he wisecracked: make sure, however, not to get them into your bureaucracy!

Like the prime minister, he had arrived at the realisation that India's future, both in terms of prosperity and poverty reduction, required economic reforms. And he worked tirelessly to translate that understanding into policy. When the full story of our reforms is written, Abid will share the glory with the prime minister as a hero of our historic transformation.

This article was first published in the *Times of India* on 26 June 2012.

2

NITIN DESAI

The Perfect Bureaucrat

Abid Hussain, the much loved and widely admired administrator and diplomat, passed away in London on 21 June. Abid bhai, as many of us called him, was everything a civil servant ought to be and embodied many qualities that are sadly missing in today's bureaucrats.

His bureaucratic experience was wide-ranging. He started in community development and this phase left him with a lifelong concern about poverty and rural development. But when he came back to India after a UN stint, he became a pole star guiding the way in economic administration. His major contribution was the orientation of trade policy where he argued for growth-led exports as the strategy for India rather than export-led growth. This focus on national development can be also seen in his seminal work in the committees on small industry development and scientific research that he chaired. All of this came together when he became a member of the Planning Commission, which is when I worked most closely with him.

Abid bhai was born in Hyderabad on 26 December 1926 and belonged to a group that I call 'Midnight's Adults'—people like him, Lovraj Kumar and George Verghese (happily still with us), who were young adults around 20 years of age at Independence and who retained their idealism and the hopes that Independence inspired throughout their very active and dedicated lives. They were the ones who were the instruments of Nehru's vision of a secular, rationalist and democratic India.

There was a second burst of idealism after the 1971 Bangladesh War and a bunch of us—myself, Yoginder Alagh, Vijay Kelkar and

Montek Singh Ahluwalia—came in laterally into the government. Abid bhai and Lovraj were the ones who made us feel welcome. There were others who came in later, Jairam Ramesh, Rakesh Mohan and Shankar Acharya to name a few, who also benefited from Abid bhai's openness and enthusiastic welcome for new blood.

Abid bhai's personal qualities were exceptional. Always warm, he would greet you with a "*mere pyaredost/beta/beti*" and would happily plant a kiss on your cheek. He made a point of dressing informally, even jauntily, and that itself put one at ease when meeting him.

Abid bhai had two qualities that made him a joy to work with. Unlike many of his IAS colleagues, who think no end of themselves, he was not just open but enthusiastic about the views and experiences of outsiders, lateral entrants like us, advisers, consultants and even journalists.

That led to a second great quality—an ability and willingness to listen rather than to lecture. He was a careful listener who would provoke with a question or two and then take detailed notes as his interlocutor spouted wisdom. And the notes were worth seeing. They were not linear. He would write the ideas and thoughts that struck him as valuable in little bubbles scattered through the page linked by lines and arrows to show the structure of the argument. Often, the structure was made even more explicit with the use of multi-coloured pens.

Abid bhai's transparency and patent integrity meant that he was never afraid to take decisions. Throughout a long career in the most sensitive part of economic administration, there was never even a whisper of scandal around his name. Not for him the safety of saying 'no' simply because a 'yes' could lead to questions. Abid bhai was always conscious that his job was to promote development and this meant supporting public and private sector proposals when they served that purpose. He was a liberaliser long before others climbed onto that bandwagon.

Today's bureaucrats must learn from his example. Their effectiveness will depend on their reputation for probity, which they must establish convincingly. They must be much more open to ideas from outside, be good listeners and, above all, not be afraid to take decisions. Many tributes have been paid to Abid bhai over the past few days. Perhaps, the best way of celebrating his life and work would be to recognise and reward in some form these qualities of transparency, openness and decisiveness in today's bureaucracy.

This article was first published in *Tehelka* 28(9) on 14 July 2012.

3

PRATAP BHANU MEHTA

The Power of His Example

There are individuals whose achievements we can measure. But some individuals themselves become the measure of a life well lived. Abid Hussain, distinguished civil servant and diplomat, was one such individual. It would take pages to describe his extraordinary contributions to Indian public life. As a thinker, he was ahead of the curve in so many respects: a reformer, before reform became fashionable; a liberal, even when the word was a source of political embarrassment in our culture; a believer in opening India up to the world in a climate where our fears often got the better of our hopes. He served in a number of key ministries, committees, the Planning Commission and as ambassador to the United States at critical junctures, always leaving a legacy for the better. He was a consistent reformer, well ahead of his colleagues on a range of economic issues from trade liberalisation to industrial reform. His contribution to a range of social and educational institutions is enormous. But a measure of his achievement is that he was far more important to India than the sum of his administrative actions.

No one who knew Abid sahib could resist the force of his personality. His unmatched charm, generosity, curiosity, ability to incandescently light up a conversation, clear-eyed analysis of facts, acute insights into the moral psychology of power, and his belief in a better future for India, even in the darkest moments, were always like a fresh breeze energising the soul. His wit was legendary, often a laconic window on the working of government. A distinguished official once told the Government of India, "Reform or Perish." Abid Hussain's quick admonition to the official was something to the effect, "The grammatical form of the sentence 'Reform or Perish' will lead the government to think they have a genuine choice between two alternatives. And they will choose perish."

But the void that he leaves behind is all the greater for the fact that he represented an ideal of India that is fast dwindling. That ideal was not an ideological project; it was embodied in the power of his example. He firmly believed that India can be held together only by *samanvaya* (synthesis). That would require a politics that would reach across party lines, and openness to the idea that no one has the monopoly over truth. He probably paid a huge price in his public career by choosing generosity of engagement over narrow and partisan loyalty. He was ready to serve, but never clamoured for power.

His secularism was not a dogmatic shibboleth to cut down opponents; it was practised in his being. In an age when the powerful trade on badges of identity to secure more power, he refused to opportunistically play the minority card. He had ideals of high culture without being elitist. He could combine a passion for poetry with a nose for more banal facts. There was no wall between people that humour could not breach. He had a rare sort of intellectual integrity. In a culture where too many people have too many certainties, he was always thinking, in the genuine sense of that impoverished word. This gave him an uncanny ability to understand how times change, and allowed him to be ahead of the curve, whether in economics, or international relations.

He would never surrender his intellectual judgement in the face of his other compelling instinct to be generous. But he would always cloak his criticism in such a constructive vein, that it was all the more effective for being gentle. His sheer enjoyment of human nature and human diversity was infectious: he never admonished people for being who they are, or wishing people different from him would conform to his views. Rather, he would focus on their strengths, enlist their energies in what they could do rather than what they could not. He had a fine sense of judgement: a realist who never gave up on the inspiring power of ideals, nor succumbed to the low depths of cynicism.

These may seem like personal virtues. But these personal virtues were also deep political statements of sorts. They diagnosed more clearly than reams of abstract analysis what it will take to get India to flourish. He was an irredeemable believer in India's prospects, and was eternally youthful in his optimism about what India could achieve. Although his loss, particularly to his extraordinary family, is hard to fathom, there is something emblematic about the suddenness with which he passed away. It is hard to imagine him fussing or fretting over life, and when the time came, he decided to let go and not resist. But he has left a gaping hole, in a context where few understand that an ambitious nation needs to be generous, and a diverse one, expansive in its sympathies.

This article was first published in the *Indian Express* on 23 June 2012.

4

DEEPAK NAYYAR

Master of the Public Sphere

Abid Hussain, a distinguished citizen of India, passed away on 21 June 2012 at the age of 85. He was in London for a meeting; a sudden heart attack snatched him away from his family, friends, colleagues and admirers. Abid Hussain was a superb civil servant, a diplomat par excellence, a natural leader in the public sphere and a concerned citizen. He was held in great esteem by his peers, much admired by the young, consulted by national leaders, respected by corporate bosses, invited to speak by universities, and sought after by the international community. And his loss is bound to be felt nationwide. For me, Abidbhai was a close friend. And I have not quite come to terms with the reality that he is no longer with us.

Abid Hussain was born in Hyderabad on 26 December 1926, where he lived during the formative years of his life. As a young student, his politics was very much on the left. He was selected for the Hyderabad Civil Service. But it was not to be. The police action came. And an examination in Telugu intervened as an obstacle. It was not long before he was selected for the IAS in 1951. A chequered career followed. In Andhra Pradesh, he served as a legendary Collector of Visakhapatnam, where he is remembered with much affection. For the United Nations, he worked in Ankara and Bangkok. In the Government of India, he was Secretary, Heavy Industry, and Commerce Secretary.

I first met Abid Hussain almost 30 years ago, in June 1983, when I was appointed Economic Adviser in the Ministry of Commerce. We had never seen each other before, but we must have been destined to meet. It was the beginning of a lifelong friendship. It was also a learning experience, with Abid as mentor, in the corridors of power. We had differences. Abid believed that the licence raj had become counterproductive so that it was time to rely far more on markets, while I believed that there was a critical role for the State in terms of strategic trade policy and industrial policy. There were fierce debates. Yet, in the process, there was openness, dialogue and persuasion. The reform of trade and industrial policies was an outcome of that process in which there were many actors but Abid was the catalyst and a leader. Outside the world of work, our friendship blossomed. We were in and out of each other's homes. Our families became close.

For Abid Hussain, life after retirement provided exciting opportunities. He served as a Member of the Planning Commission, from 1985 to 1990, when Rajiv Gandhi was Prime Minister, where he exercised significant influence. He was appointed Ambassador to the United States, in 1990, when V.P. Singh became Prime Minister. It was a challenging period, when the relationship with the United States was beginning to be redefined following the end of the Cold War juxtaposed with the macroeconomic crisis and political instability in India. During this period, I was Chief Economic Adviser to the Government of India. We worked together closely once again. I saw, at first hand, the networks he had developed with the government, industry, media, academia and society. He was a superb Ambassador who helped build our relationship with the US in a changed world and in difficult times. On his return to India, he joined the newly established Rajiv Gandhi Foundation to lead the Institute of Contemporary Studies and create a remarkable meeting space for people with different, sometimes polar opposite, worldviews, to debate contentious issues in economy, polity and society. I recall a fierce debate on the demolition on the Babri Masjid where the widest possible cross-section participated. This was altogether new and it imparted a high profile to the Rajiv Gandhi Foundation. In theory, he retired after that. In practice, he never did. He continued to read, write and speak as a public intellectual.

There are some attributes of Abid Hussain that deserve special mention. First, he had remarkable leadership qualities embedded in delegation, trust and loyalty. If things went well, he gave the credit to those who worked for him. If things went wrong, he accepted the responsibility. There is a splendid story worth narrating. Prime

Minister Indira Gandhi once said to him: "AbidSaheb, I gather that you are partial and select only those whom you know or are your friends." In reply, Abid Hussain said: "Yes, Madam, that is correct, but I assure you that everyone I choose is better than me." Second, he searched for and nurtured talented young people, so rare in India. I was one of them. So was Jairam Ramesh. And there were others. Third, his relationships were never a function of office which is so characteristic of Delhi. Prime Minister Rajiv Gandhi was very fond of Abid. In 1989, when he lost the elections, many of those allegedly loyal to him chose to stay away. But Abid met him regularly. Indeed, when Prime Minister V.P. Singh, who was also very fond of Abid, appointed him Ambassador to the United States, he told the then PM that he would meet the former PM, to consult him for advice. And so he did, several times, during his tenure as Ambassador. Fourth, Abid was secular in the real sense of the word both in belief and in practice. Indeed, his family is living testimony and proof of secularism in India. I recall his perceptive hypothesis when he said: "Deepak, we will be truly secular as a society only when you can attack Muslim fundamentalism and I can attack Hindu fundamentalism".

Abid Hussain epitomised the liberal intellectual tradition. He was not simply a good listener. He had the capacity to learn from others. More unusual, he had the ability to unlearn from experience. Yet, he remained a person of strong convictions and uncompromising integrity. For all his attainments, he was unassuming and modest. Above all, he was a wonderful human being. The Abid I knew was a man of many parts: the admirable family person, a caring husband for Karki and a doting father for Suhail, Vishakha and Rana; a gem of a friend, warm affectionate and loyal; and a person with a zest for life, whether it was cuisine, clothing or parties. Abid Saheb was someone you could trust with your life. He will be sorely missed.

This article was first published in *The Hindu* on 23 June 2012.

5

ARVIND PANAGARIYA

Abid Hussain

A Man of Many Parts

On 21 June 2012, precisely a year to the day after Suresh Tendulkar passed away, India lost another of its leading light of economic reforms, Dr Abid Hussain.

Affectionately known to his friends as Abid Bhai or Abid Sahib, he was a warm, wise and witty gentleman. His conversations and speeches were peppered with humour and memorable anecdotes.

Those who came into contact with him or heard him speak invariably came away with interesting material for future conversations.

My own first substantive interaction with Abid Sahib followed a brilliant speech he delivered at the World Bank in 1990, soon after his arrival in the United States as India's ambassador. The speech narrated how protectionism and licensing had hurt India.

Among other things, he noted the detrimental effect the controls have had on the quality of products, graphically illustrating the point by reference to Indian-made fountain pens that flowed more like fountains than pens. But his message was filled with optimism and hope for India.

That inspired me to send him a note the same day stating that his speech had been electrifying, but would our politicians and bureaucrats let go of the controls? He wrote back saying that the two hundred million strong middle-class would force the change. In retrospect, I wonder if even he thought at the time that his prophecy would come true so soon.

A man of many parts, Abid Sahib began his career as a civil servant. He joined the prestigious Indian Administrative Service in

1951 and rose to the top, serving as secretary in the ministries of commerce and heavy industry before formally retiring.

Such were his diplomatic skills that the government felt compelled to eschew the normal practice of appointing a member of Indian Foreign Service or a politician as the Ambassador to the United States and chose him for the post instead.

His command of economic policy making earned him a membership in the Planning Commission at a time when such appointments were reserved for the best in the trade. Then again, he wrote prolifically on such diverse subjects as trade policy, the role of bureaucracy in Indian democracy, science and technology, and attributes of a good society.

Abid Sahib practiced liberalising reforms well before most civil servants became converts to them. Two key committees had guided some of the earliest trade policy reforms in India: P.C. Alexander Committee on Import-Export Policies and Procedures in 1978 and Abid Hussain Committee on Trade Policies, 1984.

While the former led to some piecemeal liberalisation of imports of selected capital goods and raw materials through the Open General Licensing, the latter advocated measures aimed at expanding India's exports and making trade policy more predictable.

Recommendations of the Abid Hussain Committee led the government to adopt the policy of announcing the export-import policy for three years at a time instead of annually. The first such policy, covering the period 1985-1988, was announced in 1985. The report also led to the introduction of several East Asia-style export incentives in 1985-86 and 1986-87. Complemented by substantial depreciation of the rupee, these measures more than doubled India's exports in the second half of the 1980s.

Abid Sahib remained involved in catalysing reforms after they became systematic in 1991. In the second half of the 1990s, he helped push one of the most difficult reforms: effective end to the Small-Scale-Industries reservation.

The 1997 Abid Hussain Committee Report on Small Enterprises provided the intellectual foundation as well as a practical roadmap for this important reform. Recognising the political sensitivities in this area, the report carefully balanced its unequivocal recommendation of the abolition of the reservation policy by a strong case for support to the small and medium enterprises through alternative instruments.

The process of trimming the list of reserved items got underway soon after and greatly accelerated under PM Atal Bihari Vajpayee and his finance minister Yashwant Sinha.

Abid Sahib effectively deployed his wit to silence India's critics. Once, when visiting a Middle Eastern country, a member of the royal family asked him if it was true that Muslims in India were an unhappy lot.

Unperturbed, Abid Sahib replied that this was indeed true but went on to add that in India Hindus were equally unhappy! On another occasion, confronted with particularly hostile questioning on a foreign TV channel, he could diffuse the situation by remarking, "Gentlemen, there seems to be some confusion here. I am Abid Hussain from India, not Saddam Hussain from Iraq".

My wife and I last met Abid Sahib over a memorable lunch this past March. He discussed serious matters such how India could build up its academic institutions while treating us to his trademark humour.

A gem from the afternoon: "When a highly successful man was asked what his greatest strength in life had been, he replied that it was his wife. When asked to name his greatest weakness, he answered it was his neighbour's wife!"

With the passing away of this great son of hers, India has been left poorer in wisdom, wit and much else.

This article was first published in *The Economic Times* on 25 July with the title, "Wit and Charm were Traits of Dr. Abid Hussain, One of India's First Practitioners of Economic Reforms".

6

JAIRAM RAMESH

Recalling Abid Hussain

Abid Saab was a liberal in every sense of the term, a wonderful product of the Nehruvian era, a man with a great capacity to listen

I cannot imagine that Abid Hussain is no more. Even at 85 he was so full of life, ever smiling and zestful, nattily dressed as always, brimming with ideas and spreading hope and good cheer.

After two fleeting encounters in 1984 and 1985, I first met, in any serious way, Abid Hussain in August 1986. I had just finished my assignment in the ministry of industry and, sensing that I was at a loose end, he asked me to join the Planning Commission. This launched a very intimate personal and professional relationship—a relationship that, in many ways, shaped my subsequent career. I worked very closely with him for a little over three years, and it was he who got me together with Sam Pitroda as well, roughly over the same period. Working with both of them simultaneously was an extraordinary experience and gave me whole new capabilities that were to come in useful later.

Abid Saab was a great mentor and there are not many of that breed left in government. Lovraj Kumar, a contemporary of his, was another such person. And he was a mentor who did not become a tormentor, as quite a few end up becoming. Both spotted youngsters, created openings and gave them opportunities, and protected and projected them without feeling threatened in any way. All the "laterals" then in government—Montek Ahluwalia, Vijay Kelkar, Nitin Desai, Rakesh Mohan, Arvind Virmani and Deepak Nayyar, to name some of them—were part of Abid Saab's orbit in some way or the other. His room in Yojana Bhavan would be a veritable intellectual *adda*, embracing people of diverse ideologies. He would be getting ideas from an Isher Ahluwalia in the morning, an S.K. Goyal in the afternoon and a Mohit Sen in the evening. He was among the most easily accessible people I have ever known, and the younger you were, the greater the attention he lavished on you.

Abid Saab was among the very first to roll the dice on industrial policy reforms that finally reached their apogee in July 1991. Prime Minister Rajiv Gandhi had asked him to coordinate the preparation of a policy paper on this subject for consideration of the full Planning Commission. This paper was approved by the then Deputy Chairman of the Planning Commission Dr Manmohan Singh sometime in March/April 1987. Presumably, subsequent political developments precluded the type of changes recommended in the paper. Between April 1987 and September 1989, he delivered a number of lectures at different forums in which he anticipated much of the reforms that were to come later. I said to him after he had given the final touches to the text of the J.N. Tata Memorial Lecture at the Indian Institute of Science: "Sir, I have one request. In return for my helping you with the preparation of these speeches, please allow me to be the first one to deliver the Abid Hussain Memorial Lecture." His reply was quick and vintage Abid Saab. He said: "Babu, tuh pehle jaa sakta hai par jaane ke pehle draft de kar jaana!"

Abid Saab was a legendary Collector of Vishakhapatnam. The love was reciprocal. There is an Abid Nagar in that city and his only daughter was named Vishaka. He was commerce secretary at a time when Indira Gandhi wanted to make changes in trade policy to provide a fillip to exports. The process of simplification began during his tenure. It was this work that led to another great line of his. When V.P. Singh, as commerce minister, told him that he was thinking of an exhortation, something along the lines of "export or perish", Abid Saab replied: "Sir, choice mat dijiye. Given a choice, Indian industry would rather perish".

His contributions were not confined to industry and trade. He authored a landmark report on restructuring of the Council of Scientific and Industrial Research and on textile policy in the late 1980s, with his role extending to being much more than the titular chairman of the committees.

I saw Abid Saab interact with politicians from across the spectrum. And it was a real lesson. He used to tell me of his interactions with S.K. Dey, the man Jawaharlal Nehru picked to implement the community development movement in the country. He spoke often about his association with K. Brahmananda Reddy, the Andhra politician who did much for that state's industrial development. Rajiv Gandhi was fond of him, but so was V.P. Singh. It was the latter who appointed him as our ambassador to the US. When he became prime minister, one of the first things P.V. Narasimha Rao asked me to do was to speak to him and get his ideas on what needs to be done to deal with the financial crisis of 1991.

I once heard P. Shiv Shankar, who became deputy chairman of the Planning Commission after Dr Manmohan Singh had left for the South Commission, describe Abid Saab as a quintessential Hyderabadi, epitomising the best of the city's secular and cosmopolitan traditions. I recall Abid Saab's great ability to laugh at himself without taking umbrage. He used to tell me: "Young man, take your work seriously but don't take yourself too seriously".

He could never be brief in public speeches and would often meander and lose all sense of time. Once I told him: "Sir, if I was ever chairing one of your speeches, I would begin by saying Abid Hussain needs no introduction but badly needs a conclusion." He laughed uproariously and would often repeat that line in public, of course, not failing to mention where it came from.

Abid Saab was a liberal in every sense of the term, a wonderful product of the Nehruvian era, a man with a great capacity to listen, a man with an unparalleled capacity to reach out and communicate, a man who never harboured a grudge or a grouse, a man who always thought positive and wanted to bring out the best in people—even in those who did not necessarily share his ideas.

This article was first published in *Business Standard* on 27 June 2012.

7

Y.V. REDDY

Abid Saab

A Tribute from a Trainee

Mr Abid Hussain (Abid Saab) initiated me into civil service by training me in Vishakapatnam in 1965-66. He was my Collector and I was Assistant Collector under training. In those days, the Assistant Collector was treated by the Collector and his family as sort of a younger brother, and was usually guided through the professional, social and family life of a Collector.

On the day I reported for duty and called on Abid Saab in his office, he received me with surprising warmth and welcomed me profusely. Within a couple of minutes, he was reminded by his assistant that he had another appointment for which he had to leave the office. Simultaneously, he was reminded that he had to hear a very important irrigation dispute (obviously there were three appointments fixed for the same time slot). He called the advocates into the room and said that the hearing of the dispute would proceed, but it would be undertaken by the Assistant Collector (me) on his behalf. He added that Reddy is young, bright, impartial and knowledgeable, and therefore, can certainly be trusted. The advocates consented (perhaps, they had little choice). Abid Saab went away for his other appointments. I was, thus, initiated into the complexities of hearing an irrigation dispute from day one.

After I heard the dispute and prepared the draft order, Abid Saab simply wrote 'Excellent' on the note and signed the draft order without even having a glance at the order. When I protested, he smiled and said, "What else can it be but excellent, of course". I thought that it was a brilliant way of efficient delivery and charming way of managing time and handling controversial matters. It was obvious that behind the charm and casual approach, there were elements of a shrewd and purposive personality.

Abid Saab wanted me, as Assistant Collector, to accompany him for a dinner being hosted by a rich and influential person. I mentioned to him that I was uncomfortable accepting hospitality from such people. He explained that being anti-rich was as bad as being anti-poor. I always remember those words of wisdom.

Mr Jairam Ramesh a common friend worked under Abid Saab, and during that period, he was virtually a permanent fixture in Abid Saab's room. Jairam used to say that Abid Saab needs no introduction, but only a conclusion. In other words, Abid Saab was not pre-disposed to any particular ideology or outcome. He was not too bothered about the fruits of his efforts. He always believed in continuous action through goodwill to one and all.

It is widely believed that Abid Saab was instrumental in an important policy decision in Government of India. Mrs Indira Gandhi was in a meeting, considering a proposal to discourage brain drain from India. An argument was made that people in IITs and medical colleges had been trained in India at considerable expense to the tax payer. These expenditures could have been spent on drinking water or public health. However, the individuals preferred to move out of the country and serve other countries. It was, therefore, felt that such brain drain could be discouraged by some measures, including taxation. Towards the end of discussion, Abid Saab is supposed to have quipped: "Madam Prime Minister, it is better to have brain drain than have our brains in our drains". He had a special and effective way of getting across his point of view without offence, in many meetings and conferences.

He made everyone with whom he had contact not only comfortable in his company, but made him, and more particularly her, very special. He felt and expressed his warmth without reference to position, wealth, creed or anything of that sort. I am a witness to his transparent warmth in equal measure, to his *Duffedar* (attendant on the Collector) and the Chief Minister. He was not unduly concerned about content or consequences of his interactions, but was a leader in his own manner. His greatest quality has been that his very presence added to happiness all-around in every moment of his life.

I had the honour and privilege to be trained and to be proximate professionally and personally for almost half a century.

He has left a permanent imprint on some of my attitudes and style of work.

This tribute was delivered by the author at a memorial meeting organised by the Administrative Staff College of India and Apna Watan, on 8 July 2012, in Bella Vista, Hyderabad.